JOHN HANCE

JOHN HANCE

*The Life, Lies, and Legend
of Grand Canyon's Greatest Storyteller*

Shane Murphy

THE UNIVERSITY OF UTAH PRESS
Salt Lake City

The Defiance House Man colophon is a registered trademark of The University of Utah Press. It is based on a four-foot-tall Ancient Puebloan pictograph (late PIII) near Glen Canyon, Utah.

Library of Congress Cataloging-in-Publication Data

Names: Murphy, Shane, author.
Title: John Hance : the life, lies, and legend of Grand Canyon's greatest storyteller / by Shane Murphy.
Description: Salt Lake City : The University of Utah Press, [2020] | Includes bibliographical references and index.
Identifiers: LCCN 2019044433 (print) | LCCN 2019044434 (ebook) | ISBN 9781607817536 (paperback) | ISBN 9781607817543 (ebook)
Subjects: LCSH: Hance, John, 1840–1919. | Grand Canyon (Ariz.)—Biography. | Storytellers—Arizona—Grand Canyon—Biography. | LCGFT: Biographies.
Classification: LCC F788 .M875 2020 (print) | LCC F788 (ebook) | DDC 979.1/3204092 [B]—dc23
LC record available at https://lccn.loc.gov/2019044433
LC ebook record available at https://lccn.loc.gov/2019044434

Errata and further information on this and other titles is available online at UofUpress.com

Printed and bound in the United States of America.

IN MEMORY OF *Jane Allen Murphy.*

"I shall be pleased to say I have seen God's greatest and most stupendous natural wonder—the Grand Canyon. But the greatest satisfaction of all will be the remembrance of having shaken hands with the greatest liar on earth."

—President Theodore Roosevelt, May 6, 1903.

CONTENTS

ACKNOWLEDGMENTS

I've been quite fortunate to have benefitted from the encouragement and enthusiasm of many people during the years it took to compose this book. I put the small pieces they gave me into a larger reserve and hope to have done it well enough to please them. This book is the product of their interest, patient assistance, and attention to seemingly small yet undeniably important details. Everyone involved in this project helped make it whole.

"Babs" Monroe, of Camp Verde, Arizona, and the Camp Verde Historical Society.

Ruth Hance Thayer and her gracious daughter Amanda, descendants of George Hance's son Harvey, corresponded with me long after their patience should have allowed them.

Jennifer Walker, a distant cousin of John Hance, is tracing the family tree. I hope she writes a book.

Gary Hance of Dandridge, Tennessee, was a welcoming descendent of John Hance Jr. and an enjoyable companion while exploring the Dandridge countryside.

Bob Jarnagin, Jefferson County historian, drove during that same expedition. Bob knows the county records inside out and has visited Glendale Springs.

The Jefferson County Genealogical Society in Dandridge is made up of dedicated individuals working in a comfy upstairs room in the old courthouse.

The Phelps County Genealogical Society in Rolla, Missouri, also on the second floor of a historic courthouse, gave me an understanding of Green Berry's move to Missouri, and the county recorder put me on the road to where he lived.

John Bradbury of the State Historical Society of Missouri supplied notes and leads on the Hickok brothers.

R. Hugh Simmons of the Fort Delaware Society, Delaware City, Delaware, was key to my rudimentary understanding of what the Civil War meant to John Hance.

George Elmore, then chief ranger at Fort Larned National Historic Site, Kansas, provided access to post returns and sutlers' files.

Tammy Mower, Beth Scully, and the "boys in the basement" at the secretary of state's office in Augusta, Maine, put copies of the surviving Hance Asbestos Mining Company documents in my hands in only five hours.

Bruce Dinges of the Arizona Historical Society published one of my first essays on Hance while, in Flagstaff, Joe Meehan let me explore the society's Pioneer Museum papers. The society archives in Tucson houses "John Hance's Visitors' Book."

Brad Dimock, Dan Cassidy, and Bill Bishop are Grand Canyon boatmen, explorers, and bibliophiles who are part of this, in conjunction with geologist Wayne Ranney, historian Mike Anderson, and Hance trails expert Doug Nering—and everyone else I've met driving shuttles or on the river or rim, as well as during history conventions, guides' seminars, and symposiums over what's now almost fifty years.

Richard Quartaroli is a boatman, historian, author, speaker, editor, and emeritus special collections librarian at Northern Arizona University, who gave me his interest, time, and knowledge.

Earle Spamer, the keeper of all things Grand Canyon at RavensPerch .org, contributed to this book in ways even he cannot imagine.

Tom Martin, Grand Canyon long-walker, speaker, boatman, and publisher, the man with the tape recorder, provided me with more encouragement than he knows.

Don Lago and Roy Webb are Colorado Plateau historians and authors who reviewed the manuscript and offered criticism and guidance.

Diane Boyer, a descendent of the Sykes brothers, is a researcher, author, and photo archivist.

Stuart Rosebrook of *True West* magazine took a day out of his schedule, starting with a three-hour plane ride and car drive, to show me around John's old Ash Creek homestead.

Verde Ditch administrative judge David McKey allowed me to inspect files concerning Verde Valley water allocations.

Kathleen Jacobs is descended from Murray McInernay and kindly supplied photos and information.

Someone wishing to remain anonymous provided me with encyclopedic, unimpeachable knowledge of Verde Valley's remarkably colorful history.

Vincent Randell, the Yavapai-Apache tribal historian in Camp Verde, offered warmth, stories, and guidance in tracing the Yavapai-Apache Removal from the Camp Verde Reservation.

Coleen Hyde, Kim Besom, Ron Brown, and a lot of other folks at Grand Canyon National Park were willing accomplices to my research.

Marieke Taney at Northern Arizona University, Flagstaff, rows a dory named "Betty Boop" and knows a lot about George Flavell.

Richard and Sherry Mangum authored *Grand Canyon–Flagstaff Stage Coach Line—A History & Exploration Guide,* an indispensable chronicle of early rim visitation.

Sheila Stubler at Fort Verde State Historic Park in Camp Verde provided microfiche post returns and allowed me to photograph the Head & Co. ledgers in her archives.

Judy Mathe Foley, a lifetime friend (along with her sister Nancy), edited my first couple of drafts of this book. "She done good," as my mother would have said.

I also want to recognize and thank the many individuals who work in the academic institutions I visited, but that is a double-edged sword. There's no way I can now recollect everyone I spoke with. My memory works off faces, not names, as many will attest, so please accept my apologies for the shorthand to follow.

Librarians at the National Archives and Records Administration in Washington, D.C., and Riverside, California.

Everyone at Northern Arizona University's Cline Library, Special Collections and Archives, Flagstaff, Arizona.

The Grand Canyon Historical Society.

The Museum of Northern Arizona, Flagstaff, photo archives and library staffs.

Everyone at the Arizona State Library, Archives and Public Records, Phoenix, Arizona.

The small but dedicated staff at the Mohave Museum of History and Arts.

The Billie Jane Baguley Library and Archives staff at the Heard Museum in Phoenix.

Everyone at Slusser Memorial Philatelic Library, Tucson, Arizona. Thanks for the coffee in the "Jane" cup.

The Rare Books and Manuscripts overseers at Arizona State University Library in Tucson.

The Fray Angélico Chávez History Library and photo archives staff, Palace of the Governors, Santa Fe, New Mexico.

The reading room "crew" and those supplying photo research and reproductions at The Huntington Library, San Mateo, California.

I always felt welcome at the Mohave, Coconino, and Yavapai County recorders' and assessors' offices, meaning in courthouses, warehouses, and vaults spread far and wide, where I was permitted to independently root out original documents.

The online archive at ChroniclingAmerica.loc.gov at the Library of Congress in Washington, D.C., gave me some 10GB of fascinating newspaper pages to download.

Finally, a few years ago I was having lunch with Christa Sadler, talking about submitting "the manuscript" to a publisher. She suggested the University of Utah Press, and I *think* I want to thank her—not because she sent me to the wrong place, which she didn't, but because she gave me too much work to do.

John R. Alley at the University of Utah Press accepted my manuscript; it was in such tatters that I'll forever wonder why he did that. Tom Krause is the acquisitions editor into whose hands the manuscript eventually and unfortunately fell. I have appreciated his attention and guidance in bringing this project to fruition. Copyeditor Kellyn Neumann, with her close attention to detail, applied the final coat of polish.

Thank you all.

ABBREVIATIONS FOR ARCHIVAL SOURCES

AzSLA&PR—Arizona State Library, Archives and Public Records, Phoenix, Arizona.

CVHS—Camp Verde Historical Society, Camp Verde, Arizona.

CCAzAR—Coconino County, Arizona, assessor's records.

CCAzRR—Coconino County, Arizona, recorder's records.

GRCA—Grand Canyon National Park Museum Collection, Grand Canyon, Arizona.

MCR—Mohave County Recorder, Kingman, Arizona.

MNA—Museum of Northern Arizona Research Center, Flagstaff, Arizona.

NARA—National Archives and Records Administration, Riverside, California, and Washington, D.C.

NAUSCA—Northern Arizona University, Special Collections and Archives, Flagstaff, Arizona.

PCGS—Phelps County Genealogical Society, Rolla, Missouri.

SHMA—Sharlot Hall Museum and Archives, Prescott, Arizona.

THL—The Huntington Library, San Marino, California.

USDIKNF—U.S. Department of the Interior, Kaibab National Forest, Williams, Arizona.

YCAzRR—Yavapai County, Prescott, Arizona, recorder's records.

YCAzAR—Yavapai County, Phoenix, Arizona, assessor's records, Arizona State Library, Archives and Public Records.

Hance, his dog, and burro on Hance Trail. "Hance's Trail down," 1892. Photo by
William Henry Jackson, History Colorado, no. 86.200.3104.

One

INTRODUCTION

"An Old Acquaintance of Mine"

At Grand Canyon, where I led river trips in large motorized pontoon rafts for over twenty years, Hance Rapid at river mile 77 requires close attention. There are plenty of rapids above and below Hance, all storied in their own way. But with its twisting, rock-bound course and thirty-foot drop, Hance is the canyon's longest piece of serious whitewater. The Colorado River's other "big boys" are Crystal and Lava Falls, and they await discovery downstream, but a boat must safely navigate Hance to get to them.

Hance's entry features a circuitous move around a partially submerged rock to a downstream wave that providentially surfs the raft left, toward midstream and deep water, in place to run the "gut" or main current. That means a big, bumpy ride at Hance, with huge "haystacks" and mammoth "holes" when the releases from Glen Canyon Dam are enough to alleviate the worry of parking on a midstream boulder. When the releases are low, however, Hance is a rock garden capable of significant damage to both equipment and a boatman's pride.

I led trips that covered 280 river miles on a six-night, seven-day schedule—not much time to get from Lees Ferry at the head of Grand Canyon to Pearce Ferry at its end. Interpretation of flora, fauna, geology, and history was a key component of these journeys, but because of my schedule there was only time for a quick John Hance tidbit as we approached the drop.

"We're coming up on Hance Rapid, folks. You'll need good handholds for this one! Hance is named for an old storyteller who lived up on the

Hance Rapid. Red Canyon Trail enters from the south (left) at the head of boulder-strewn Hance Rapid. The large pontoon boat holds fourteen passengers plus two crew and is thirty-seven feet long. Tailings from "John Hance's asbestos mine" can be seen in the upper left portion of the image. Courtesy of James Kirchner.

rim years ago, Captain John Hance. One day the Cap'n decided to ride over to the North Rim to visit a friend. But he didn't want to travel all the way 'round to Lees Ferry, get shuttled across the river, continue up the mountain to Jacob's Lake, and then head south to the lodge where his friend was. That's two hundred miles; it would've taken him a week, easy. But it's only eighteen miles by air. So Hance saddled up his strongest, fastest horse, got on, backed up, and took a long running leap. But when they got 'bout halfway across, Hance saw they wouldn't make it, so he turned around and went back."

A few mild chuckles and into the maelstrom we'd drop. Flushing around the last corner at the bottom of the drop, with everybody soaking wet, I'd point to Hance's asbestos mine high above us on river right as we flashed past beneath it. "Next rapid, Sockdolager!" I'd bawl over the motor's roar. "That's where Hance saw a fish so big it took all day to pass."

That was John Hance for me for at least one hundred trips: mostly ignorance. To be honest, I knew Hance Rapid was the terminus of New Hance Trail, but I had no idea Sockdolager Rapid was the terminus of Old Hance Trail. Rather, I thought New Hance Trail was the latest iteration of Old Hance Trail—or something.

Then, one winter morning, leafing through a weathered old Arizona atlas, I noticed a place named Hance Spring twenty miles from where I live in central Arizona's Verde Valley. I'd heard Hance spent time around Camp Verde before he got to Grand Canyon and wondered if the place was named for him. I drove over there using a one-lane, dusty and narrow road with cattle trucks roaring past me at reckless speeds. Finally, I located Hance Spring, a quaint perennial puddle beneath a couple of tall old cottonwoods. My thought was it could water one man, his dog, and a mule—if they didn't drink all that much.

At the Camp Verde Historical Society I learned the spring was named for George Hance, John's younger half-brother. George Washington Hance was a prominent Verde Valley figure for nearly five decades. He was the area's first civilian postmaster, notary public, school board secretary, majordomo, census enumerator, and longtime justice of the peace at his ranch. The society had a folder of reminiscences he'd sent to friends and others like Arizona historian Sharlot Hall, and he would sometimes mention John in references to their time on the plains, Indian attacks, and a wagon trip to Arizona in 1868. That information was more than compelling, and I can't thank George enough for sending me on the mission he sparked.

George described Verde Valley when he and John were among its early settlers, and by training the Hance brothers' magnifying glass on the area much of its initial white social history can be visualized in theoretical Venn diagrams. In this, I was extraordinarily fortunate to meet a lifelong Camp Verde resident who, appreciating my desire to learn everything I could about the area's early history, offered me unreserved access to a collection of hand-recorded store ledger books from the town's only mercantile outlet. As it turned out, the books spanned the years John Hance lived in Camp Verde. The first page of the first book I opened had John Hance's name on it. Talk about hog heaven! I began to photograph and index every page and after a year had 5GB of information, copies of which I donated to the Arizona State Library and, because of their connection to Hance, to Grand Canyon National Park.[1]

These revelations sent me further afield, to records vaults and warehouses, collections of hotel guest registers, county indexes, deeds, and mining claims. In all of this I made an unexpected discovery: the information showed Hance to be even more incredulous than the stories he told. Those tall tales of his paled in comparison to the real life he lived.

I found that John Hance had become his own folklore, about as close to living fiction as you can get. We know less of him as an actual person than we do of the stories he told. Here, Hance and his gelding Darby rank right up there with Paul Bunyan and his blue ox, Babe—except Hance and Darby were the real-world manifestations of an imagined frontier. John Hance actually lived the life portrayed in his colorful tall tales.

John Hance's time on earth spanned twenty-one American presidencies, beginning with Martin Van Buren and ending in Woodrow Wilson's second term. Those eighty-one years saw drastic change in the course of humankind, from the daguerreotype to the Autochrome Lumière process, plate cameras, and moving pictures; from the lone dispatch rider to the international telegraph; from the Civil War to the conclusion of World War I; from the flintlock rifle to the machine gun, airship, and even airplane; from whale oil lamps to Edison's 1,200-hour lightbulb; and from the horse-drawn carriage to automobiles. Hance cared little for these lifestyle advances. He was from the back woods and it was there his mind remained. The only mechanized sort of transportation Hance ever owned, albeit briefly in 1901, was a bicycle.

In photographs we see Hance seated backboard straight on a horse, mule, or wagon, in a chair or on a slab of limestone. That was his pose, his shtick, but even late in life he is identifiable by his posture. He walked the same way, on his heels, as if marching, and he was once observed heading down a trail "putting his heels down hard, looking back over his shoulder and saying to those behind, 'Yaas, yaas, yaas.'"[2] We know he was an imposing man when whiskey was flowing, sometimes with terrible results, and that he talked. About anything. For hours.

Hance is shorter than others standing with him in most photos. His height, averaged from Coconino County voter registration rolls between 1912 and 1918, was five feet, five and a half inches. However, as when reporting his age, there'd be no telling what he'd say to the man holding the pen; he once claimed he was five feet, eight inches tall. The same images also show him as slim, about 135 pounds, an estimate that agrees with the same averaged documents. We read that his speech was a thick Appalachian drawl, an American brogue of sorts, that his voice was high pitched and nasal (becoming "squeaky" when he closed in on a punchline), and that he sang in high, harmonious tones. A variety of sources confirm Hance was missing the tip of an index finger, which stories say he'd worn off pointing at Grand Canyon. If true, it happened after 1903—several photos taken that year clearly show all his digits intact.

Though it's not certifiable since color photos of him are unknown, Hance's German ancestry points to his eyes being blue—all his living kin are blue-eyed—and those eyes were keen. Hance was a crack shot with his rifle, by his brother's account killing seven turkeys with as many bullets on Thanksgiving Day 1868. Another time, "he dropped a deer so far away that the meat spoilt 'afore he could git to it."[3] But tall tale–telling aside, Hance really did find water for a military wagon train during a nasty Kansas snowstorm.

Hance's imaginative stories began innocently enough, with a gentle tug at common sense, then trended due south to end in utter absurdity. For example, it seems Hance was down by the Colorado River one bright day, and mighty thirsty. Dropping to his knees he bent over, stuck his mouth in the river, and sucked down its wonderful coolness. But, as frequently happens, the river was carrying a heavy load of silt, so thick it lodged in his throat like a log—John Hance began to choke! He tried biting off the mud's flow, he said, but his teeth were in poor repair. So he drew out his Bowie knife, cut the stream of mud in half, swallowed down what was left, and called it good.[4]

The honorarium of "captain" completes the man we know best, Cap'n John Hance. That story comes in two varieties, woeful fiction and true grit. Here's the fiction. On a horse tour along the rim, a lady[5] inquired how Hance had become a captain. He was given that title, he replied, because he'd led a gang of horse thieves on a raid to Mexico. After phenomenal early success, the gang grew careless and rode into an ambush. All night and most of the next day, vaqueros chased them across the barren wastes of northern Chihuahua. Late the second afternoon his group scattered, but the vaqueros doggedly pursued Hance. Frantic to shake them, he ran into a vast buffalo herd, jumping on the lead bull in the dust and confusion to make his getaway. It was a tactical triumph, but also a strategic error. Once underway, the startled bull refused to stop, first charging west before heading north. Much as he wanted to, Hance couldn't jump off for fear of being trampled in the stampede. At the end of the third day, the vaqueros, choked by dust, gave up. However, nothing slowed the herd's flight across the Southwest, until Hance was jerked awake early one morning as the herd skidded to a halt. He flew off the bull and landed feet first, right there at Grandview Point.[6]

Contrast that with an honest accounting by John Miller Stotsenberg. From Indiana, Stotsenberg graduated from West Point in 1881,[7] participated in the Wounded Knee massacre in December 1890, and died in action at Quingua, Luzon, Philippines, in 1899. In the summer and fall of 1882, during Hance's concluding days in the Verde Valley, Stotsenberg was stationed at Fort McDowell with the Sixth Cavalry. Post returns show him in and out of Forte Verde and Whipple several times.[8]

Stotsenberg and his friend, Lieutenant John "Black Jack" Pershing (who later commanded the American Expeditionary Force during World War I), visited Grand Canyon in June 1889 and were photographed talking with Hance next to his cabin, perhaps its earliest image. Stotsenberg's reminiscence of this visit turns some odd corners but is also brutally informative. There's only a quick reference to Hance as a freight conductor. At the time, "conductor" meant "captain," or a wagon train's boss.

[Our Indian guide] tried to explain to us that we were approaching a house where, he said, there was a bad white man named Hancey. After a long time I finally concluded that he must mean the man who lived on the edge of the Grand Canyon, an old acquaintance of mine named John Hance. He was a freight conductor at Fort Verde and a good whole-souled fellow when sober, but a terror when drinking. I knew him well and felt that our welcome would be hearty.

Before we came in sight of the cabin we were greeted with the sound of loud and violent swearing. It was evidently Hance in a rage at someone. When we drew near, we saw him rush out with a rifle and take aim at a small squad of Supai Indians watering their horses at his spring, and he was cursing them for muddying the water. For a moment we expected to see bloodshed, as Hance was known to have an ungovernable temper; but the Supais began to make some apologies, and Hance, accepting them with poor grace, told them to go off.[9]

Hance at his cabin speaking with John "Black Jack" Pershing, summer 1889. Standing next behind Hance is John Stotensberg. The man seated closest to Pershing could be Bill Hull. Courtesy of The Huntington Library, Otis R. Marston Papers, V059/0027.

"When he saw us," Stotsenberg continued, "he gave us a more cordial welcome than I had anticipated. It seemed a wonder that a cabin so small could hold a heart so large. His outburst had subsided, and he began at once to get us something to eat."[10]

The next morning Hance packed them a lunch, took two dollars for their use of his trail, and they descended into the gorge. Hance had installed signs to help guide the way, one reading "Fifth Avenue." Both men were deeply impressed by their visit, Stotsenberg predicting, "This point will in no distant day be world-famed, and this poor cabin will give way to a fine hotel."[11]

Before all of that, however, Hance spent over twenty years raising crops and tending livestock on backwoods Tennessee and Missouri farms before enlisting in the Confederate army. He fought in two Civil War battles, was captured, and starved through twenty-two months in Union prisons. He took three years freighting across the plains to reach Arizona, where he spent twelve years farming, freighting, and bidding military contracts before settling on Grand Canyon's East Rim and practically inventing Grand Canyon tourism.

However, Grand Canyon tourism wasn't John Hance's brainchild. Someone would have become its first tour operator if Hance hadn't established a camp that people could get to. The only road to the rim, which he and two others carved out, ended there, at a log cabin with a few army wall tents in the yard. Hance's cabin was the only structure anywhere along the rim south of the river for a decade. From there, Hance led tourists down to the Colorado River using a precipitous trail he'd built, and like his road, it was the first.

Then his stories took over. Between the mid-1880s and early 1900s, "John Hance" was another way to say "Grand Canyon." The two were so entwined you couldn't have one without the other. To miss either, as someone remarked in his guestbook, was to miss half the show. One journalist wrote,

> All the way from Albuquerque you have heard of John Hance. You have read about him in all the guide books you have bought. People whom you meet tell you about the flapjacks he will cook for you at the canyon camp. You constantly hear references to "Hance's Peak," and "Hance's cabin," until you wonder if John Hance owns the Grand Canyon of the Colorado River. When you get to Flagstaff, the air is still filled with confused murmurs of Hance. You come to have a sort of "See-Hance-and-die" feeling and are a little uncertain whether you have come thousands of miles to see the Grand Canyon or John Hance, of Arizona.[12]

Two

BEGINNINGS

"Chinamen Eating Rice with Their Chopsticks"

Deep in southern Appalachia lies eastern Tennessee's Great Valley. Carved into southwestern trending mountain ridges by intervening river troughs, it is pushed eastward by the Unaka Mountains, on the north by the Cumberland Plateau, and to the south by the Great Smoky Mountains.

The French Broad River rises near Rosman, North Carolina. The river's name comes from a wide, flat, navigable waterway that flowed, before the Louisiana Purchase, into territory claimed by France. After a northerly arc through Asheville, North Carolina, the French Broad enters Tennessee and trends northwest some eighty miles before suddenly veering southwest at its confluence with the Nolichucky River. Near Knoxville it joins the Holston River to become the Tennessee. About two-thirds of its course winds through Jefferson County, the birthplace of John Hance. There it passes Dandridge, the county seat, first called Dandridge Spring because a quaint freshet of pure water rose from a fragrant glen just west of the river bottomlands. Early Scottish immigrants used the spring to make whiskey. The small cemetery girding the spring, which dates from the Revolutionary War, became a crossroads where boatmen gathered and camped. That meeting spot grew into the community of Dandridge, the first permanent white settlement in eastern Tennessee and the second anywhere in the state.

Jefferson County's official records are held in a vault on the second floor of its historic courthouse, which also houses a small, but informative rustic museum. The collection includes David Crockett's 1806 marriage bond to his first wife, Polly Finley. Crockett's legend would have been at high tide when John Hance was born, the year after Crockett famously declared, after losing a rigged congressional race, that he was done with politics and headed to Texas.

East Tennessee is the homeland of many North American cultures. Archaeological evidence of human activity dates back fourteen thousand years, early enough to demonstrate interaction with megafauna. The timeline of Native American history is distilled into the Archaic, Woodland, and Mississippian periods. The final two span the last five thousand years, ending in 1540 when the Spanish explorer Hernando de Soto possibly stood within sight of the old courthouse (some accounts of de Soto's first march across the South place him nearby). By the 1700s, Cherokees controlled much of the area. They lived in hamlets, though they had a large trading center, remembered as Overhill Towns, where the first white settlers sowed their seeds in about 1775.

Land across the river southward of Dandridge was then called "Territory South of the French Broad" and colloquially referred to as "Lesser Franklin." Administratively, Lesser Franklin had no sure footing. Shuttled back and forth between jurisdictions, the area assumed desultory independence after its attempt at statehood failed in 1786. Its people lived outside the law, settling wherever they wished, mostly on lands legally granted to the Cherokee Nation by treaty. The Cherokees revolted, skirmishing fiercely until the concluding days of the Trail of Tears (about the time of John Hance's birth), when the Cherokees and other tribes endured the long and deadly journey to lands west of the Mississippi River.

Because of Tennessee's vague political designations and surrounding circumstances, who owned what and when in Lesser Franklin is sparsely documented. To further the confusion, deeds of the place and time didn't use the township and range survey method—i.e., "the northwest quarter of the southeast quarter of township 16 Range 9 East." Instead, Lesser Franklin deeds followed the metes and bounds system, which described the physical scene as measured in chains. One example reads, "From a poplar [tree] on William Gibson's line running thence South Eighty four East one hundred and sixteen poles to a white oak [at] Lichlyter Corner thence with his line crossing the road leading to [Cowan's] Ferry to [a] New Post South twenty six poles."[1] That deed, illustrated by a one-dimensional diagram scaled at one hundred poles to the inch—the equivalent of one hundred rods—was recorded in October 1825 by someone named John Hance.

That was John Hance's grandfather. Numerous John Hances exist in Captain John Hance's lineage. They're all related, and the captain is the youngest of the lot. John's great-grandfather was, evidently, born sometime around 1760 and raised near Hesse, Germany. He was shipped to America as one of thirty-five thousand Hessian mercenary troops for Britain in the Revolutionary War, afterward settling in South Carolina with his German wife and beginning a large family. Among the sons born to him in South Carolina was John Hance Sr. in about 1783, who fathered John Hance Jr. in 1801.[2]

In the Old World, Hance's great-grandfather's name would have been spelled and pronounced something like "Jon Hans."[3] A John Hans was recorded in Spartanburg, South Carolina, after the Revolutionary War, and later near Edgefield. Then, in 1810, again in Spartanburg, on the only known U.S. Census page identifying him, there is a John Oldhance. This man also had a son and grandson named John Hance. It would have made sense for officials to designate the elder John Hans as old Hance, or Oldhance.

John Oldhance next appears in several early Lesser Franklin deeds, starting with his original ten-acre plot "South of the French Broad" granted by Tennessee in 1815. In 1819, William Gibson sold John Oldhance steep, heavily wooded hillsides in the same area. A decade later Tennessee granted John O. Hance eight acres on the road to Sehorn's Ferry; neighbors included a William Hance. In 1829, William Gibson again sold land to John Hance. This was probably John Jr., but it's impossible to be sure, since the records grow more and more confusing. Most of the information connected to John Hance of Grand Canyon occurs along lower Indian Creek, but that turns a blind corner when, by the 1840s, "John Hance" owned over eight hundred acres along the brook's heavily timbered, abrupt limestone hollows.

John Hance Jr., recorded as "John Hants Jr.," married his German neighbor Catherine Rinehart in 1825. When he died in 1834, Catherine's father bequeathed $600 ($14,400 in 2015[4]) "to my daughter Catherine Oldhance."[5] And in 1832, when twenty-two-year-old Elizabeth Hance married her German neighbor Martin Bunch, the bond papers were marked, not signed, by Bunch and "Oldhance JR." This almost certainly indicates John Jr. was descended from John Oldhance.

Green Berry Hance, "G. B." or "Green B." on deeds and other legal documents, was John Jr.'s younger brother by eighteen years, born to John Sr. and Rachael Daulphin Laight (later the name became Light) in 1819. He was his father's tenth child, the second born in Tennessee. Green Berry married three times and, like his father, produced over a dozen children, some dying in infancy. In 1837, when he bought fifty acres from his brother-in-law neighbor Martin Bunch, Green Berry's second son John—Cap'n John Hance—was born to his first wife Elizabeth James. Green's second wife, Rebecca Ann Hill, produced two living children, the first being George Washington Hance in 1848, who went to Arizona with his brother John in 1868.

Green's land was near today's intersection of Upper Rinehart and Shropshire Hollow Roads, off Indian Creek Road south of Dandridge. Interestingly, on Upper Rinehart road (a half-mile south of Lichlyter Lane) sits a period-built, three-room, dovetail-joined log cabin and cantilever barn, a structure peculiar to the times in east Tennessee. The presentation is so realistic that one almost expects to find the cap'n standing out front with his broadax. When shown a photo of this cabin, Jefferson County historian Bob Jarnagin, whose family dates back to the first days there, fairly erupted, "Wow! That's exactly what John Hance's cabin would have been like!" After running through a bank of ancient deed books, Jarnagin concluded that the house had probably belonged to John Hance's uncle, John Jr.

The intersection of Rinehart Road and Indian Creek was ground zero for John Hance's childhood. Life in the hollows was rough-hewn and subsistence driven, its workload determined by gender. Men did the heavy lifting and only the very young and infirm were exempt; young John had little time to play with crawdads in the rock-lined springhouse. The imagined scene is of a small, hand-built log cabin with sleeping lofts, a slight porch in front, a cast iron wood-burning cook stove in the kitchen, and a fireplace and wooden benches in the small "front" room. An outhouse sits in the downhill yard.

Common amenities were foreign by today's standards. Soap was made from lye by adding ashes from the fireplace; lye was also employed to render hominy from corn, Green Berry's most important crop. After harvest, the corn was stored in a crib to feed livestock and ground into

Home of John Hance's uncle, John Hance Jr., on Indian Creek, south of the French Broad River near Dandridge, Tennessee. Author photo.

meal at a community gristmill to make bread. Pork was the most important meat, since pigs were easy to raise and also provided leather. Butchered in cool fall weather, the meat was either salted or smoked for a week or more in the meat house, after which it was buried in a cask of cornmeal where, protected from insects, it "flavored" during the humid summer months. Livestock required daily attention, hillsides were cleared and furrowed behind a mule, firewood was cut into rounds and then quartered, and crops were planted, tended, and harvested. Even such rudimentary necessities as horseshoes and their nails were manufactured onsite, pounded out in a crude blacksmith shop burning locally mined coal. All this was done on top of tending gardens, plucking chickens, gathering eggs, harvesting walnuts, picking berries, and building fences "horse-high, hog-tight, and bull-strong."[6]

The story of John Hance's origins is not so easily told, however. According to George Hance, his brother John was "born at Cowan's Ferry on

French Broad River on September 11, 1838."[7] Owned by Andrew Cowan on the south side, Cowan's Ferry was at the southern tip of Beaver Dam, a yawning curve in the French Broad four river miles downstream of Sehorn Creek. Coal miners and farmers, the Cowans were early settlers who dedicated land for the area's first cemetery, where John Oldhance was possibly buried—it was either there or Reinhart Cemetery, now completely overgrown and heavily forested with only a few unmarked headstones in evidence. The crossing is illustrated on an 1835 facsimile map that also shows teepees along lower Indian Creek. Later, during the Civil War, Cowan's Ferry Road led to Indian Creek from Blant's Hill battlefield. The northside landing was called Elliott's Ferry after its land-owner, and today in Dandridge the narrow Elliott Ferry Pike traverses a quiet residential neighborhood on its downhill course to the French Broad. It's still listed as a public right-of-way.

To George Hance of Camp Verde, writing many years later, Cowan's Ferry was a childhood waypoint, though he would have been too young to remember it. In 1919, he placed John's birth there because, he thought, people could find it on a map. Cowan's was the only prominent landmark near his father's farm, four tumbling narrow dirt miles to the southeast. By the 1940s, however, the Tennessee Valley Authority had impounded the French Broad, and Cowan's Ferry lay beneath Douglas Reservoir. When the reservoir is at full capacity, it laps nearly at Green Berry's old doorstep.

George was off by a year and a few days on John's birthday, but it was an innocent mistake. On two recorded occasions John claimed beginning life on September 7: on his eightieth birthday and in an 1898 guestbook.

"The Diggin's" was an area of Lesser Franklin between Chestnut Hill and Dandridge. Today it reaches westward a few miles from a Bush's Beans factory, visitor displays, and a store and cafeteria complex. Its name is derived from the road connecting Chestnut Hill to town that crossed Hickory Ridge, a stubborn slate barrier that had to be blasted and dug out with long hours of hard labor.

John Hance's most formative years were spent in the shadow of the Diggin's. Diggin's people were even then known as exceptional storytell-ers. Alexander Barn Dickey (1848–1926), known as "Barn," is the best remembered of them—except for John Hance, who was ten years his senior and gone by the time Barn was born. Like Hance, Dickey was called the biggest liar in seven states. One of his tales involved a cow wearing sunglasses with green lenses so she could eat "sage." Then there was the one about the man so old he shriveled up until there was hardly anything left. When his kids needed advice, they'd drop him in a glass of warm water to rehydrate him until he got big enough to talk.[8] The town of Dickey is a tiny rural community, and Dickey Road, about a mile long, is an enjoyable backcountry glide in an old truck at sunset. Barn's birthplace is known, but the building is gone.

Barn Dickey was a mirror-perfect image of John Hance. Speaking to a group about Grand Canyon, Hance said, "a mile and a quarter you go into the solid earth, and if you put your ear to the ground by the river you can hear Chinamen eating rice with their chopsticks."[9] The day after that, rustlers ran off with some of his mules. John tracked them for three days and found their camp at sunset. By then, one of his animals had been turned into an outsized bowl of chili. The rustlers were rough, heavily armed men, and the situation needed fast thinking, so Hance waited in the shadows as the moon rose and the grub was ladled out. Just when the cowboys began to swallow, he yelled out, "Whoa, mule!" and those rustlers nearly choked to death when the mule stopped itself from being swallowed.[10]

Dickey was a part-time casket maker who roamed Lesser Franklin on his days off. He'd arrive unannounced, take a meal, tell some stories, spend the night, and move on at daybreak. That, too, was John Hance in a nutshell. Census records continually locate him at the home or workplace of others rather than his own, supposed, domicile. And just like Barn Dickey, John Hance told stories wherever he went.

Today, Hance stands prominent among Appalachian yarnspinners. His trailblazing hard work put him on the map, but his tall tales are his legacy. Imaginative storytelling was imprinted on him from his days in the Diggin's, and it fit his personality well. Hance's verbal confabulations contained all the elements of the classic yarn: snake oil salesmanship, a clever twist or two in the storyline, and cadenced delivery and mannerisms to match the event. Hance had them all. His guests were entranced by his stories, and one can't help but wonder if the way he told them didn't lend a burnishing luster to his own hardscrabble story.

By 1850, only John Hance Jr. and his immediate family remained in Jefferson County.[11] Many others had relocated to Pulaski County in Missouri's central Ozarks.

Gary Hance is John Jr.'s great-great-grandson. Gary is a slim, fit, erect, five-feet, seven-inch, blue-eyed man who has spent a lifetime around Dandridge. He believes Green Berry and the other family members left Tennessee beginning about 1845. "As far as transportation," Gary Hance claims, "I always thought horse and wagon, although there was river access in Knoxville and river boats that came to Dandridge. But moving household as they did, they probably wouldn't have gone by boat or rail." Getting all the people, stock, tools, and farming implements to Missouri by barge and train would have been an enormous and expensive undertaking, so they went by road. According to Gary Hance, the men made several wagon journeys to construct buildings and work the fields before the women and younger children came across.

Whatever prompted the five-hundred-mile move—a family feud, economic necessity, or better prospects on the western frontier—is unknown, but a contributing factor may have been Tennessee's population, which had doubled during Green's time there. Family illness could have also played a part. Gary Hance's great-grandfather once remarked that "Green Berry & Rebecca moved to Rolla after mother's illness."[12] His mother died in 1908, so it's evident he was referring to his grandmother, Rachael Laight.

Green's Missouri land was remarkably similar to the land left behind in Tennessee. Today, as on Shropshire Hollow Road, Bridge School Road west out of Rolla remains largely unfettered by modern concerns. Five miles south of town, Little Beaver Creek is as small and intimate as Indian Creek, its bridges are still narrow, and some of its pathways remain one-lane gravel. Close to Green's former property, Bridge School Road meets narrow, two-lane Historic Route 66. The surrounding forest is predominately hardwood with pine woodlands to the south. The humid summer hollows are not so close, dark, or steep around Rolla, but that is the only pronounced difference between the two places. In winter, because it is a bit more exposed, Rolla is correspondingly more frostbitten and windswept. For Green and his older brother Crowfert—called Crow—Missouri meant larger, flatter fields with greater corn and wheat harvests.

The 1860 Phelps County census identifies two remarkably similar individuals named John Hance from Tennessee: one was twenty, the other twenty-one. Neither attended school during the year or claimed an estate, but only one rode racehorses for income.[13] The younger man was a farm laborer who lived with Crow and his wife, Mary, ages sixty and forty-seven respectively. The other John Hance, also a farmer, lived one house away with a day laborer from Tennessee named William Bohanon and his wife, who were both in their fifties.

Except for John fibbing about his age, it doesn't matter who is which—and they could certainly be the same person. But that's John Hance. Backwoods animal husbandry was his heritage and mindset. He was slight, strikingly erect, literate to a useful degree, unshaven, and most often clothed in frayed overalls. Raised well outside mainstream American society in steep, heavily wooded ancient limestone canyons, he was sent alone into the forest with a flintlock rifle to shoot wood pigeons and fox squirrels[14] for dinner as early as eight years old, and his father would have considered it an honest beginning. From infancy, Hance knew barnyard animals like a scientist knows his chemicals, and he understood farm tools and their maintenance as well as the turning of the seasons. And even in youth he relished vibrant tall tales told in the language of everyday events.

Three

A SALTED FISH

"They Knocked the Wax Out'en Us"

For much of the Civil War, Missouri remained a violent, politically confused border state. It sent representatives to both the U.S. Congress and the Confederate Congress. Not surprisingly, many Missouri families were torn apart by divided loyalties.

After the southwest branch of the Pacific Railroad reached Rolla in 1860, the threat of war stopped its further progress, and Rolla became headquarters for the Union's Army of the West. That is where, barely a teenager, George Washington Hance joined the Union's quartermaster department. Because he started as a civilian contractor, much of his early military-related work is undocumented, but he perhaps began as a "cavvy boy," or a person who superintended broken-down pack animals. George was reliable and good-natured, able to work extended hours without undue effort. It surely would not have taken long for a superior to notice his enterprising spirit. He was soon outfitting teams and driving them farther afield before being promoted to dispatch rider, which put him beside people who would later facilitate his and John's move to Arizona.

John favored the Confederacy, afterward telling writer George Wharton James he ran away from home to join the cause. He may have been surreptitious enough about it that official records do not reveal his earliest involvement. More than once he remarked on riding with William Clarke Quantrill, mentioning to James in 1895 that "Bill Columbus' regiment . . . was the first outfit I struck, so I joined him, and I assure you we were a great lot of fellows, wild, woolly, and full of tricks!"[1] William Columbus Anderson rode briefly with Quantrill in August 1861 and would have been the man Hance was referring to,[2] but Hance's name is not on muster rolls describing Quantrill's accomplices or activities. The oversight could be explained if Hance accompanied only one raid. Perhaps that was the event he described to a campfire gathering at Grand Canyon's Bright Angel Hotel, telling of a night when horse nippers were used to extract a banker's toenails one at a time until he opened his safe after losing four toenails.[3] It could also be that Hance was mistaking one man for another, in this case Bill Columbus for William O. Coleman.

Hance's Combined Military Service Records (CMSRs) indicate he was enrolled August 1, 1862, in Oregon County, Missouri, on the Arkansas border well south of Rolla. He enlisted for three years of service in Coleman's Regiment Missouri Cavalry. Coleman, however, was already in command of eight cavalry companies and overly busy. When he failed to complete the organization of Hance's unit, those men were dismounted and reassigned.[4]

Hance explained these events to James: "By and by, I joined [Lieutenant] Colonel [John Adams] Schnabel's band of cavalry, a respected outfit under General [Sterling] Price. But 'hoss feed' and man feed were often scarce, and many a time I took a share of the hoss feed for myself. After a while I was dismounted."[5] Hance's CMSRs indicate no association with Schnabel, so he seems to have been speaking of Coleman. But the service records make quite clear that, following the dismounting of Coleman's unit in September, Hance was transferred to Company D, Tenth Missouri Infantry, under the command of Colonel Alexander Early Steen.[6]

Evidence suggests John Hance marched agreeably to war, which says something about him—he didn't have to fight. The Confederacy instituted military conscription for men between the ages of eighteen and thirty-five in April 1862, but it had no way of enforcing its authority on the western frontier. In Missouri, Confederate ranks grew only because recruiters set up temporary camps and scoured the hills for sympathetic, able-bodied men. All a volunteer needed was two feet, four front teeth (to work a powder bag's jess) and enough fingers to handle a shovel and pull a trigger. Hance was qualified, able, and felt duty bound.

The Tenth Missouri Infantry mustered with 650 men at Camp Mulberry, Arkansas, just east of Fort Smith, on November 10, 1862.[7] Like Hance, five out of every nine recruits were farmers, dressed in overalls, armed with their own fowling gun or squirrel rifle, a Navy revolver, and an "Arkansas toothpick," also known as a Bowie knife. Many were illiterate. If, on the off chance Hance was issued a uniform, one of numerous Confederate styles produced, he would have had to make do with what he got—chances were slim the uniform fit him. Hance took what clothing he could get when he could get it, sometimes from a corpse, and that is the awful truth of it. He was also poorly trained and outfitted for the long haul. As the war progressed, he was lucky to have shoes on his feet, if he started with them at all. One-fourth of his battalion did not.

Within a month of the Tenth Infantry's formation, the Battle of Prairie Grove resolved the question of who controlled Arkansas's northwest hill country for the remainder of the war. On December 7, 1862, the Union Army of the Frontier, under Brigadier Generals Francis Herron and James Blunt, numbered some eight thousand soldiers from Arkansas and Missouri, along with men of the Cherokee and Creek Nations. The force was bolstered by forty-four cannons that fired flesh-shredding canisters. The Confederate Army of the Trans-Mississippi consisted of some nine thousand men from Arkansas, Missouri, and Texas; Cherokee and Creek warriors also fought for the South that day. Twenty-two Confederate cannons were commanded by Major General Thomas Hindman, whose troops were noted as "a makeshift force of volunteers and unwilling conscripts . . . malnourished, poorly clad, and lacking in training and equipment."[8]

The end of the story at Prairie Grove is that Hindman initiated events. For much of the battle Colonel Steen's command was perched on a wooded hilltop, today the locus of Prairie Grove Battlefield State Park, overlooking the bottomlands from which Union forces tried to advance. As daylight faded, the rebels mounted several charges in an effort to prevail. In their final attempt, a huge surprise to Union troops, the Tenth Infantry and other units swept "out of the timber in solid column . . . lifting their guns with fixed bayonets above their heads. They came downhill with a yell, like 7,000 demons"[9] (the famous "Confederate yelp" from the Battle of First Manassas).[10] When the Confederate units were within three hundred yards of Union lines, the Eleventh Kansas Infantry's cannons opened fire with double-shotted grape and canister, ripping yawning holes in Steen's column. Steen died instantly from a head wound. John Hance would have been only yards from him.

After the bloody day-long engagement, a thirty-six-hour truce was arranged to attend the wounded, gather dead, eat, rest, and prepare for the next round of fighting. Having joined the battle with ammunition sufficient only for the day, Hindman was short of armament, rations, and other supplies; his supply train was broken down thirty miles away. After building decoy campfires, his troops sneaked off in the darkness, their wagon wheels muzzled by blankets tied around them. The number of killed, missing, and wounded at Prairie Grove was nearly 1,300 on both sides. In John's regiment, thirty-one died, sixty-two were wounded, and three went missing.

The Tenth Missouri Infantry retreated unpursued to Van Buren, Arkansas, and then retired until the following May to winter quarters near Little Rock.[11] The encampment was laid out along military lines, with privates like Hance along its outer perimeter and other privates in tents or small wooden enclosures close by. A nearby field was used for drills and maneuvers, with company wagons, armament, and stock also assembled there. That winter the Tenth Missouri Infantry kept time to military standard with bugle calls to announce events. Days were spent as follows: gathering firewood and tending fires; standing inspections; performing drills; maintaining stock, equipment, and firearms; walking sentry; playing cards; partaking in religious services or private prayers; and singing Confederacy favorites such as "Bonnie Blue Flag," "The Wearing of the Gray," "Red, White, and Blue," "Dixieland," and the popular love song "Lorena."

Breaking camp in May, the Tenth Missouri Infantry proceeded to Jacksonport to join other infantry units. In late June, these combined forces moved southeast to attack Helena, Arkansas. The Tenth Infantry was commanded by General M. M. Parsons, under General Sterling Price. Price's long military history included service in frontier New Mexico protecting Bent's Fort, afterward turning to the Confederacy and leading a horse-borne renegade outfit on raids across Arkansas, though he lost that round to John Charles Frémont. Price knew how to organize and move people. His conscripts, however, were not up to the task. From Jacksonport they made an agonizingly slow twelve-day march across flooded river bottoms, arriving in Helena uncomfortably wet, tired, hungry, and disheveled late on July 3.

Helena's riverside hilltop batteries guarded Union freight headed downstream to the siege of Vicksburg. Union general Benjamin Prentiss, although vastly outnumbered the following morning, superbly defended the hilltop fortifications, including: Rightor Hill with Batteries A and B north of the city, Graveyard Hill immediately west of town with Battery C, and Hindman Hill with Battery D located south of Helena near the home of General Thomas Hindman.

Confederate commander of the West, Edmund Kirby Smith, with Lieutenant General Theophilus Holmes, planned the attack. Holmes sent his eight thousand men into battle with the cry, "The invaders have been driven from every point in Arkansas save one—Helena. We go to retake it."[12] It seemed a sure thing. Helena's heavily armored garrison had only four thousand defenders because sixteen thousand men had been dispatched to the Vicksburg campaign.

Parson's attack on Graveyard Hill began at four o'clock in the morning. The Tenth Missouri Infantry quickly overran Battery C—only to discover its cannons had been disabled before the Federalists withdrew. Now disadvantaged, the Tenth Infantry came under continual heavy fire. Regrouping, its men charged the star-shaped Fort Curtis entrenchment shortly downslope in town. The attempt failed, with heavy casualties. While this was going on, the Confederate assaults on Rightor and Hindman Hills were beaten back, all while the Union's timber-clad USS *Tyler* cruised the shoreline, laying down over four hundred exploding shells. It wasn't long before the rugged battlefield was littered with rebel bodies. Survivors retreated to the closest steep ravines for cover. "We attacked Howard," Hance told James, "but he was too strong for us and beat us and knocked the wax out'en us. Yes, they sure knocked us back. Out of eighty-nine that 'started the fight' (as we call it), we only mustered out sixteen."[13] At ten thirty that morning, realizing he would not prevail, Holmes withdrew, trapping large numbers of his men where they lay sheltering in Helena's precipitate defiles.

Union losses were 57 dead, 146 wounded, and 36 captured or missing. Confederate losses were exponentially higher: 173 killed, 687 wounded, and 776 captured or missing. In the Tenth Missouri Infantry, 11 died, 141 were wounded, and 237 were captured, with John Hance among them.

Hance's CMSR card describing this event simply reads: "Hance, John [and 724 other Confederate prisoners]. The above-named Prisoners of War were forwarded to Memphis, Tennessee, July 4th, 1863, on steamer

'Tycoon' [under the charge of Major Edward Right] and sent from Memphis to Cairo, Ill., July 5th, 1863, on steamer 'Silver Moon,'"[14] and from there transferred farther upstream to Alton Federal Military Prison.

Alton was the place its former POWs visited after the war, to acquire rocks for use as their gravestones. John Hance survived eight months at Alton. All he saw of the town on his arrival that overcast, windswept, and rainy evening was the jetty from which he marched one hundred yards directly into the compound. Alton was described as an "old State penitentiary [1833–1860], which was [put out of use] on account of the unhealthiness of the place. The privates are crowded into the old workshops, which are more filthy than the worst negro cabins in the South, and they have no way to remedy it. Water is scarce and very bad, although the upper Mississippi is flowing within one hundred yards, it is far beyond the reach of a prisoner as if it was a thousand miles off."[15]

When brought out of mothballs in February 1862, Alton was planned for 800 prisoners, but within days of opening its population exceeded that with the capture of Forts Henry and Donelson in northwest Tennessee.[16] For the remainder of the war, Alton housed between 1,200 and 1,500 prisoners, and more than 1,600 when Lee surrendered at Appomattox in 1865.

Alton's central feature was a three-story brick building with 256 cells, each measuring four feet by seven feet; longer rooms divided by wooden partitions went to officers. Imposing stone buildings and outsized wooden sheds dominated the yard where the latrines and tainted drinking water were located, all surrounded by a high, impregnable series of buildings and stone walls that left only sky to the west and little else to the north, south, and east. The only way out was up a tall stepladder.[17]

Summer days were hot, with intense lightning bursts and heavy downpours. As the months wore on, only stagnant humidity prevailed. Winter days were short and cold, with overcast skies and damp snowfalls. Smallpox was the most dreaded disease, presenting itself in October 1862, and by the time Hance arrived months later it had reached epidemic proportions and spread to town. Because of transfers and other alignments in military rotation, it quickly sprawled throughout the entire prison system. Pneumonia, scurvy, typhoid, rubella, malaria, chronic dysentery, and anemia were also prevalent at Alton.

Hance spent three weeks in Alton's hospital. His CMSRs offer no diagnosis, only stating he began treatment on December 17, 1863, was returned to quarters after two weeks, and was back in the hospital between January 11 and 18, 1864. He survived while up to a dozen a day did not.

Hance's transfer to Fort Delaware Prison on Pea Patch Island was initiated February 9, 1864. In legend, Pea Patch Island raised its slight head after a shipwreck washed peas onto a shoal in the middle of northern Chesapeake Bay south of Wilmington. The peas took hold and flowered and a sandbar developed. Its actual history is less romantic. An 1813 earthen breastwork had to be dismantled in 1821 because it was sinking into the river. A second masonry installment then burned in 1832. The massive stone structure now in place was begun in 1835 and completed in 1848. A protective moat, outer moat, and series of canals were added in 1859. During Hance's stay on Pea Patch Island, the island comprised 178 acres, 128 of them bogs, with the remaining 50 acres covered by prisoner barracks, post hospital (600 beds), the fort, and its ancillary structures.[18]

Fort Delaware was called "a perfect Hell on earth" and "the Death Pen" by POWs.[19] Its commandant during Hance's confinement was Albin Francisco Schoepf, a deaf general brought out of retirement. One of Schoepf's rules was "one man, one blanket." If by slim chance a prisoner owned an overcoat *and* a blanket, he had to surrender one of them. Schoepf's attention to detail was especially egregious because he allowed his staff to mete out discipline as they saw fit. With this freedom, his guards transformed Pea Patch Island into a brutal environment.

Fort Delaware began March 1864 with 2,600 prisoners. By the first of April, 3,218 more had arrived, Hance among them (on March 5 after a four-hour steamboat ride from Philadelphia). Many of his fellow prisoners were abnormally thin, dressed like him in tattered, threadbare clothing. Marched off the ship from the island's eastside landing, they crossed the wooden pier, proceeded down a rock causeway beside the inlet moat, walked around the enormous granite fort in a southern semicircle (Hance would never be inside it), and then headed directly north to a set of long wooden barracks called the "bull pen," a series of tall, one-story dormitory structures festering on stilts. There sat and slept John Hance, already a "salted fish" with eight months behind him, for twelve more months.

Fort Delaware's numbers continued to rise after Hance's arrival, once peaking at just under 9,500. At war's end, some 7,000 prisoners were

Erected over the footprint of an original building, the recreated prison barracks at Fort Delaware State Park give a realistic feel to where Hance lived, slept, and sat as a Confederate POW. Author photo.

confined there. Enlisted men were separated into "divisions" of about one hundred men led by an informally elected non-commissioned officer and fellow prisoner. This "chief" played the role of an ordinary first company sergeant, leading his men to meals and roll calls or on rare work details.[20] Hance was accountable to Division Sixteen, made up of privates like him from Missouri. It's not known where the Division Sixteen dormitory was located, but a facsimile barracks has been built on the footprint of one of the original buildings. It's only a small part of what was a very long, roughly boarded series of one-floored, two-story structures joined together. The new building would house about two hundred men. The "furniture" in that enormous room consisted of two long walls of three-tiered wooden bunks, two coal-burning cast iron stoves, two small card tables, and three chairs.

John G. Wilson, a private in Company F, Russell's Fourth Alabama Cavalry, arrived at Fort Delaware in March 1864 and was housed in

Division Ten, a few doors from Hance. "Our barracks were more comfortable [than Camp Morton, Indiana, where he was imprisoned during the winter of 1863–64], but the rations were miserably insufficient, and prisoners who could not obtain money from friends with which to procure extra supplies from the sutler suffered the pangs of hunger day and night and reduced to skeletons, and eaten up by scurvy from scantly and unwholesome food, fell ready victims to disease, and died by the hundreds."[21]

Hance spent three continuous months in the Fort Delaware hospital. From November 22, 1864, until February 23, 1865, his illness was again unrecorded. Hugh Simmons of the Fort Delaware Society believes he "suffered from chronic diarrhea and from congestion of the lungs (catarrh, pneumonia, etc)." In going through the fort's files, Simmons discovered a "Hanie" in Company D, Tenth Missouri Infantry. "I found no one surnamed Hanie in the 10th Missouri CMSRs," he noted, "so by the process of elimination this record belongs to John Hance." Other corruptions to John's name occurred during his time in prison, but the poor conditions generally preclude the notion he was having fun with words—it's more likely his southern drawl was given to unreliable transcription.

News of General Lee's surrender swept the Fort Delaware yard on April 10, 1865. That same day, Hance was sent by train to Cairo, Illinois, and from there to New Orleans on a paddlewheel steamer,[22] but it wasn't because the war was ending. Rather, it was due to the long-standing exchange imbalance between the federal Department of the Gulf at New Orleans and the Confederate Trans-Mississippi in Shreveport. Because Hance was from a Trans-Mississippi unit, he and others were chosen to make the numbers right.

Abraham Lincoln was assassinated four days after Lee's surrender. While we don't know how Lincoln's death played with Hance, there is a record of its aftermath at the prison he'd just left: "We were informed privately by a sentinel that if more than three of us were seen together . . . we would be fired upon. But before many hours elapsed the commandant learned we were in sympathy with Mr. Lincoln, abhorred the assassination, and were horrified at the thought of falling into Andy Johnson's hands. The order to shoot us was at once countermanded."[23]

Beginning at Cairo on April 26, Hance traveled downstream under the confinement of Colonel C. C. Dwight, federal agent of exchange. On May 4, he was transferred from New Orleans to the mouth of the Red River, Louisiana (near Simmesport, Pointe Coupee Parish), where his exchange would take place.[24]

While there was no longer a Confederacy, what remained of the Tenth Missouri Infantry and surrounding units was subsumed into the Tenth Consolidated Regiment, Missouri Volunteer Infantry. Hance was assigned to Company One of this new regiment. Because its commander, General Edmund Kirby Smith, was in Texas at Galveston Bay, the war-concluding papers were not signed by him until three weeks later. Those same documents had to make their way back to Camp Allen before Hance was paroled—a second time—on June 8, 1865.

"Bleached and softened,"[25] Hance and so many emaciated others like him boarded the steamer *E. H. Fairchild* and returned upstream to St. Louis. From there he went overland to his home in Rolla.

Four

ACROSS THE PLAINS

"Water You Could Shake Like a Blanket"

According to his brother George Washington Hance, John Hance returned to Rolla at the close of the war. By one account, George "was at that time field messenger, carrying dispatches for Major E. B. Grimes, chief depot quartermaster, district of Rolla, Missouri. John hired to L. B. [Lorenzo] Hickok, a brother to 'Wild Bill' Hickok, scout during the war, later on the plains, and came to Fort Leavenworth, Kansas [with George], in September 1865."[1]

John gave it more bounce, reported by a Grand Canyon guest in wonderfully depicted Hance-speak. John left Missouri, he said, because he stole a rope. "When told 'that was no reason fer a man ter haf ter leave,' John, he said, 'Wall, thar war a mule tied ter the other end 'o the rope.'"[2]

George worked with Lorenzo and James Butler Hickok for three years during the war and two years in Kansas.[3] George was John's principal biographer during John's life on the plains.[4] With rare exceptions, most of what we know about John's life during this time is what George offers up, and there is not much of it: "John served on the plains as teamster and also as dispatch carrier for over two years, then came to New Mexico in November, 1867 [and] was on the Navajo Indian expedition from Fort Sumner on the Pecos River, N. M., to Fort Defiance, Arizona in the summer of 1868. He [and George] left Fort Union, N. M., the first of November 1868, and arrived at Prescott December 4, 1868."[5]

Following his long imprisonment, hiring on to Lorenzo Hickok was the best thing that could have happened to John Hance. He was fed, clothed, paid, and busy, without time to think about when his body was thin as a rail and his clothes were rags. Heading to Leavenworth, Hance probably didn't start out with much except his bedroll, a Navy revolver, gloves, a waxed rain slicker, a satchel of papers, a few photos, husbandry tools, a knife, some blankets, a tinderbox, and fishing line. It's reasonable to picture him clothed in a buckskin jacket and chaps, with a six-shooter and knife sheathed at his waist, buying whiskey and axle grease at the sutler's store. His hair was long, greasy, parted in the middle, and down past his shoulders.

Lorenzo Butler Hickok, long obscured by his younger brother's fearsome reputation, deserves more attention in America's frontier literature. Known as "Shanghai" because of his supple six-foot, two-inch frame, or sometimes "Tame Bill," his sister considered him "the very opposite of James. His word was always the law because he was never known to tell an untruth nor did he ever have to shoot a man to enforce obedience." Her brother Howard agreed: "I have never met his equal in the homely character that go to make good citizenship honorable, thoughtful, unselfish, brave, and unassuming. He was a bachelor, a plainsman, and in early youth was called 'Billy Barnes,'" a Texan whose name he and James sometimes assumed, hence "Tame Bill" and "Wild Bill."[6]

Moreover, Lorenzo Hickok "was celebrated as one of the best wagon masters in charge of the great Government trains with all their responsibilities. He became famous for his courage, ability to command men, to defend the interests of his employees, to stand off the Indians and bandits that preyed on the wagon trains." Respected for his jurisprudence by the men who worked for him, "Lorenzo came home after spending ten years in government service with supply wagons. Strenuous work with little glory and less appreciation."[7]

A teamster was normally up at three o'clock in the morning, on the road by daybreak, and in camp by three in the afternoon. That meant rising in the middle of the night, eating breakfast, outfitting teams with a confounding array of leather accrument, and connecting chains by the aid of strong lanterns, sometimes in terrible weather. A military supply train consisted of a wagon master and his assistant wagon master(s), blacksmith(s), a packmaster and his cargadores (or baggage handlers), and a cook and his swampers, normally accompanied by mounted cavalry. Infantry soldiers also attended Hickok for part of his first outward journey. Each wagon was supervised by a man who either walked beside, rode on, or sat abreast his wagon. The miles-long conveyance was made up of freighting wagons, some dead-weighted to as much as four thousand pounds, their back wheels tall as a man, with sturdy brake blocks two feet long. With a large interior capacity, they could haul massive loads depending on the span of mules or oxen used.

Enormous danger lurked in that sort of work, a lot of schlep and muck and rough-handed midnight toil. And after being worn down by long dark hours patrolling camp perimeters, the glory only came in brief, dusty patches, assuming a man lived until morning. Hance did his job with that in mind, either saddled to a horse or mule or driving one of many teams stretched long across the wide Kansas hill country.

Hance told a story about his time on the plains to Hamlin Garland. Garland, the product of a homesteading family like Hance's, pioneered agrarian realism when recording Midwest farm life as he experienced it. Garland understood John Hance's mindset better than most, and he did a good job describing his subject. He first visited Grand Canyon in 1896, using it to inform several amusing pieces that explored Hance's storytelling in vibrant detail. One of these articles was titled "Were Drunk on Water."

Hance led Garland, along with an army lieutenant and his wife, to the Colorado via the Red Canyon trail on a hot summer day. Arriving at Hance Rapid, Garland fetched a pail of "Colorado Red" river water and hauled it back to camp. The lieutenant's wife asked if he would drink it. Garland replied in the affirmative, saying it "was only good, wholesome diet" and that he'd been forced to drink water "corrupt with carrion" on some of his patrols.

Though the lieutenant's wife shuddered, Hance came to life, and the story he told describes the events loosely associated with the Battle of Beecher Island in September 1868—and most of his particulars are actually accurate. Said Hance: "I was guide to old [Brevet] Colonel [Henry C.] Bankhead [captain, Fifth Infantry, commanding Fort Wallace] in an expedition against the Cheyennes, and I just reckon you ain't got anything worse in Arizony, lieutenant. There was no water fit to drink for plum 200 miles."

Then an emergency intervened and the men garrisoned at Cheyenne Wells, Colorado, required the Fifth Infantry's immediate assistance, so without refreshment they set out. Along the route they had to "drink water that was stinkin'," Hance said. "When hit come to haulin' out dead buffalos ... why we thought we'd reached the limit, but when it come to usin' water that you could take hold of an' shake like a blanket.... We biled hit and rebiled hit and skimmed hit like you would suet and thickened hit with coffee, but we had to drink hit at last. Hit were skunk at the beginnin' and skunk at the end."

Hance's commanding officer, knowing he couldn't control his men's thirst, told Hance to ride ahead and "pull in a good hour ahead of us and tell the commanding officer to have every damn thing that will hold water filled up, for these boys are sure goin' to stampede when they smell water."

John pulled out across the sand. "My life and soul! But hit was hot. I could hear the red hot iron hiss and spatter off my horse's shoes," he claimed, "but I rolled the rowel into him cruel an' we kep' movin'."

Finally, Hance spotted vegetation: "I hope Canaan will look as good to me when I die as them green trees did. The horse broke for hit an' I let him go. My tongue was as big as your arm an' scalin' off like a sick pickerel. When I rolled off my horse he was up to his eyes in water an' the sergeant splashed me with a bucketful. Elijah's God! I couldn't get near enough of hit.... I laid there soakin' water and my horse walked like a carpenter's bench."

When Hance could "set [his] teeth on the outside o' [his] tongue," anything that held water was filled and set out for use. "Pretty soon we seen a line of alkali a-flyin' on the swell.... The horses had nostrils on 'em like the bass horn in a brass band a reekin' with sweat an' dust, an' a-squealin' like they was plum crazy. The men were leanin' forward and a-poundin' for life—seemed like their necks was a foot long. They tumbled into one hidgous mass at the wells," Hance remembered, with twenty men at every barrel "fightin' the horses back an' tearing at each other like wildcats."

That night, the colonel told him, "John, no use tryin' to put out pickets. You and the sergeant just keep an eye out, an' we'll let the boys camp around the water bar'ls an' trust to luck."

Hance closed his story with the following: "The boys was just plum drunk on water—water drunk. They yelled and grunted and cussed in their delight ... All night long you'd see a clum o' men 'round a bar'l drinkin' an' a-gruntin'—'Oh, that's good!' and such like things. They were sure 'nough cotton dry, an' it did seem like they would get soaked up ag'in—but they was all right in a couple of days."[8]

Time and again, however, John and his brother delivered the supplies and messages Uncle Sam gave over to their care. They and the people working beside them were the main cogs in the westward-spinning wheel, one that moved quickly. So quickly, in fact, that the quartermaster general was unable to report the number of freight wagons used on the frontier in 1865 (meaning anywhere west of Fort Leavenworth, Kansas). He could, however, cite the total cost of transporting stores between Leavenworth and Fort Union, New Mexico Territory: nearly $26 million in 2017 dollars. The grain alone delivered to Fort Union cost $69,100 in 1865; the fare for just one bushel of corn was $9.44.

According to George Hance, Hickok's Leavenworth expedition departed Rolla on September 5, 1865, with two hundred wagons of government supplies to support the upcoming western Indian campaigns. The wagons were towed by six-mule teams with six hundred loose mules following. Military wagon trains traveled two to three miles an hour—up to thirty miles a day under ideal conditions, but a more conservative average would be about eighteen miles a day due to the enormity of the train. With this in mind, Hickok's 250-mile journey to Fort Leavenworth would have taken some two weeks.

At Leavenworth, George Hance continued, "an expedition was organized the last day of September to establish permanent military garrisons along the Smokey Hill River. We had one hundred and eight six-mule teams. These were to haul forage and rations for four Companies of the First United States Calvary and four Companies of the First United States Infantry."[9]

The seven hundred–mile Smoky Hill Trail began near Atchison, Kansas, and trended south to Leavenworth, where it turned west, eventually ending at Denver, Colorado. Laid out in September 1858, it was the shortest route through Kansas to the gold rush then sweeping Pikes Peak. Paralleling the Smoky Hill River for much of its course, the trail was rich in verdant grasses, enormous buffalo herds, timber, and dependable water.

The Butterfield Overland Despatch (BOD)[10] began operations along the Smoky Hill in June 1865. Choosing from an offering of tri-weekly departures, voyagers endured every dust-filled bump of that twelve-day journey for one hundred dollars. But the influx of whites, compounded by grievances suffered during the Sand Creek massacre of 1864 in Colorado, brought BOD stations and stages under continued Indian attack. It wasn't long before a dozen or more wagons with military escort was considered the minimum outfit for safe transit. And it was no accident that army forts and outposts quickly grew up beside BOD stations. That the Hance brothers were on the plains was in large part due to both the BOD stage and the Union Pacific Railroad, also called the Kansas Division of the Union Pacific and renamed the Kansas Pacific in 1869,[11] its tracks inching farther westward every day.

Resupplying at Leavenworth, Lorenzo Hickok coursed westward to Fort Riley, a presumed eight-day journey. Since 1852 Fort Riley had guarded nearby portions of the Oregon and Santa Fe Trails from Indians, horse thieves, and bandits. Located 140 miles from Leavenworth near Manhattan, Kansas, it stands at the confluence of the Republican and Smoky Hill Rivers.

In the fall of 1865, Fort Riley amounted to a few city blocks of red brick and gray limestone buildings. Reassigned from Rolla, the assistant quartermaster brought along Wild Bill Hickok, appointing him deputy U.S. marshal. He would be back and forth across Kansas during the coming months in a variety of roles, visiting Lorenzo and the Hance brothers in passing.

Lorenzo's outfit next proceeded ninety-five miles west to Camp Ellsworth, near today's town of Ellsworth, described then as "forty men, four women, eight boys, and seven girls. There are also fourteen horses, and about twenty-nine and one-half dogs. There is neither a cow, hog, cat, nor chicken around, but there are plenty of rattlesnakes, gophers, owls, mice, and prairie dogs."[12]

After relocation, Camp Ellsworth settled into the present-day wayside community of Kanopolis and was renamed Fort Harker. John and George Hance would have witnessed the change in locale. When they first hove into view, to drop half of their accompanying cavalry and supplies, Fort Harker was also a BOD base station with a small bank of people, equipment, and stock.

Mark Twain's *Roughing It* describes a BOD station: "The buildings were long, low huts, made of sundried, mud-colored bricks, laid up without mortar (adobes, the Spaniards call these bricks, and Americans shorten it to 'dobies). The roofs, which had no slant to them worth speaking of, were thatched and then sodded or covered with a thick layer of earth, and from this sprung a pretty rank growth of weeds and grass. It was the first time we had ever seen a man's front yard on top of his house."[13]

The railway arrived at Fort Harker that fall. Beside telling the end of BOD's local enterprise, this brought with it an increase in Indian hostilities. Comanches destroyed the heavy iron rails, scattering them about. Repair crews hastened to the field but they, too, came under attack.

Lorenzo Hickok and company next moved sixty miles farther west to deliver Fort Fletcher's first supplies and foot soldiers. During their travels over the following months, John and his brother saw Fort Fletcher morph into a relocated compound renamed Fort Hays—and they may have been present during the Big Creek flood of June 23, 1867, which necessitated the change in location. According to witness Jennie Barnitz, "Oh! what a night. At about 3 O'C a.m. Gen. Smith came to our tent and screamed, 'For God's sake Barnitz get up, we are under water.' I was obliged to look for my things and got dressed soon. With one shoe & one of Albert's boots & took my watch, jewelry & money and went out.... The ladies were out half dressed, with hair over their shoulders, & to add to the terror of the scene, drowning men went floating past us shrieking for help."[14]

Lorenzo's train proceeded 130 miles west to arrive at Camp Pond Creek, today called Wallace, then went another 130 miles west with about sixty teams to Fort Wise, Colorado. Wise was created in 1860 at a location that, like other forts in the West, changed due to floods, unsanitary living conditions, and, especially, malaria. In 1866, Fort Wise was relocated a third time and became Fort Lyon.

At Fort Lyon, Lorenzo reloaded with supplies for the infantry back at Fort Wallace. From there, wrote George Hance, "most of the transportation returned to Fort Leavenworth except for Hickok's train that again reloaded and proceeded to Fort Hays, Fort Harker and Fort Riley."[15]

That winter Lorenzo and company were caught in such a terrific blizzard that landmarks were obliterated and his men burned wagons to keep from freezing at night. Hickok thought they had strayed from their course and called a meeting with the commander of his military escort. The officer thought little of it and ordered them straight ahead. Hickok reluctantly agreed, and they pressed on another day without signs of Smoky Hill River. The next morning, Hickok changed course. He picked Hance to lead a small group and find the river, setting them in relays on a route contrary to his escort's direction.

When the officer noticed this, he confronted Hickok. "What the hell do you think you're doing? I am in command of this outfit and they go as I say." Hickok countered that the officer was mistaken, that he was simply an escort and that he, Hickok, was responsible for the safety of his men, mules, and cargo. The captain retorted, "You order these men to change their course and follow me or I will have my men overpower you and lead you behind the wagon from here to Fort Riley." Hickok told him directly, "If you give that order I will kill you before you can countermand it."[16] The officer relented. "All right," he said, "we will try your way for a day." Eight stormy hours later, Hance sent word that he had found trees bounding the river. "The news had scarcely been conveyed when the mules smelled the water and with one accord all raised their heads and brayed lustily."[17]

Back at Fort Riley, George Hance rode dispatch. He also worked out of Fort Hays and Fort Harker in Kansas, and Fort McPherson in Nebraska, in early 1868. Before becoming an assistant wagon master at Fort Union, George was back and forth with mail, telegraphs, and dispatches for George Armstrong Custer's chief of staff. John offered a similar, if vague, resumé when interviewed by George Wharton James.[18]

By mid-October 1867, Hickok and his party had recrossed the plains westward and arrived at Fort Union, New Mexico,[19] an enormous complex nearing completion after six years of construction. Spread across four hundred acres, the "third" Fort Union was one hundred miles northeast of Santa Fe at the junction of the Santa Fe Trail and Cimarron Cutoff. It was easily the largest military presence anywhere in New Mexico Territory. With enormous quartermaster and ordinance depots, it functioned less to pacify natives than as a transportation and warehousing hub where supplies and provisions were stored for deliveries farther west. It was at Fort Union that a plan to quit military work and emigrate to Prescott, Arizona Territory, seems to have crystalized with the Hance brothers.

Except for the Mexican War adventures of Stephen Watts Kearney and Kit Carson along the Gila River, Arizona Territory was so far west as to be off America's cognitive map. In 1868 there was nothing to it except

Apaches, cactus deserts, and Tucson, a sleepy little town. As relayed in the press, Arizona was fractional and monochromatic, about a quarter of it "fit for agriculture and grazing, about one-fourth a barren, sandy waste, about three-eighths is covered with lava from extinct volcanos, and almost one-eighth may be put down as mineral, or where the bed rock is of primitive formation, and would by its appearance induce a miner to look for mineral."[20]

All that was true. However, because John and George Hance lived in the underbelly of western expansion, they knew it was swelling with military activity that required support services. A deciding factor in their move may have been the railway's ever-westing terminus, as teamsters were no longer needed where the train went, and it chased them farther toward the setting sun every day. They must have envisioned opportunities greater than what they were used to, and they do not seem to have hesitated in making the choice.

First, however, in the late spring of 1868 they made their way south with Lorenzo Hickok to Fort Sumner, New Mexico, and Bosque Redondo (the Round Forest) near the lower Pecos River.

Between 1864 and 1866 over fifty forced marches along various routes delivered eighty-five hundred Navajos to Bosque Redondo. Collectively, these forced migrations are remembered as the Long Walk. About five hundred Apaches from southern New Mexico were also rounded up. All were put to work constructing irrigation canals, planting corn, and making and laying adobe bricks. By 1867, however, beetles had destroyed the crops and floods had erased the irrigation dams. As a result, some three thousand Native Americans died from disease and starvation.

On May 28, 1868, with Kit Carson five days deceased and Fort Sumner's flag at half-staff, General William Tecumseh Sherman arrived at Bosque Redondo. On June 1, Sherman, acting as an Indian peace commissioner and agent, signed the Treaty of Bosque Redondo with Navajo (Diné) leaders. The document granted the Navajo a reservation, education for their children, seeds, agricultural implements, and other provisions, as well as "rights of the Navajos to be protected, establishment of railroads and forts, compensation to tribal members, and arrangements for the return of Navajos to the reservation established by the treaty."[21]

The return from Bosque Redondo began in mid-June with some seven thousand Navajos ushering forty-five hundred sheep, one thousand goats, and fifteen hundred horses northwest along the Pecos River, escorted by four U.S. Cavalry companies under Major Charles J. Whiting.[22] Lorenzo Hickok, with George Hance as his assistant wagon master, was responsible for the progress of fifty-six wagons that carried the halt, infirm, and blind, as well as food and supplies. John Hance drove one of those wagons.[23] The ten-mile-long column reached the Rio Grande at a late-season meltwater high on July 6. To get across, one writer claimed, "Preparations were made for ferrying the expedition over the river ... in which three cables were twisted into a hawser 21 inches thick and some six hundred feet long, for swinging the boats across."[24] Getting all wagons, people, and stock to the other side took a week. After passing Mount Taylor, one of four Navajo sacred mountains, the column arrived at Fort Wingate, New Mexico, in late July, where dispersal began. The return "ended" at Fort Defiance, Arizona.

Jeremiah William Sullivan was energetic, widely traveled, accomplished, and successful in his many pursuits. Born in Picton, Ontario, Canada, in 1843, he was lumbering in Pennsylvania's Susquehanna Valley by 1865. By 1867 he was a Fort Leavenworth carpenter, and in 1867 he accompanied the Hance brothers to Fort Union. "Hon. Jerry W. Sullivan drove team for me when I was government wagonmaster. The Indians killed 8 and wounded 4 of the lot the first year," wrote George Hance, describing life shortly after arrival in Prescott. "That white spot on J.W. Sullivan's neck is an Indian souvenir."[25]

In early 1868, Sullivan hauled army supplies from Fort Union to Fort Bowie, Arizona, where he supposedly heard stories of gold discoveries made near Prescott and decided to have a look.[26] In Albuquerque with the Hance brothers after they had returned the Navajo to their homeland, Sullivan recalled, "there were only four of us had enough to buy riding animals, so we bought ponies for the rest of the fellows as we had to have a large party for protection" against Indian attack.[27]

George Hance supplied a manifest of this party and it corrects a long-standing misconception about his younger brother Jim. In George's hand, John holds top billing, probably in deference to his older sibling. George comes next. William Breed and the others, among them a family of four, follow him. Jim Hance is absent[28]—nor is he mentioned in George's other notes concerning the emigrant journey. From this it appears Jim did not travel to Arizona with his brothers in 1868.

Sullivan's personal outfit included a wagon team, two mules, four big cavalry horses, and ponies condemned by the U.S. Cavalry, all acquired for eighty dollars at Fort Union. He reportedly added five thousand pounds of rancid bacon in Albuquerque, allegedly selling some of it on the spot and saving the best cuts for Prescott.[29] Folklore, possibly via John Hance, relates this same pork fortifying the ramparts at Fort Craig, New Mexico, when the fort was attacked by Confederate forces six years earlier.

The Hance-Sullivan party[30] departed Albuquerque in early November. By horseback and wagon the group proceeded to Zuni Pueblo, where, a month earlier, trader Solomon Barth and his group had straggled in naked and famished after a horrifying confrontation with the Chiricahua Apache leader Cochise. All would have been murdered had Pedro, one of Cochise's party, not known someone in Barth's group.[31]

Four years later, Al Doyle and his group followed the Hance-Sullivan party along the same route to Sunset Crossing—today's Winslow, Arizona—before turning south on a new road to Camp Verde. Conditions had not changed much, as Doyle noted. "We never saw a white man," he said, "and it was a lonesome, dreary old tramp, as we were compelled to travel mainly at night on account of the activity of the measly Apaches who seemed to bob up at any old place, any old time, with a strong hankering after our top knots."[32]

After Zuni, the Hance-Sullivan group turned west, toward the San Francisco Peaks, traveling on Edward Fitzgerald Beale's route along the thirty-fifth parallel. They passed Navajo Springs, east of today's Petrified Forest National Park, and Register Rock just west of the Little Colorado River near Leupp, Arizona. That day, Register Rock framed the San Francisco Peaks in striking, snow-clad allure, but they apparently passed through before people started chiseling their names and dates into that house-sized chunk of orange sandstone. Continuing straight on toward the mountain along the rutted furrows of Beale's road (still easily identified today), they gained elevation, working through two feet of snow in the high pines around Antelope Springs, today's Old Town Flagstaff. There they camped[33] and celebrated Thanksgiving with seven turkeys, all shot by John.[34] The previous day he'd killed as many deer with a Henry repeating rifle, a breech-loading, lever-action "sixteen-shooter" much revered during the Civil War. It came into wide use while John Hance was in prison.

The party proceeded westward through Garland Prairie to an old government trail called Overland Road. Created as an expeditious short-cut to gold discoveries along Lynx Creek near Prescott, the route veered southwest of Bill Williams Mountain, where the party slogged through four feet of snow,[35] then trended almost directly southwest and down into Chino Valley, a small community of some thirty rough-hewn farms fifteen miles north of Prescott on a plain of tall grass, ephemeral streams, and towering cottonwoods.

"About the first white man we struck on our trip was old man Bang-hart," Sullivan told one writer.[36] George Banghart was Canadian, a farmer from the old country who settled with his wife and mother-in-law in Chino Valley.

George Hance noted their Prescott arrival on December 4, but Sullivan quotes John as saying they landed in Prescott about December 2.[37] Regardless, the event was reported in the *Weekly Arizona Miner* on December 12: "Since our last issue, about thirty single men, and one family have arrived from the East, and most of the men are preparing to go to Black Canyon Diggings" in the eastern Bradshaw Mountains.

But the Hance brothers were not interested in prospecting. A month after arriving they bought land and began furrowing. George joined the Prescott Masons, listing his birthplace as "Swinesville, Tennessee,"[38] and his residence as Granite Creek. Nor did the gold diggings attract Jerry Sullivan. In Prescott, because horses and mules were at a premium, he is said to have sold two mules for $500, two of the cavalry horses for $400, and the other two for $450.

What Sullivan really did, however, was go work for C. C. Bean in Williamson Valley. Born in 1828 in New Hampshire, Curtis Coe Bean was schooled at Exeter Academy and Union College. In New York City during the early 1850s he worked in the federal custom house and also for a brokerage firm. He studied law and was admitted to the bar but lost interest. In 1864, he moved to Columbia, Tennessee, then to Nashville. Living in Prescott by June 1868, he became of one John Hance's longest running Yavapai acquaintances.

A short, bald-headed man, Bean was busily engaged in mining, farming, raising stock, handling military contracts, and playing the Prescott real estate market. His wide swath across Yavapai was mentioned in the local press as gossipy, informational tidbits. One day he'd be returning from a mine, while the next week he was home in Williamson Valley planning improvements to his ranch. Then he was giving a speech, riding a train, or walking down the street. He was also a member of the Territorial Senate in 1879 and a one-term Republican nonvoting member in the forty-ninth United States Congress.

Sullivan's first job for Bean was herding cattle, but Apaches continuously stole and killed the animals and that enterprise was abandoned until conditions improved. Sullivan also cut trees and hauled them to a lumber mill when working a contract for 1.5 million shingles.[39] Headed into town one afternoon, he was ambushed by Apaches, took an arrow in the neck, survived, and afterward wore the arrow's mark, as George Hance noted.

Five

APACHERÍA

"Eighty Dollars for Boulders"

According to his writings, George Hance went to some effort to assert residency in Verde Valley soon after he and John arrived in Prescott. While other sources do not verify this, the Hance brothers were early enough on the scene that George could later note, with authority, "when [John and] I first came to Verde Valley there were two ranches, two ditches, two hundred acres under cultivation, and barely a dozen citizens."[1]

In the above quote, George was describing irrigation ditches constructed by the area's first white settlers, the James Swetnam party.[2] A mud-soaked two weeks slogging across the mountains from Prescott took its toll on the group. Arriving in Verde Valley in February 1865, the party splintered into two factions. Those staying with Swetnam settled near the mouth of Clear Creek Canyon on the Verde River, strengthening and fortifying an Indian compound discovered there. They intended to grow and sell vegetables to Fort Whipple and the burgeoning Prescott community, but Apaches stole their crops and killed their livestock. That should have been expected. Clear Creek Canyon was an idyllic area overshadowed by tall sycamores, a superb summer camping spot for Apache families.

In August, Swetnam petitioned the U.S. Army for protection. A month later the first detail of seventeen men inbound from Fort Whipple lost its commissary wagon when Apaches attacked and burned it the night before its intended arrival.[3]

When a year of tribulations returned some of the party to Prescott, Joe Melvin remained behind. From Pennsylvania, he was a Copperhead, against the Civil War because he thought the Union could make do with slave states. When the news of Lincoln's assassination reached him, Joe was picking grapes along Clear Creek. He "jumped up, popped his heels together, and said it was the best thing that ever happened. Mr. Boblett took the matter up with Joe and they went at it fist and skull," according to Boblett's wife, Lois, who kept a diary of the settlement. "Joe was found on the bottom in the sand. . . . The army 'Camp on the Clear Fork of the Rio Verde' was renamed Camp Lincoln that December in a pointed reference to Melvin. The Copperheads among the local settlers owe their protection to a post bearing the name they abused."[4]

By the time John Hance knew him, Melvin's house was the polling place for Camp Verde's small band of denizens. His small but sturdy residence, built from homemade adobe bricks, may be Verde Valley's oldest structure. Some of John Hance might have worn off on Melvin, or maybe it was the other way around. Joe once said it rained so hard his cornstalks were driven into the ground "clean down to their ears."[5]

In search of farmland, George Hance (and presumably John) visited Wales Arnold in Camp Verde shortly after their Prescott arrival. With hoes, George wrote, they harvested gramma hay[6] for Camp Lincoln. They may have visited Montezuma Well, even then a tourist attraction, perhaps leaving their signatures in a bottle containing "paper and cards on which the names of many visitors" were placed.[7] The Hance brothers would have done business at Arnold's sutler store, a small adobe building located on a short uprise in the grassy river bottomlands a mile upstream from the confluence of Beaver Creek and the Verde River. Camp Lincoln was relocated there from Clear Creek in early 1866 and renamed Camp Verde shortly before the Hance brothers arrived.

Upon landing in Arizona Territory, the Hance brothers settled a few miles north of today's Prescott Regional Airport. Yavapai County's 1869 census shows them residing with fellow immigrant John Bullard on Lower Granite Creek, downstream from a high stone pinnacle named Point of Rocks. Their residence was one of an estimated five hundred white dwellings in Yavapai County. At the time, Yavapai County covered nearly all of northern Arizona—from the Salt River northward to Utah, west to what became Mohave County, and east to New Mexico, fully one-third of the state.

In February 1869 the brothers bought 640 acres of farmland from James Giles for $2,500, and then purchased adjoining property owned by Giles and Bowers that November.[8] As independent contractors, teamsters on the plains earned about $25 a month, equivalent to about $450 in 2017. John and George Hance, if paid continuously at base teamster wages beginning at Rolla in August 1865 and ending at Fort Union in September 1868, would have collectively earned some $1,900. If using their own stock and wagons, the amount could have been upwards of $3,500. As dispatch riders they would have made up to $75 monthly. Further assuming, for lack of John's records, a conservative estimate of ninety days of dispatch riding between them, the amount for that alone would have been about $450. George later earned $90 a month as Lorenzo Hickok's assistant wagon master, accumulating another $360, give or take. All of it lumped together would be around $3,000, with George having more money than John. Add a few questionable side enterprises, such as inflating the scale weight for military deliveries or playing a shell game with their stock when the county assessor appeared, and it seems they had the cash for a sizable down payment and the wherewithal to handle the mortgage.

One summer day in 1870 a U.S. Census enumerator recorded the people living in Chino Valley and Lower Granite Creek. Working south from northern Chino Valley at Del Rio Springs, one first encounters George Banghart (age forty-four), his thirty-eight-year-old wife, Mary, and their four children. Below him lived Englishman Robert Postle. Postle arrived in 1864 with his children and bought what remained of the original Whipple Barracks.

Continuing south toward Point of Rocks, David Wesley Shivers comes next. Shivers's grandfather fought in the American Revolution under George Washington. His father fought in the War of 1812, and David was such a deadly shot that the Arizona territorial government awarded him a Spencer carbine to more efficiently kill Indians. Born in Missouri in 1826, he married Sarah Ann Roberts from Tennessee in 1849 and headed west. Arriving at Del Rio Springs in September 1866 after a circuitous wagon journey, he met Postle, who convinced him to stop where he was. He did, purchasing some of Postle's land and installing Chino Valley's first gristmill. People came from all over the area to use it.

The page ends at the fourteenth residence, that of John and George Hance, farmers from Tennessee. They would have occasionally visited Shivers on the Sabbath, normally a day of rest. "We started for Chino Valley and had a delightful ride over one of the best stretches of road in the Territory" read the *Weekly Arizona Miner* in early 1870, continuing that "[we] arrived in the settlements where we encountered Mr. and Mrs. Geo. Banghart [and] Mr. and Mrs. Shivers. Next day, Sunday, a party of the boys went down to the [Upper] Rio Verde—which is about two miles from the ranches—cast their lines upon the waters and succeeded in 'lacerating the mouths' of several big and little fishes. They brought back with them about thirty pounds of fish—as a result of an hour's devotion' on the Sabbath."[9] The fish were roundtail chub (*Gila robusta*), locally called "Verde trout."

The Hance brothers' first Prescott newspaper tidbit appeared that August: "What Our Farmers Have Put in the Ground" read the tease. In Chino Valley, Banghart was working one hundred and fifty acres of corn; Shivers had four acres of wheat, and forty more in corn. Postle had seventy acres of wheat under cultivation, five acres of corn, and forty peach trees. The Hance brothers had the largest spread on the page, working three hundred acres in corn, fifty acres in millet, and twenty acres of beans.[10]

"Indian trouble" in Arizona was not the Indians' fault. Nor is Arizona's Monument Valley–style silver screen scenery an accurate portrayal of Verde Valley's chalky limestone cliffs. Camp Verde, though, did play a central role in the Apache Wars.

The Apaches and Pai (those of Lower Colorado River Yuman descent: the Yavapai, Hualapai, and Havasupai) were simply asserting their rights to ancestral lands occupied by settlers moving west. Wales Arnold's place near Montezuma Well serves as an example, and it's no wonder he faced hostilities there. Montezuma Well was the Yavapai's sacred birthplace, where they emerged from the underworld to live in wickiups and hunt and gather with the seasons. The Yavapai, "people of the sun," are linguistically related to the Havasupai of Grand Canyon who traded with the Hopi, direct descendants of the Ancestral Puebloans. Although quite opposite in appearance, Montezuma Well (a gymnasium-sized limestone hole in the ground) and the Hopi Sipapuni (a room-sized limestone dome with a hole in its top) supply nearly identical spiritual needs for the Yavapai, Hopi, and other Native Americans—as a primal birthplace.

The *Weekly Arizona Miner* reported shortly before the Hance brothers pulled in:

> A week ago today the Indians who infest this country commenced the most daring, vigorous, persistent and, we may add, successful raid against the whites of this section that we have ever known or heard of them to make, for in that short space of time they have made four successful attacks upon as many different parties, and, in every instance have come out winners in the game of life and death, having killed two men and wounded five others, three of whom are not expected to live. These startling events have crowded upon us in such rapid succession that we scarcely know what to think.[11]

The situation required more attention than Lieutenant Colonel George Stoneman, commander of the Military Department of Arizona, Division of the Pacific, Fort Whipple, could manage. He never billeted there and was not in touch with the barracks' maintenance, Indian affairs, or other pressing matters. As the *Weekly Arizona Miner* put it on June 10, after the Camp Grant massacre at Aravaipa Canyon "our rascally reds have started the summer campaign in dead earnest, and, thanks to General Stoneman's blind policy, there is not a cavalry soldier at Fort Whipple to pursue them."

George Crook, a man the Verde Apaches called "Old Woman Face,"[12] replaced Stoneman. Crook was a smart, sober, respected, career military man of enormous ego and energy. His mount was saddled long before anyone else's, and he did it himself. Crook had great respect for the Apaches, terming them "the tigers of the human race."[13] He believed the only way to quell them was to force economic catastrophe upon them, keeping them on the run yearlong and denying them normal access to foodstuffs, comfort, and rest until they surrendered. In early 1872, when mounting this nonstop campaign, Crook was improving and expanding Fort Whipple to house more troops, messengers, staff, stock, and supplies. Camp Verde underwent a similar transformation, as did the wagon roads connecting them.

Still, without strength in numbers, survival outside white outposts was uncertain. In their journeys between Prescott and Verde Valley, John and George Hance would have traveled with Joe Melvin, Wales Arnold, and others. A small cavalry detachment normally accompanied Arnold. As the post trader, he supplied Verde Valley with soap, mirrors, needles, thread, whale oil, and other cherished household items extremely dear on the frontier.

Military escort, however, was no guarantee of safe transit. In August 1869, when "Arnold ... two soldiers and one citizen were returning to [Camp Verde] with a wagon, they were attacked by Indians. Mr. Arnold and a soldier named Whitcomb were about two hundred yards in advance of the wagon, when the Indians ... fired their first volley. Mr. Arnold was thrown from his horse but succeeded in reaching the wagon unhurt. Whitcomb's horse carried him into the bushes, and he was not seen afterwards."[14]

In his distinct, curious style, George Hance relates that John "was slightly wounded skin deep on one side in the center of ribs under one arm, on the other about same depth of wound on opposite arm." Where the attack happened George couldn't say, "as [John] was on the go in the early days," but he implied it occurred within a year of the Prescott journey.[15]

No account of a man named John Hance wounded by Indians is found in the territorial press, where small Indian skirmishes were reported almost weekly. In fact, it's odd to not find these encounters described in detail. While the participants were not always named, later statements by Jerry Sullivan and Hugo Richards may shed some light on the wounds George described.

Hugo Richards was an early Yavapai financier who knew Hance throughout his Verde years, from all angles, and their relationship may have gone back to 1859 and the Pike's Peak gold rush, assuming Hance was there as his brother once said. Richards told the *Weekly Arizona Miner* about two friends, one of whom was possibly Joe Melvin, attacked by Indians in 1869, and described "the strong propensity in some people for a joke no matter how serious the surroundings may be."[16] Both men were escaping the ambush on mules, the Indians at their heels and arrows flying past thick as grasshoppers in Kansas. The lead mule was leaving the other behind, its rider naturally alarmed for his friend who couldn't keep up. In a frenzy, the lead man roared, "Joe, why don't you come along?" As another arrow flitted by Joe's ear, he sang out, "Do I act like a man that was throwing off [attempting to divert attention from myself]?"[17]

It's also possible Hance was hiding in plain sight, disguised by his Appalachian drawl, misidentified as John Couch and wounded by Indians near Lynx Creek in early 1869. "He had a narrow escape, and but for a large dog which accompanied him, would have fallen into the hands of the Indians. Rolla, for that is the dog's name, charged on the reds, and occupied their attention while Mr. Couch succeeded in getting away."[18]

Hance sold his share in Granite Creek to George's partner Sam Renslow for eight hundred dollars in late December 1870[19] and headed some sixty miles southeast to homestead 160 acres near the present-day intersection of I-17 and Orme Road.

Signed into law during the Civil War, the Homestead Act allowed "free" settlement on federal lands by any adult American citizen or intended citizen. Involved was a bit of labor, a ten dollar filing fee,[20] yearly taxes, and an official government survey. "Buyers" filed an application, improved the land, and documented their progress to published standards for five years, afterward being awarded title in the form of a government patent. Prospective owners were supposed to live onsite, seed the land with sustainable crops, and build a structure measuring "12 x 24"—the measurement was intended as linear feet but some interpreted it as inches.

Explaining his move to George Wharton James, Hance said he'd been "raising corn for the government, which I sold to contractors for 7 1/2 cents a pound. They delivered it to Fort Whipple and got 12 1/2 cents. Oh, yes! those fellows knocked the bottom out of old Uncle Sam in those days, and they haven't quit yet. At the end of my second year's farming, drought and frost made me disgusted, so I went to freighting and contracting."[21]

Hance's homestead was in Arizona's expansive central highlands, on Ash Creek, a quaint perennial stream issuing from a small limestone wash about twenty miles south of Camp Verde. He settled a few hundred yards below its junction with Osborn Creek on flat, tillable land capable of producing grains and forage for his stock. The countryside was expansive, wide beneath the stars, and softened into sandy plains overlaid with patches of high desert vegetation. Deer, antelope, and beaver crowded the draw. During his time there, Ash Creek's drainage ran beside a primitive, little-used road joining Turkey Creek (an early Black Canyon diggings supply dump to the south) with the Orme–Dugas Road, which intersected the Verde–Prescott route near Bower's Agua Fria Ranch, in the present-day community of Dewey-Humbolt.[22]

As a place to overnight while in transit, his isolated yet central location gave Hance and John Ricketts, who lived on an adjoining homestead, the chance to contract freight between Black Canyon, Prescott, and Camp Verde. It also shows something of their pioneering fortitude to settle where they did, alone and along an ancient Native American trade route that joined northern and southern Arizona.

John received his government patent to Ash Creek in May 1878, by which time the Black Canyon route ran all the way to Phoenix. With an eye toward commerce, George Hance bought the property for $1,000 a year later. A girl who knew George when he used it as a sheep camp said he stayed in a little log cabin.[23] Nothing remains of the structure, but it would have been built in partial fulfillment of John's homestead agreement and in all likelihood was similar to the small cabin he later built at Grand Canyon. Today a younger, larger, somewhat rustic building stands on the suspected site of the original, beneath a tall span of old cottonwoods along the creek's grassy floodplain.

Life was harsh along Lower Granite Creek. Apaches attacked in February 1871, nearly killing two men who escaped as their home was destroyed. In May, "during the prevalence of heavy gales of wind, the barn of George Hance" was destroyed by a fire. George lost a new $400 freight wagon, his stores of seed and grain, farming implements, and other supplies for a total worth more than $2,000. George was "badly burned" in the fire, his mules ran off, and he offered to "reward and thank any person leaving the animals at Brooks & Linn's Livery Stable, Prescott."[24]

With a continuing drought around Prescott, Granite Creek a bare trickle, and suddenly bereft of supplies and possibly bankrupt, George Hance was at loose ends. In the Verde Valley, however, crops were thriving, as the *Weekly Arizona Miner* reported, in "a manner quite unprecedented. This is owing to the fact that farmers there [are] not, as elsewhere, obliged to depend upon the very uncertain rains for irrigation, the [Verde] river affording abundant water for this purpose, at all seasons.

Joseph Melvin, who has some 300 acres under cultivation at the Verde, returned [to Prescott] from a visit to his farm on Monday, and brought along some of the largest onions ever exhibited in the Territory."[25]

A year after that, "a mule bucked [George] off and the wagon run over me and broke my leg and I stayed alone [hiding from Indians under a hay pile] at Ash Creek where the accident happened, for two days and nights while my partner, Sam Renslow, delivered hay to Cherry Creek and returned with help."[26] George was on crutches for months afterward, sequestered behind the counter of Hugo Richards's new store in Camp Verde, his move noted in the paper: "G. W. Hance has gone to Camp Verde on business for C. P. Head & Co. George is a good 'boy.'"[27] George's leg did not heal properly, and he was left with a slight limp.

Hugo Richards bought Wales Arnold's business contract and had just put up the adobe building in an empty field a quarter mile southwest of the growing military compound and its parade grounds. In business for only a year, he sold to the Head brothers of Prescott. George started with Richards and continued with Head & Co. while recovering from his injury.

"[Head & Co.] had the Grain Contract of every Military Post in Arizona and they took me out of the store and made a runabout man out of me," George wrote, "and during the fall and summer of 1872, I visited every military post in Arizona except Camp Apache. In January 1873 I returned to Camp Verde and went to work in the sutler's store again."[28] All told, he worked that countertop for twenty-two months and thirteen days. While there, he applied for homestead on land where he and Head were running one thousand cattle under the HH brand at the top of the long grade south of town. His patent was granted in late 1877, a year and a half after John secured his Ash Creek patent. George called his ranch the "Cienega."

A significant aspect of George's move was Camp Verde's relocation from the Verde River's malarial summertime bottomlands to a high cut bank just below its confluence with Beaver Creek. General George Crook was building his operations when George Hance worked behind Head's counter. George came to know Verde Valley and its small but growing population inside and out. He was appointed notary public by the territorial governor, then ran for justice of the peace at the Cienega and was elected, serving for forty-eight years.

John's first solo newspaper appearance occurred October 26, 1872. According to the *Weekly Arizona Miner*, "John Hance and another gentleman arrived here recently from New Mexico via the Thirty-fifth Parallel route." Instead of the Lynx Creek diggings, "they say the diamond question was the main one when they left New Mexico." At first glance, John seems to be making fun of all the miners scurrying around the Bradshaw Mountains, but a short-lived diamond rush "150 miles north of Prescott," an event later termed the Great Diamond Hoax, was in full swing that summer.[29]

The 1872 census has John in Wickenburg, then the only gateway to Prescott from Phoenix. The town began as a supply dump for the Vulture Mine when Henry Wickenburg discovered gold there in 1862. Ten years later, some five hundred people lived in the area. Most worked for or supplied the mine, which during its lifetime produced $16 million in bullion. During the early 1870s Wickenburg was a bustling place, busy enough that large flour deliveries from the Salt River mills were noted in the local press. John may have done some of those runs.

Or maybe he was traveling with George. When Head & Co. put George on the road, he did more than visit military installations. By one account, "The Indians were so bad in killing and robbing on the highways that Wells Fargo and Company would not take any chances in shipping money or other valuables in or out of Arizona. Head and Company wanted to use greenbacks." The company put George on a U.S. mail buckboard from Prescott to Ehrenberg on the Colorado, where he met a Wells Fargo messenger who delivered to him "$20,000 in greenbacks," which Morris Goldwater helped him count. George then rode on top of the mail sacks to Grant's Station, Wickenburg, "and from Wickenburg to Phoenix on horseback and delivered the money to Colonel [Cotsworth] Head."[30] George made several of these risky journeys, and John may have been riding shotgun for him.

By late October 1873 John had returned to Ash Creek, although the *Weekly Arizona Miner* reported him ready to create a station on the road to Camp Verde.[31] This indicates a location along the Camp Verde–Prescott road, not John's lower Ash Creek homestead, and points to George's Cienega, where Head Hance & Co. was constructing corrals and buildings. The notice presumably describes a stagecoach rest and resupply stop, all of which the Cienega became when George secured his patent four years later.

John next appears in print on New Year's Eve 1874: "Messrs Price Behan, John Hance, and J. W. Johnson, arrived [in Prescott] from Verde day before yesterday. Mr. Behan informs us that the contract of Mr. Geo. Hance, to deliver 900 tons of hay at Camp Verde, has been fulfilled."[32] John Ricketts was also involved. After the delivery, Ricketts said, he and Hance partnered up to buy George's bull team of forty oxen and six wagons and "went freighting on the road."[33]

In early December 1875, Ricketts and Hance camped at the Cienega on a layover. "We always turned the oxen loose at night to graze—plenty of grass everywhere. The next morning, we went out to round-up the oxen and found the Indians had come in the night and drove off ten head. We were sleeping only a short distance from them, and why they didn't kill us was a miracle."[34] Thirty oxen remained. The rest of the story goes like this:

> We contracted to take a load of freight to Fort McDowell and had to go via Phoenix. It was July, the cattle could not stand the heat to travel day time, so we had to lay over in daylight and travel all night. The rattlesnakes were so numerous we had to ride on wagon tongues. On that trip John Hance had quite an unfortunate accident. We were breaking in some wild steers. One day we were camped in cactus country and some of [the] steers were on the fight and one of them made a lunge for John. The ground was covered with ball cactus and John fell onto a bed of cacti. Oh boy, I never heard such moans and groans. He was covered with cacti thorns. His pants were pinned to his body. We had to lay over there until we got all those thorns off.[35]

Multiple spells of poor weather occurred in 1875. Deep snows and frozen nights gave way to warm days, causing floods along Beaver Creek, Oak Creek, and the Verde River. More snow followed. Then warm weather returned, sometimes with heavy rains that caused more freshets.

Crook's cavalry, foot soldiers, and numerous Indian scouts were on the move in the winter of 1871 and throughout the following spring. The operation was a tactical success, cemented by the Battle of Muchos

Canyones, where forty or so Apaches were ambushed and killed. Crook's policy brought Shuttlepan, chief of the Tonto Apaches, into the Verde Valley, where he surrendered with twenty-three hundred of his people in May 1873. This meant retooling a community of some twenty self-reliant farmers and ranchers into one capable of feeding that many indigenous people in a matter of days. It required a lot of beef, flour, corn, and beans—exactly what the Hance brothers needed to make good money.

Twenty miles wide (ten miles on each side of the Verde River) by forty miles long, the Camp Verde Indian Reservation arched north and west from Camp Verde to Chino Valley and Paulden. Chino Valley was well suited to farming and livestock while Verde, a rich bottomland with grass as high as a horse's belly, was given to all manner of agricultural pursuits.

As early as 1873, government contractors suggested moving the Verde Indian population south to the San Carlos Apache Indian Reservation east of Globe. San Carlos was halfway to Tucson, where reservation foodstuffs and supplies were delivered by rail, then hauled north. Cutting the delivery distance in half would reduce travel time and increase profits. John Gregory Bourke, Crook's on-scene biographer, called the actions of the U.S. government and the Tucson businessmen "an outrageous proceeding, one for which I should still blush had I not long since gotten over blushing for anything the United States Government did in Indian matters."[36]

By February 1875, the contractors had won out. "John and I owned a bull train of eight teams [eight wagons, each pulled by two or more oxen]," wrote George Hance. At Camp Verde, Special Commissioner L. E. Dudley "hired us to haul the 'baggage' and the helpless Indians to Hayden's Ferry [Tempe] on the Salt River and to the San Carlos. They numbered about 3,000 and several hundred of them were helpless women and children, aged, lame, and blind. The rest of them went by way of foot and by way of Payson."[37]

While John was known for tall tales, this one belongs to George. The actual number going by foot was 1,476 according to army surgeon William Corbusier, who accompanied the 180-mile, 36-day ordeal. Undertaken between February 27 ("The Day the Boulder Fell" according to Yavapai-Apache historian Vincent Randell) and April 3 during raw winter weather, the march entailed crossing snow-packed mountain ridges, dangerously swollen freezing rivers, and later, on lower ground, a long flat stretch of barren desert wasteland.

Oversight personnel included Special Agent Oliver Chapman in command with fifteen troopers under Lieutenant George O. Eaton. Along were Al Sieber, Dr. Corbusier, Chief Packer Harry Hawes, and other mule skinners, one of whom legend identifies as Tom Horn, a cowboy, Indian scout, and Pinkerton National Detective Agency gumshoe suspected of seventeen killings. The official report read, in part, "It was a sad duty to compel men, women, and children, to wade through the cold water, even though they were Indians."[38] Because Yavapai, Hualapai, and Apache families were moved as a unit, the ordeal was strained by tribal animosities. Food ran out as the supporting livestock died of starvation and hypothermia. A revolt was threatened but avoided after twenty-five live cattle and one thousand pounds of flour were delivered from San Carlos to the Salt River. However, 115 Indians perished during the frigid undertaking, many of them infants born en route. One broken down old man carried his crippled wife the entire distance in a basket on his back.

According to the *Weekly Arizona Miner*, the wagon train undertook its journey with twenty-five souls, not the hundreds George claimed. Written late in life following a stroke, George had confused the Navajo Return and Verde Removal, but independent corroboration that the Hance brothers were employed is substantiated by Randell. He also named two individuals who rode in the Hance wagons: "Billy Smith's father had been bitten by a rattlesnake and was unable to walk," and "a small girl too young to walk who lived to be 117."[39]

It's interesting to note that although Corbusier knew the Hance brothers and had originally recommended using wagons to his superiors, he did not mention John and George's involvement over a different route. According to post returns, Corbusier accompanied Lieutenant Eaton's Fifth Cavalry soldiers and Hualapai scouts "en route to Camp Apache, A. T. moving (?) Indians."[40] That is sufficiently vague to disguise what was actually happening. Additionally, independent contractors like the Hance brothers were paid off the books—if at all.

In a letter to Indian Commissioner Edward Smith, Commissioner Dudley complained,

> You have refused to send me funds necessary to pay for the move. I have made the move for as little money or maybe less than any similar move was made. Myself, the Indians, employees

who were with me, the military escort, pack train, all took their lives in their hands and all knew that at any time during the journey they might be in danger of losing their lives. You can sit in a nicely carpeted office and forget more in one day about this miserable place than those of us who came over it ever knew. I feel aggrieved that you should fail to give me the small amount of money that was necessary.[41]

Before John Hance's stories were widely remarked, Corbusier was one of the few who obliquely mentioned them: "John Hance delivered hay and other supplies at [Fort Verde] and the [Haskell Springs] agency," today's Clarkdale. "Each load was delivered with tales taller than any grass known, and it was from this amusing and entertaining accomplishment that he earned the name 'Honest John.'"[42]

Abraham Lincoln "Linc" Smith had a different take on those hay deliveries. Smith was born in 1864 in Humansville, Missouri. Twelve years old when his mother died, Linc sold her house for forty dollars and hired someone to deliver him and his twin brother, Ulysses Grant Smith, to Verde Valley. Linc attended the first Camp Verde school in 1877, a class of thirteen,[43] and told a story about John lining his wagon bed with limestone bricks for hay deliveries. He knew that because his brother cut John's hay for two years, loaded it in his wagons, and saw what happened next. After it was weighed on Fort Verde's scales, Hance would tip the soldier a dollar, saying, "When you git down so fur," said John, motioning to a place in the wagon bed, "you can quit. I can't get out of post tonight. I'm going to leave some hay for *my* steers." Every ton of hay John sold cost the army forty dollars. Linc thought that was hilarious. "Eighty dollars for boulders," Smith laughed. "He sold boulders more than hay."[44]

Six

THE SUTLER'S STORE

"Al Sieber, John Hance, and Mr. McInernay"

The Head brothers purchased Hugo Richards's business while George Hance's leg was mending. William Stanford "Boss" Head, a staunch Republican who earned his moniker when later appointed to the territorial legislature, was in charge. His brother, Cotsworth, "C. P." or "Colonel" through prior service to the Confederacy, was a Democrat and company overseer in charge of the Prescott store. Together they controlled a sizable portion of central Yavapai County's early mercantile business. They also bid contracts to the military for hay, grain, and cordwood, sometimes in competition with the Hance brothers.

As Verde Valley's only mercantile outlet until mid-decade, Head & Co. was the focal point of the small community. The store supplied grain, groceries, canned and dry goods, mining tools, guns, ammunition, boots, and even bottled water from Florida to soldiers and settlers alike. Head & Co. was the only post office, telegraph station, bank, and trade, collection, and bartering agency within fifty miles. With the addition of a large barn and corral with mules and other stock animals for rent at one dollar a day, it was a full-service enterprise.

In the contemporary American West, only a handful of buildings remain in which a particular person stood at a countertop to do business for a decade over a century ago. Head's store is one of them, and twelve of its handwritten debit-credit ledger books document every purchase John Hance made there for ten years, especially in the latter 1870s when he lived only three miles away.

The Camp Verde sutler's store today. Author photo.

Much can be learned about a man by studying his grocery list. Among so many curiosities is that in one ledger, Hance was twice that day's first customer, on both occasions purchasing only one item: "pain pills" and "quinine." And later, when the quinine supply ran out, he substituted whiskey and added more pills.

While several of Head's books are missing, one yearlong tally of Hance's purchasing habits has fortunately been preserved. Between May 12, 1875, and April 26, 1876, Hance did business at Head & Co. eighty times, occasionally several times a day. On average, he was in the store once every five days, but most of his activity occurred between the fall of 1875 and the following April, when that volume ends and the following ledger is missing.

These were his purchases: One hat, one white shirt, another shirt, an "Under Shirt" and "Over Shirt," three pairs of pants, two pairs of overalls, one jumper, two pairs of "drawers," four pairs of lace-up ankle boots, seven pairs of socks, two towels, two combs, two bars of soap, one roll of thread, and one needle. He drank eight bottles of whiskey, accumulated $3 in bar tabs, and spent $2.50 on a box of tea sweetened throughout the year with two jars of honey.

He bought 135 pounds of corn, $8 worth of corn meal, 24 pounds of coffee, 55 pounds of sugar, 10 pounds of salt, 20 pounds of turnips,

The Camp Verde sutler's store ledgers detail every item John Hance purchased for a decade. Author photo.

64 pounds of potatoes (one purchase), two cans of lard, and seven packages of yeast. He paid for 338 pounds of flour in seven purchases and 80 pounds of bacon in five purchases. The only other food items he purchased were 14 pounds of beans, two cans of oysters, and one tin of salmon. He bought tobacco products fourteen times, and one time each acquired one pencil, one box of stationery, one pocketknife, and one deck of cards. He also bought a small amount of shot, powder, and caps for his old Navy revolver, and took $240 in cash advances that he repaid. He covered a freight bill for $23, a wash bill of $2, two beef bills totaling $9, and spent $2 for one night's lodging at Head's latest addition, the small adobe hotel and stage stop across the street. His business-related purchases amounted to seventeen cans of axle grease, "1 axe & handle," and "3 1/2 Lbs Nails." Because the 1875 assessor's reports have been lost or destroyed, we don't know what equipment Hance used or his complement of livestock.

The people Hance did business with during Camp Verde's roughest, bloodiest, Indian-fighting times stood next to him at Head's counter, including Joe Melvin, Wales Arnold, blacksmith Alex Graydon, and Hance's partner John Ricketts. C. C. Bean, Jerry Sullivan, and other out-of-towners occasionally stopped by.

Perhaps the most historically prominent of Head's customers was Graydon's drinking buddy Al Sieber,[1] chief of General George Crook's Indian scouts. From his first days in Camp Verde until Geronimo's surrender in 1886, Sieber served the U.S. Army in nearly every Apache War campaign, many of them staged around the Verde, southward to Tonto Basin and east into the Mogollon Mountains. Sieber bought flour in fifty-pound bags, took his tea and coffee with sugar, and purchased tobacco, cigarette paper and matches as a unit. He also ate a lot of jam.

Like Hance, Sieber was a woodsman, marksman, and hunter, good with stock animals and able to live off the land without difficulty, the proof being his early mail runs between Camp Verde and Sunset Crossing. He and Dan O'Leary were early Copper Camp prospectors around what became Jerome's (Arizona) famous Verde claim, "the Big Hole." He arrived in Prescott at nearly the same time as the Hance brothers and, like Jerry Sullivan, worked for C. C. Bean tending fields and chopping wood in Williamson Valley. Because only a handful of people lived between there and Granite Creek, it's a near certainty Al Sieber and John Hance knew each other from their first days in Arizona Territory.

Another notable visitor at the Head & Co. store was the immigrant camel drover "Hi Jolly." His actual name was Hadji Ali, but he was known locally as "H'Jarly." He served in what was called the "U.S. Camel Corps" under Ned Beale, but there never was a formal military organization by that name. Rather, because oxen withered so quickly in the Southwest's torturous heat, Beale and others experimented with camels as pack animals. They performed above expectations but the program was never officially implemented because the secretary of war, Jefferson Davis, became involved with the Confederacy and the Civil War supervened.

Hi Jolly visited Head's store three times. George Hance bought him tobacco, matches, and a drink on one visit, and on another paid him the 2017 equivalent of $24,000, perhaps for a flock of sheep. John, George, and Jim Hance accompanied Ali each time. James Randell Hance, John's half-brother sixteen years his junior and George's younger full brother, was also in Verde Valley, having arrived by method and means unknown in 1873. If Head's books are taken at face value, it appears Jim drove cattle and did ranch jobs for George. Along with John, he is sometimes absent from the ledgers for extended periods. They may have been working together then, as was apparently the case later at Grand Canyon when John was several times misidentified as Jim in the press. Between times, Jim lived at George's new place at Beasley Flat near the river, six miles down the winding Salt Mine Road south of town. He later lived in Williams, where he worked as an engineer on the Santa Fe's Ash Fork run. After that he moved to Flagstaff and dabbled in real estate until removing to St. Louis in 1913.

What appears to be an informal voter registration roll from 1876 identifies John, George, and Jim Hance at Bower's ranch about twenty miles west of Camp Verde. Wrote one author in the *Weekly Arizona Miner*:

> Mr. Bower's house, on what is now known as the 'Agua Fria Ranch,' was erected by the Hon. King Sam Woolsey some 12 years since. It is a double stone house and is on the site of what was, in pre-historic times, a very large edifice ... built wholly of old [Native American] ruins, being flat blocks of slate, granite, and gneiss. Some outhouses were built of the same material, hundreds of loads have been drawn away for walls, stoning wells, etc., and yet there remains a large amount on the ground, and in places the debris is over five feet high. From the above, the reader can obtain some idea of the immense amount of material in the old ruin.[2]

George Hance was at Agua Fria Ranch because Parthenia Rutledge worked there, and it was a curious thing that around dusk each evening George's sheep would migrate over to the Agua Fria and he would have to go fetch them.[3] People were not surprised, then, when on April 2, 1878, George married Parthenia at the Cienega. Without mention of John, the paper termed it "an event, and one that [George's] many friends will learn with pleasure."[4]

Parthenia was of Cherokee and Euro-American descent, born in Talladega, Alabama, and late enough on the scene that people knew nothing of her. George's descendants report that she was his guiding light and kept him on an honest, respectable heading during their years together. Her mother, a Cherokee named Melissa Ann McKay (or McCoy), had impressed upon her the importance of good table manners. Known throughout the Verde as "Mother Hance," Parthenia "practiced those manners and insisted all her family use them."[5]

A popular spot, the Cienega was "the regular mail station of the Arizona & New Mexico Express Co. and headquarters for large herds of sheep, cattle etc."[6] A spring there "was referred to as the big spring, boarded around. It had an underground seepage and was where 'Old Jose,' a ranch hand, grew his marijuana, dried and smoked it as he did not care for cigarette tobacco."[7] During the Cienega's long run, "it was no unusual sight to see half a dozen old-time freight outfits, army ambulances, and the mail and passenger buck-board, all camped under the spreading box elders"[8] that George planted and nurtured. "With his fine dwelling, barns, stables, corrals, etc he can accommodate travelers with meals for themselves and animals."[9] He was also the Cienega's first and only postmaster from April 1877 to November 1892.

These were doubtless George's happiest years, and a story from this time describes him well. One of the Wingfield girls encountered him mumbling to himself on the street one day. She asked why. "I like to talk to a smart man," he replied, "and I like to hear what a smart man has to say,"[10] and muttered himself onward. John was better at it—or worse, depending on your perspective. Bob Fix, who camped with John for several weeks in 1914, verifies this. Hance needed companionship just then, but he nearly drove Fix crazy with his incessant chatter.[11]

John's Ash Creek homestead lay halfway between Camp Verde and the Peck Mining District in the Bradshaw Mountains, named for William David Bradshaw, "brave, generous, eccentric, and in simple truth a natural lunatic."[12] Bradshaw was a member of the Bear Flag party, which captured Sonoma, California, in June 1846. Afterward he started a ferry across the Colorado at Ehrenberg but, instead of tending it, accompanied Joe Walker to the Lynx Creek gold diggings. Bradshaw then coursed eastward on his own through miles of a precipitous, rugged, cactus-bound landscape to locate "good color"—gold tailings—in Black Canyon, but Apaches frightened him so badly that he never returned. By 1864, after losing a congressional bid by a huge margin, he returned to Ehrenberg and ferry operations, but the Colorado jumped its bed that year and left him high and dry. That was the last straw. In December, Bradshaw walked deliberately into a carpenter's shop, "took up a drawing knife, and with one stroke nearly severed his head from his shoulders."[13]

Despite Indian raids and livestock thefts, prospectors had been in the Bradshaws since the Del Pasco lode of August 1870 when the Prescott paper gushed, "Our miners have discovered a great thing, a big thing . . . the richest gold mine in the world."[14] By early 1871 the nearby Tiger Mine was assaying silver at $1,000 per ton, and some 150 independent prospectors were reported working the area, earning up to $20 a day with their picks and shovels. A town called Bradshaw City sprang up under the ponderosas on a saddle between the two mines. In 1871 the Prescott paper reported, "everything is lively, a crowd of men is cutting timber, teams are hauling logs, building is brisk, and everybody sanguine."[15] Today it's nothing more than a small commemorative marker.

Enter Edmund Peck, born in Canada in 1858. He came to America to join a party of California emigrants but reversed course in northern Arizona when his group was confronted by angry Navajos. He returned to Arizona in 1863, chasing Walker's Lynx Creek gold rush as Bradshaw had done, finally settling at Del Rio Springs, where he won Whipple Barrack's first gramma hay contract. He sold out to George Banghart and moved to Granite Creek, near Point of Rocks, where he babysat stock for $3 a head while working at Fort Whipple as a guide and scout after identical service at Camp Lincoln. He was all over the Bradshaws chasing Indians for the army at the time but didn't know what silver sticking out of the ground looked like. Ten years later, when learning about silver ore, he recalled the spot. Off he went with C. C. Bean and others. Within two weeks they were back in Prescott with samples assaying over $6,000 a ton. Bean returned in August, selling ten tons of rocks for $13,000.

The future looked bright. But by the following year Peck Mine was mired in a long, ongoing series of legal proceedings after Bill Cole, one of its discoverers, took himself on an extended debauch and signed over his interest to C. C. Bean's wife, Mary Margaret "May" Bradshaw Bean. After regaining consciousness, Cole brought suit, saying he'd been incapable of conducting business at the time.

The court agreed, judging the arrangement a mortgage. C. C. Bean, of course, did not agree and immediately appealed. While Bean's countersuit was proceeding, Peck removed to San Francisco and incorporated the mine in the names of himself, May Bean, Leonora Jewell, and Catherine Alexander. Jewell was the mine assayer's wife, and Alexander was Peck's mother-in-law. None of his original accomplices were mentioned. The situation was so intertwined that, even before Bean sprang to life, two other actions were running concurrently: *Peck Mining Co. v. Peck, Rowe, Anderson, and Park*; and *Peck Mine v. Peck, Rowe, and Anderson.*[16]

Into these confused legalities stepped John Hance and James Graham, defendants, through the unlikely person of Solomon Barth, plaintiff. "Jas" Graham owned the Gray Eagle Livery, Feed & Sale Stables in Prescott and also contracted cordwood to Peck Mine. In October, he hauled finished lumber to the mine's latest mill, where new stamp machines awaited a roof. By early November, Graham was readying his wagons to haul additional wood to Peck Mine.[17]

That same month he and Hance delivered flour from Hayden's Mill on the Salt River to Prescott via the Black Canyon Road. The *Weekly Arizona Miner* reported that "Hance who superintended the train ... condemns the Black Canyon route in the most bitter terms and thinks he can handle with the same teams and wagons at least one ton more freight over the Wickenburg [to Prescott] route in less time with a great saving to his stock."[18] John was swearing because steeper, rougher grades like Black Canyon required elongated strings of animals. The miles-long hill—technically a mountain because the elevation gain exceeds one thousand feet—required "doubling up." That meant leaving wagons unhitched at the bottom and adding their animals to other wagons' teams, strengthening them for the long uphill pull—but they all had to return down the grade to bring up the remaining wagons. This was mere shuttle work, grueling, time-consuming, never-preferred labor, rough on equipment and stock.[19]

Hance was making two and a half cents a pound, however, and the Black Canyon Road had quitted New Mexico as an adjunct supplier to the Verde.[20] It gave Hance increased local business and put men like his longtime associate John Yours Truly Smith in charge of territorial grain deliveries from Phoenix. Because he was the first contractor at Camp McDowell, Smith also became the first white person to live permanently in the area.[21] It's possible Hance hauled the first load of milled lumber ever delivered to Phoenix—if he did, it was used to build Smith's house.[22]

Plaintiff "Sol" Barth was from Prussia. He was about John's height but much heavier, with a broad, sheet-white mustache. He arrived in Arizona in 1863, fought Apaches with King Woolsey at the Battle of Bloody Tanks, and withdrew to Wickenburg to become a merchant. In the late 1860s he and his brothers ran stock near Sunset Crossing, and it was in that role he had staggered naked into Zuni Pueblo a month before the Hance-Sullivan party passed through.

Barth was the sort to purchase ten freight wagons and a year later trade eight of them, fifty oxen, and $2,000 for 2,500 sheep that were immediately stolen and never recovered. In 1881, as a member of the Eleventh Territorial Legislature, Apaches attacked Barth and his partner en route to an Albuquerque conference. The same Indians set upon him elsewhere; altogether, twenty whites were killed in ten days, his partner going under in the first round. That same year he saved a Mexican family from immolation by Apaches. He was once convicted of forgery, quickly pardoned, and with even greater alacrity accused of $12,000 in graft.

Barth, however, did not remain the plaintiff for long. Hugo Richards replaced him, probably buying the debt at a discount or taking it as repayment for a loan. Richards died in 1911 when, as president of the Bank of Arizona, he leaned back in his chair, remarked upon feeling queer, and expired. But in the early days, after selling his store to the Head brothers, he worked military contracts, ran cattle, and was heavily vested in the Peck and other Bradshaw mines.

In midsummer Hance was summoned to appear in the Third District Court, Prescott, regarding "Docket Number 565, Hugo Richards vs. The Peck Mining Company, James Graham and John Hance."[23] How and why Graham and Hance got involved here is unknown; they were teamsters, ostensibly partnered up to move supplies to and from Peck Mine. That aside, Peck Mine, Graham, and Hance executed a $2,600 promissory note to Barth in October 1877, payable on demand with 2 percent interest after sixty days. Before it came due, Barth endorsed it over to Richards who, aware that Peck et al. were strapped for cash, delayed action—when brought to court a year later only $200 had been repaid. Posted in November 1878, the findings declared Peck Mine, Graham, and

Hance liable for $2,937 including court costs.[24] Hance would have been responsible for about $1,000 of that.

C. C. Bean appeared as a prosecution witness, earning $103 for his troubles, but it doesn't seem to have affected his long relationship with Hance, whom he visited at Grand Canyon in the 1880s.

Fourteen years Hance's junior, Murray McInernay took the long way around to be Hance's business partner. Raised motherless, McInernay's father was an impoverished Scots-Irish cobbler. Fleeing his Brooklyn, New York, home at fourteen, he enlisted in the Union Army two days after Grant met Lee at Appomattox and was discharged one year later (to the day). His whereabouts during the following decade are uncertain. According to *Portrait and Biographical Record of Arizona*,[25] he sailed to the Amazon in company with others, worked odd jobs across Brazil for eight months, and in Peru boarded a ship to San Francisco. From there he *walked* across mountains and deserts to Fort Mojave, Arizona, where he vanishes from the record.

He reappears in late 1870, again on foot proceeding upstream along the east bank of the Colorado from Yuma to Ehrenberg and then to Prescott, much of it through thick desert creosote and cactus. Safely at Fort Whipple, he was hired as commissariat at Camp Date Creek, sixty miles southwest of Prescott. As de facto trader to the Yavapais there, he accompanied them in their move to the Verde Valley. He began working government contracts for charcoal, cordwood, and grain, and hired Hance and Ricketts to haul some of his deliveries, the first recorded load for $55 on December 6, 1876. In January 1877 he paid them $250 for a larger consignment.

In June 1877, "Al Sieber, John Hance and Mr. McInernay, all Camp Verde guests, left for home last evening after a pleasant visit of several days [in Prescott]."[26] John had sold his Ash Creek homestead patent to George for a large profit and no doubt was on holiday. But John also made the trip to proffer (and win in December) a bid at Fort Whipple for one thousand cords of wood for what would equal $116,000 in 2017. In that same bid cycle, McInernay offered $17.74 a ton for hay at Fort Verde, $4 under George Hance.[27]

A month later Ricketts sold two wagons and ox teams to James Patterson, who supplied meat to the army, since he no longer needed the equipment. As the paper put it, Ricketts and John had amicably "divided

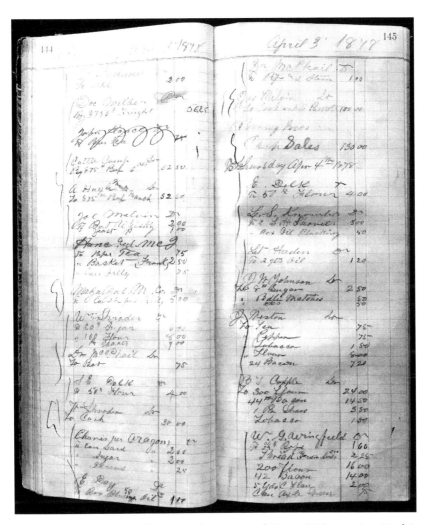

The "partnership agreement" between John Hance and Murray McInernay in a Head & Co. ledger book, April 3, 1878. Author photo.

up their teams"[28] after three years in business. In early 1878 Hance and McInernay became partners. Hance had the location, stock, equipment, and logistic know-how while McInernay, well established with crews already in place, could supply the material to fill the wagons.

While no formal agreement between them is known, Head's ledgers actually witness the partnership's inaugural day in real time on the morning of April 3, 1878.[29] Hance and McInernay had always run separate accounts until then. But that day Hance took a package of tea off the shelves and put it on the counter. The clerk wrote it down. Then John changed his mind and the entry was crossed out. After Joe Melvin bought whiskey and a package of yeast, the clerk again recorded Hance's tea, this time as the first item in a new account titled "Hance & McI." During the next few days they charged overalls, rope, a pair of shoes, two hundred pounds of flour, $1,000 worth of bacon (in 2017 currency), a shovel, an axe head and handle for it, sugar, and coffee; and a few days later matches, letter paper, more coffee, sugar, tea, candles, and plug tobacco.

These purchases align with McInernay's previous, sometimes substantial expenses to cover his work crews. At the same time, the arrangement was a giant step up for Hance, whose comparable prehistory with John Ricketts is, in context, not worth mention.

The business end of the relationship is described in an 1879 assessor's report: "Hance & McInernay Camp Verde. Possessory rights to 160 Acres of land and improvements on the Verde [River] adjoining Military Reserve,"[30] located just off the southwest corner of Fort Verde's sixty-acre garden tract. With thirty-six steers and four freight wagons, they were prepared for big loads on long roads.

The 1879–1880 contracting season became Hance's most profitable year. John won three delivery contracts: 150 tons of hay at $25.74 a ton for a gross profit of $3,861, 800 cords of soft wood at $5 a cord, and another 1,000 cords of soft wood for $5.75 a cord, $4,000 and $5,750 respectively. The grand total was $13,611.

It was a big operation, with Mexican laborers reaping hay in the fields and stacking cordwood in forests, and the ledgers show expenses the partnership incurred for these employees. In August 1879, for example, Hance bought coffee, sugar, tobacco, matches, bacon, and other items for men named Juan, Jose, and Pedro. McInernay did likewise, as did George Hance for his crews. As a general matter, however, none of them seem to have cared for Mexicans. On another store visit, some of John's workers bought a bottle of whiskey and "had a girl with them. On leaving, about a mile from town [they] got into a fight and [the] foreman killed one of the crew. [They were] tried in George's JP court with John as the jury foreman. John suggested the Jury each donate another $1 apiece and get the foreman another bottle or two of whiskey and send him out to kill a couple more."[31]

Page 307 of the fifth ledger details the purchases of March 30, 1880, when Hance and McInernay bought their normal supply of coffee, sugar, tea, bacon, and whatnot. But the first thing laid on the counter that day was a one-time purchase, a map of Arizona. Because of its cost (about seventy-five dollars in 2017), there's only one probable candidate: an outsized piece of exquisitely detailed, occasionally colored paper that folded down into an attached pocket-sized leather envelope. Titled "Official Map of the Territory of Arizona Compiled from Surveys, Reconnaissances and other Sources by E. A. Eckhoff and P. Riecker, Civil Engineers, 1880," it revealed the territory's topography, counties, centers of commerce, wagon roads, and mining districts to the particulars of the day.[32]

For instance, what's now called Marble Canyon, the first sixty miles of Grand Canyon National Park, appears to be named Echo Cliffs while, downstream, Upper Granite Gorge is mislabeled as Marble Canyon. All of northern Arizona appears uninhabited while, in marked contrast, the Bradshaw Mountains are covered with overlapping red squares to indicate mining activity. Clear Creek settlement is gone, but, interestingly, the Cienega ranch is indicated. Prescott and Camp Verde barely show. Pathways between today's economic landmarks are few, if there at all.

Neither Hance nor McInernay needed a landform map for anything except what lay to the north—they had been all over central Yavapai and throughout the southward lands for years.

Corresponding to this is that 1880 enjoyed a noticeable uptick in Grand Canyon newspaper references, heretofore nearly absent from the local press. Generated by the Atlantic & Pacific Railroad's plans to cross northern Arizona, the articles began with a dramatic telling of the Little Colorado River Gorge, saying it was deeper than Grand Canyon.

An account of the death of retired Irish sailor Daniel W. Mooney also appeared in print. While accompanying the Beckman and Young prospecting expedition to "Avi-Supai canyon," Mooney attempted descent of a sheer ninety-foot waterfall with insufficient rope. He fell the distance, "dashed to a sudden and rock tomb where he now rests as he fell, his companions being unable to rescue his body from that awful and abysmal grave." Unable to proceed, "the party retraced their steps and went ... to the Grand Canyon of the Colorado. The water is described as being 100 yards across, still, from the elevated view of the explorers, the furious stream appeared to be a silver thread of only a few inches in width."[33]

That was almost a verbatim copy of what Spanish conquistadors recorded in 1540 when García López de Cárdenas, on outreach from Francisco Coronado's expedition in search of the Seven Cities of Cibola, first encountered the spectacle. But that information wasn't published until after Mooney's death—altogether an odd set of circumstances.[34] Of special interest here is that Mooney lived in Williamson Valley. He probably knew C. C. Bean, Jerry Sullivan, Phillip Hull and his sons, and, perhaps, John Hance.

That map was purchased a week before Mooney's death was announced in the press. Did the "frontier telegraph" actually travel that quickly? Was Daniel Mooney the reason John Hance bought that map?

Also in 1880, C. C. Bean visited Topeka, Kansas, as Prescott's "envoy extraordinary," there to do business with railroad officials in the hopes of getting rails laid to Prescott. He reported home that the Atlantic & Pacific Railroad survey had progressed eastward through Beale's Springs, Truxton, and Peach Springs. The message motivated C. P. Head to explore the San Francisco Peaks region and determine for himself the future location of Prescott Junction. Once there, Head couldn't make up his mind. Jerry Sullivan fixed that the following April after discovering perennial water near the railroad's path. Sullivan went to some expense to construct large holding yards and roofed outbuildings there. His patch of ground was later named after a railway investor named Seligman.

For reasons unknown, Hance and McInernay's 160 acres were reduced to 130 acres in the 1880 assessor's rolls. During the year, they cashed vouchers for $400, $1,470, and $520, for a total of $2,390, well below their previous earnings.

That June, Hance was noted in the federal census on Beaver Creek at Luther Knowles's farm. Knowles, fifty-nine years old, was originally from New Hampshire. His property rested two easygoing miles downstream from Wales Arnold's place; it's now a community named Lake Montezuma, a slight misnomer since the lake is, at best, barely a pond, even by Arizona standards. At his 330-acre homestead, Knowles owned horses (mares, one with a colt), a cow, her calf, two tons of corn, and the machinery to bring it in. The *Weekly Arizona Miner* thought him "one of the most extensive farmers on the Verde and an excellent citizen . . . of excellent judgment."[35] Going by Head's ledgers, Knowles had known Hance since 1875.

Listed directly above "unemployed 3 months" John Hance was Robert Mack Rogers, late of Texas, "18, single, laborer, employed, Missouri," a fit young man, slight of build, with a mustache and curly hair.[36] He and Clint Wingfield, Henry Wingfield's son who also knew Hance, partnered to buy the Head & Co. store in 1897, long after John left Verde Valley. Witnessed by George W. Hance, notary public, each purchased a half share on September 20. They were in business but a short year and a half before being shot and killed at the store during the early evening of July 2, 1899.

George Hance's son Harvey rode Wingfield's chestnut sorrel horse named Fashion to Prescott to alert Sheriff John Munds, arriving at his doorstep at sunup. Fashion made the dash unshod and recuperated in Prescott for a month. A posse was quickly mounted. Five people were arrested and charged as killer or accomplice, but none went to trial. The murders remain unsolved.[37]

Camp Verde's annual patriotic parade and barbecue forgotten, Rogers and Wingfield were buried in a common grave in separate coffins on July 4. Wales Arnold, William Head, and George Hance were among Rogers's pallbearers. George penned an eloquent obituary for page one of the *Arizona Weekly Journal-Miner*[38] on July 12: "These two good and noble men were my friends and I loved them, and it is with a sad and heavy heart that I write this."

Murmurs that Fort Verde would close began in December 1880, which didn't bode well for people who depended on the military for most (if not all) of their income. Worse than that, Hance's steers had been dying since September, the victims of a valley-wide bovine epidemic.[39]

The fifth ledger expires a month after the costly Arizona map was purchased, before the closure rumors started, and the next few books are missing. Unfortunately, this is when a closer examination of Hance and McInernay's affairs is most needed. Lost are aspects of the partnership's dissolution and any possible connection between that map and Hance's removal to Grand Canyon, which has never been explained. Outside of one newspaper reference to Hance at a place named Panula, his next two years are shrouded in darkness.

Only a trace of evidence remains in county records, but there's a significant clue in them. In early April 1881, Hance mortgaged his homestead to McInernay in the form of a chattel mortgage. Not used much today, in Hance's time a chattel mortgage was a popular means of securing a loan, preferred by working men over dealing with a bank. Collateral held by the grantor was normally livestock and equipment.

The indenture begins on page twenty-five of Yavapai County's records of chattel mortgages, rambles across five pages, and at McInernay's request is repurposed on page 312. The first entry was after Hance borrowed $900, did not repay it, and after several allowances again failed to perform. "John Hance, Contractor, of Verde, County of Yavapai and Territory of Arizona" mortgaged everything he owned, except his household furniture, to McInernay. This included a strange count of "139 52/100 acres," twenty-eight head of marked oxen[40] with accoutrement, several milk cows, two mares, one horse, and five freight wagons.[41]

In May 1881, with John's mortgage in full play, supply contracts were awarded at Fort Verde. The entire feedlot went to the Hance brothers, John being accountable for 100,000 pounds of barley, 100 tons of hay and 160 tons of straw. George was in for 600,000 pounds of barley, 306,000 pounds of corn, and 300 tons of hay. Jim added a bit more straw.

In early July, Hance was in Prescott "from Verde, where he holds forth, supplying the government with hay, wood, etc."[42] The sideways glance at Hance's personality is notable, but the remainder was true only by degree. Unsaid here is that the removal of Native Americans to San Carlos, coupled with the profound reduction of military operations in the region, was wreaking economic havoc in Verde Valley. Fort Verde was abandoned for the first time two weeks later.[43] It was briefly reoccupied in October after the Battle of Cibecue Creek, then abandoned again and only occasionally garrisoned afterward. George Hance later bought some of it at auction.

In the meantime, George and his brothers, especially John, held the bag. They couldn't deliver or get paid for their goods, nor were they offered future work—that went to Shep Randol. It was his outfit that hauled Fort Verde's 100,000 pounds of military equipment and supplies to Camp Hualapai at Peach Springs in July 1881.[44] Observed the *Miner* just days before the first abandonment, "We hope that the people of the Verde Valley will not be discouraged by the breaking-up of the Post, and that they will turn their attention to the raising of hogs, sheep, cattle, etc. They have good homes and can live without a Military post if they but direct their attention in that direction."[45]

Because of his large cattle and sheep herds, George could transition into raising and selling livestock without difficulty, and that is what he did. His brother, however, drove freight wagons for a living.

McInernay was repaid in full and with interest by the close of 1881, but it took a trip to the Board of Equalization sixty miles away in Prescott to get it. He removed to an unrecorded locale, taking what he'd brought into the partnership, including wagons, oxen, mares, and a buggy and harness. McInernay hauled freight to Williams and considered moving there but instead married and started a family in Prescott. During the following years he carried the Prescott-Verde mail, operated a shuttle service to the Bradshaw Mountain mines, and was the warden at Yuma Territorial Prison. Returning to Prescott, he was Buckey O'Neill's under-sheriff, owned a bicycle shop, and retired as the longtime manager of the Prescott House Hotel.

Hance briefly remained in Camp Verde with his original premort-gage complement of stock and freight wagons before turning north. He probably left town much as he arrived, with a few stock animals, his bedroll, some tools and cooking supplies in a wagon, and his papers in a kit box. John's Verde prosperity had come from McInernay's foresight, hard work, and access to military contracts. Without those things, Hance was on his own—he was always something of an opportunist rather than an entrepreneur, which proved true at Grand Canyon as well.

Hance was last seen at the Cienega in the fall of 1882. His next mention comes in mid-1884, when he appears at Grand Canyon near Grandview Point. From there he is unknown to county assessors and tax collectors for a decade. In curious juxtaposition to this long hermitage, however, is that John's trail and hotel were frequently mentioned in the press, and Hance became a character of wide remark.

John's last visit to C. P. Head's store was on Friday, July 10, 1885. It's his only appearance in the seventh ledger, a 567-page tome spanning December 1884 through January 1886. That afternoon, John drank a fifty-cent beer on his brother Jim's tab, account number 458, and just like the old days Joe Melvin was with him. McInernay had been to the counter first thing that morning. His new account was number 567.

Seven

FIRST LOCATOR

"A Genuine Old-Fashioned Pioneer"

"Wall, I guess it was a right hard trip," Hance told George Wharton James.

It was three days o' the hardest work I ever done in my life, to get down to the river the fourteenth of last June. I was then forty-one years old, and when I got back, I was the proudest boy you ever seen. Mr. [William F. "Bill"] Hull, and a friend of mine, Mr. [Silas "Cy"] Ruggles, had been out here and had brought back strange stories of the canyon, but I couldn't find my way there. I'd never seen the canyon and hooted at the idea of there being anything of the kind they described. I asked them how long the canyon was and how far down, and when they told how far they thought it was, but that they had never been down, I laughed at them and said: "Wall, my grandmother's a pretty old woman, but if I was as old as she is, I'd go down that canyon, if I had to roll down."

Hull and Ruggles, remarked Hance, "sneered at my boast, and said I hadn't 'sand' enough" to make the trip, so he told them if he hadn't returned in four days,

they needn't look for me, but just take everything I left. And then down I went. It was awful work, but I would have taken far more desperate chances than I did to show those fellows I was not the chicken-livered dude they thought I was.

Well, Sir! it took me a little over twenty-four hours' hard tugging to reach that river. I bathed in it. I drank myself full of it! And then I washed in it! I built a monument and although I had no knife with me, I picked up a piece of hard granite and scratched my name in the sandstone rock.[1] I got back on the third day, pretty well used up, but as proud as ever a boy was in his life. I lived that three days on jerked antelope and biscuits.

"And you got to the river?" asked James.

"Yes, siree! Just sure as you are alive! I done some pretty ugly climbing, but I never allowed myself to get dispirited, even when I was through with going over and under those falls. I got drenched to the skin several times, but I kept on. I took good care not to go where I'd be likely to fall, and so I pulled through all O.K. and hunkey-dory."[2]

Most of Hance's stories were obvious, deliberate falsehoods that didn't need verification. But this one makes a claim so significant it warrants a second look. If proven true, an important piece of Grand Canyon history could be placed where it belongs.

The easy part is that Hance turned forty-one in 1878, so it would pay to examine 1878 from as many perspectives as possible. Hull was twenty that year,[3] Ruggles forty-three,[4] but 1878 is otherwise a problem. Because neither Hull nor Ruggles appear in the territorial voting roll or Yavapai County assessor's books, it can't be verified either was nearby until February 1880, which, according to Hull's later note in "John Hance's Visitors' Book," was his first visit.[5]

What did Hull mean by "first visit"? Was it his first time at Grand Canyon—ever—or was it his first trip to see Hance, who was already there? It's certainly possible he was visiting Hance, who had been in the Hull family's orbit since John and George farmed at Granite Creek. Bill Hull's father, Phillip, owned a sheep dipping station in Mint Valley a few miles west of Granite Creek. He also owned Prescott town lots and land described by the assessor as "stock range in Bill Williams Mountain,"[6] which was sheep country at the time. The Hulls were among northern Arizona's early principal sheepherding families.[7] Like John Hance reporting his age, Phillip, sometimes appearing as Philip, never seems to have been on target.

In the early 1880s, Phillip's son Philip (Phil Jr., occasionally identified as Phillip in news reports)—who was born in Illinois and arrived in Arizona by way of Sacramento, California—oversaw the family's Coconino Forest operations from Challender, a small logging community nine miles east of Williams built up around a sawmill named for a railroad man. According to newspaper references, Phil was a "genial, courteous young gentleman, and an efficient and trustworthy guide."[8] In fact, he seems to be the lead man in the rim's earliest sightseeing activities. But he died at forty-one in November 1888 from a heart attack. That unfortunate event resulted in John Hance's rise to sole prominence on the rim and begs the question of how the story might have turned out had Phil Hull lived to tell it.

George Wharton James knew Hance even then, "long before he had dreamed that the Canyon would help make him famous. I ate venison stew with him when he was but a cowboy in the employ of the proprietor of the Hull Ranch."[9] It's difficult to say where or even when that happened, but it fits comfortably enough in the late 1870s or early 1880s. This timeframe is supported to some extent by Day Allen Willey, who studied Hance for an article published in 1910. John Hance, Willey wrote, came across Grand Canyon "hunting for some grazing ground in the desert for a few steers."[10]

We can also test the veracity of Hance's claim for the proposed date by consulting an unimpeachable witness, the Head & Co. ledgers. Charges at Head's store by Hance and McInernay in June 1878 were posted when Hance was presumably at Grand Canyon. On June 13, pants, plates, fifty-eight pounds of corn, and a one dollar knife were purchased, and on the seventeenth a pair of overalls and forty cents' worth of plug tobacco left the store. McInernay smoked a pipe. Hance both smoked and chewed.

But could Hance have returned from Grand Canyon to Camp Verde in time to be at the store that day? Not in 1878. If a man knew where he was going, a horseback journey from Camp Verde via Beaverhead Station and Stoneman Lake to what was then called Flag Staff required two days. It would have taken three more days to reach what's now Grandview Point. With the addition of a rigorous, days-long scramble from the rim to the Colorado River and back to the rim, and with a speedy return to the Verde, the absolute minimum time away from home would have been at least two weeks. Hance could not have returned to Camp Verde until June 21 at the earliest.

As a tourist attraction, "Grand Canyon" didn't exist before the Atlantic & Pacific Railroad laid tracks across northern Arizona. Prior to that, the place was largely unknown to Euro-Americans save for the exploits of John Wesley Powell on the Colorado River during 1869. In 1881, for instance, the *Arizona Weekly Citizen* quoted the *Miner*, "our people who go out and visit the San Francisco mountain country, through which the railroad is being [surveyed], come home perfectly astonished that such a grand and magnificent county exists to the north of Prescott, of which little has been said heretofore."[11] And as late as 1886, articles describing Grand Canyon included guidance on its whereabouts with reminders like, "the Grand Cañon of the Colorado, north of Flagstaff."

Two early newspaper articles identified Grand Canyon as the home of ancient civilizations. Another piece, well ahead of its time in 1876, termed it "the crowning wonder of the natural world."[12] A long article the following year, titled "Grandest Scenery in the World,"[13] described the adventures of John Moss, a "distinctive character, peculiar in many respects," known in "nearly every mining camp from British Columbia to Mexico."[14] In April 1877, Moss claimed a boat journey down the Colorado from Lees Ferry to Fort Mohave, some 360 river miles, taking a scant four days to complete it. An anonymous correspondent with an astonishing knowledge of Grand Canyon geography took him to task two issues later.[15] Looking back, Moss, with his oft-remarked transparent fibbing, could easily be confused for John Hance, save that Moss died in 1880. His death notice termed Grand Canyon an "unfrequented and difficult place."[16]

Railroads changed that. Before they crossed northern Arizona, Victorian-era travelers couldn't visit Grand Canyon without undue hardship and large expenditures of time and money. The rails reached Flagstaff from the east on August 1, Williams on September 1, and Seligman on December 6, 1882. By March 1883, they were in Kingman, and that put Grand Canyon within travelers' reach. After reading Powell's powerfully evocative descriptions, all they needed was transportation from a train depot and lodgings.

Peach Springs, Arizona, is located fifty miles east of Kingman on Historic Route 66. Today, it is barely a wide spot, but in 1883 it was a bustling, vibrant community, poised expectantly to become northern Arizona's largest commercial center. Located near the depot were the H. J. Young & Farlee feed corral, saloon, and restaurant. Farlee and Young began their tour business in January 1883[17] and in March advertised "accommodations at the river for sight seers, and boats for a short trip in the Cañon."[18] This was something fresh and completely new. Their hotel, over twenty miles north of town and three thousand feet below the rim at the dusty, sun-scorched confluence of Peach Springs Wash and Diamond Creek near the Colorado, was termed "a rude little house, roughly boarded, called by convenience Grand Cañon Hotel."[19] But it was Grand Canyon's first, and only, tourist accommodation. To get there required a rugged six-hour buckboard ride from Peach Springs down the road Farlee recorded at the Mohave County courthouse on April 2, 1883—which perhaps should be recognized as the birthday of Grand Canyon tourism.

Diamond Creek was suddenly "full of sight-seeing" with more folks on the way.[20] The Atlantic & Pacific even granted layover courtesies to passengers so they might visit Diamond Creek, or at least that's how it was couched in the press. In truth, the rails had problems on the King-man end, and passengers needed something to do while the train was stopped. Grand Cañon Hotel was the only attraction at hand.

H. J. Young married and moved to California in late 1884, leaving Farlee on his own. Julius Farlee could have succeeded well beyond expec-tations but failed through level of care, as told so well by a German visitor: "The proprietor, expecting us for several days, was ready with an excellent meal: cabbage."[21]

Farlee was too busy to worry about the menu. Between 1883 and 1893, he ran another boarding house and a saloon, blacksmith shop, feed lot, and stable in Peach Springs—while also maintaining the road, driving the stage, and acting as interpretive guide and cook at Diamond Creek. During this time, he was paid coroner's fees by Mohave County and performed duties as a notary public. He ran for the House of Representa-tives, losing by three votes when the polling place was his home. In 1887, he divorced one wife (Ellen) and wed another (Cecelia or "Celia") the same week. He then sold Celia the Grand Cañon Hotel to avoid losing it in an action for debt. Generally, Farlee was short of funds to satisfy either the assessor's bill or the mortgage or surety bond arranged to pay the assessor's bill. He was also arrested twice for cattle theft and tried and acquitted three times, at one point acting as his own attorney. He spent several months in jail when unable to post the required $1,500 bond, probably because Mohave County had assessed his Diamond Creek toll road at the 2017 equivalent of $26,500 and Farlee was flat broke. At the same time, Peach Springs' anticipated role as northern Arizona's premier commercial center amounted to nothing. By early 1884, the *Arizona Champion*, Yavapai County's newspaper of record, had moved to Flagstaff.

Farlee and Hance were cut from the same cloth. Farlee was five years younger but, like Hance, came from a large family, growing up in Michigan, where his father was a cabinet maker. Both men were Civil War POWs. Both identified Grand Canyon's sightseeing potential, building hotels far removed from civilization in locations available only by roads they fashioned and maintained. Farlee encouraged patrons to climb Prospect Point, or Diamond Peak as it's now called. There, with a magnificent view high above the river, his guests found "a cairn to which each . . . was asked to add a stone." Located on that growing stack of rocks was a "large bottle" into which visitors were kindly requested to slip their visiting cards.[22]

Both men also kept guest registers. However, Farlee's was lost in a fire after his death.[23] Its only known signatories were botanist Samuel Mills Tracy, who transcribed notes left in it by fellow botanist Asa Gray in 1885,[24] but a list of prospective others can be drawn from newspaper accounts and other writings. These include: E. E. Ayer; Fred Harvey; W. W. Bass; General Sedgwick (accompanied by John W. Young and others); a group comprising Lawrence Jerome, E. F. Searles, John Travers, M. R. Schuyler, and W. B. Murray; and a Frenchman named Felix Frederic Moreau in 1886. Moreau devoted a chapter in his book, *In the United States: Travel Notes*, to Peach Springs and Diamond Creek, describing Farlee's operation without ever mentioning his host's name.[25]

Conducting his seminal work on life zones based on the distribution of plant communities found in northern Arizona, C. Hart Merriam was at Diamond Creek in 1889. He also visited Hance that September, collecting a new species of snail—now called *Sonorella coloradoensis*—on Hance Trail. In tow was Frank Hall Knowlton, who took a cutting from a tree near the camp that turned out to be a new species of the birch family (*Ostrya knowltonii*), now commonly called the "Knowlton hophornbeam."[26]

Farlee was also an amiable host, storyteller, and guide. Mary Wager Fisher, a prominent American author and journalist, found him "chatty, social, offhand and direct. He talked to [his mules] Pop and Rowdy as if they were intellectual beings. The buckboard was without cover, the sky was cloudless, the sun blazed down in full splendor, and, after the first few miles of comparatively level, dusty road, it was impossible to hold a sunshade, as both [gloved] hands were required to keep one's body from being bounced off the 'tallyho.'"

Farlee told Fisher stories that Hance might have approved of. One went like this:

Oh, this air, madam! I should have been a dead man if it hadn't been for this Arizona air. I came here now three years gone, given up for as good as dead—lungs bleedin' and generally banged up anyway. You see I had been in the war, in Libby prison—a hell, you know—I've a rifle ball now in one leg; the lightning struck my gun once when I was on picket and cut the muscles of them two fingers so I can't lift 'em voluntarily—but you see now that I am as well and hearty a feller as you'll be likely to find anywhere.

Fisher wrote that Farlee "told us the names of the flowers, the trees and the stones, and the altitudes of peaks made by Government surveys, and was full of anecdotes of the famous people whom he had piloted into the Cañon." Then, like many a truth-torturing guide, Farlee told Fisher there were no rattlesnakes at Diamond Creek. Fisher quickly spotted one. "Christopher Columbus!" exclaimed Farlee. "If that ain't a rattler! It is the first varmint of that kind ever seen in this Cañon!"[27]

Hance knew all about rattlesnakes as well, those "pecooliar things," and he "uster wonder how in thunder they made a livin' out on the desert." One day, he found out. "I hadn't taken a drink for over three months— now, laugh, you durned fool, but it's a fact," claimed Hance at the start of his story. After long days of slow travel on the way back to the rim, Hance and party arrived by the side of a shady knoll and took a break. "We hadn't been settin' there long till we heerd a kinder 'chug, chug, chug' noise of the earth pretty reggler like, and we sot thar wonderin' what in thunder could be 'round thar. The other fellers got scart almost ter death, and spishoned it was ghosts on the desert or sum other durned thing, because it was so pecooliar and onaccountable noise."

At this point, Hance, "fearin' nothin' and bein' a man of uncompromised disposiihun," crept slowly forward with his rifle. "When I got jest under the brow of the knoll I heerd sounds like this: 'B-r—r, chug!' I got more and more morterified. I'll be gol-daned if all the nice curly rinkles didn't sorta come out of my hair, and my scalp kept curlin' up till my ears got tired of tryin' ter shove my hat off." But Hance kept crawling forward, using all his "morrel courage" to do it.

Then Hance saw the source of all the commotion:

> Wall, sir, may I be tuck fer a millionaire 'er a parson the rest of my days if there wan't big snakes, little snakes, and mejum sized snakes, all in seemin' great excitement, doin' some kind of game.
>
> Thar was a big rock that run up slantin' like, and the other end was riz up severll feet frum the ground. Well, sir, them snakes was com up' up ter the top of that rock from the slantin' side and thay was a big rattler settin' up ter one side, with his tail in the air. When he would ring the signal with his tail—'b-r-r, b-r-r, b-r-rupt,' kind of a one, two, three business—away would go one of them air snakes over that rock till he struck the edge. Then he would jump up and out and stiffen up his hull boddy and come down with a chug, tail end first, on the ground.
>
> I'll be everlastin' unsoaked if thay wasn't drillin' fer water, fer every snake hit in the same hole with his tail, and the hole was as straight as an arrow, too. I never knowed before whut made so many short, thick snakes, but here was the hull mystery solved.[28]

While making his transition to Grand Canyon from the Verde, Hance may have worked for the A-1 Cattle Co. at Fort Moroni eight miles northwest of Flagstaff. Originally called Leroux Spring, today the area is known as Baderville.

John Willard Young was son and counselor to his father Brigham Young, president and prophet of the Mormon Church in Salt Lake City. A small party guided by John Young built a cabin at Leroux Spring in 1877. In 1881, Young established a permanent camp there for his sixty-five-man team that supplied railway ties for the Atlantic & Pacific's westward course. Suspecting trouble from loitering Apaches, he joined the sides of his one-story log sheds together, then added three outreaching walls to form a large enclosed structure. Prentiss Ingraham, who was there in late 1892, described Fort Moroni in *The Girl Rough Riders*: "The buildings were all built of massive timbers and were located in the center of a plain-like valley. Around them was a high stockade, built of huge logs, standing end on end and close together, forming a wall of from five to ten feet high, with a platform on the inner side on which men could stand and fight back a foe."

After losing his railroad tie contract[29] to Ayer Lumber Co. in 1882,[30] Young reorganized his business. Although the timeline is vague, Fort Moroni's transition into Moroni Cattle Co., the Arizona Cattle & Wool Co., and, later, the A-1 took place during the time Hance was leaving the Verde. In historical literature, these several outfits have become commingled as the A-1. Hance's association with Fort Moroni is confused to a similar degree.

Evidence of this relationship begins and ends with a single letter written by Andy Ashurst, then seventy years old.[31] Andy's father, William Henry Ashurst, had maintained a close association with John Hance for as long as two decades. They were best friends, and their association continued even after both of them had died.

Born in 1844 in northeastern Missouri, Bill Ashurst learned to hunt as a boy and by twelve was supplying game while crossing the plains to California in a covered wagon with his family. In the late 1860s he mined around Red Bluff, California, and again in Nevada when he married Sarah Bogard, with whom he had ten children. The best remembered child is Henry Fountain, born in 1874 in an "uncovered wagon"[32] near Winnemucca, Nevada. He became a Democratic politician and one of the first two U.S. senators from Arizona, widely remarked upon for his sesquipedalian vocabulary. Even as a young man Henry was termed "the Boy Orator of Williams mountain."[33]

Henry Fountain could tell a story as well, such as this one:

Mr. Jerome J. (Sandy) Donahue operated the Senate Saloon; Donahue was of tremendous personal charm, red headed, handsome, athletic, humane and generous; sometime sheriff of Coconino County. Into Donahue's Saloon walked Mr. William

G. (Mickey) Stewart, also red headed, weighing 110 pounds, of Prussic acid wit, born tragedian, brilliant orator who played upon human emotions and human prejudices as a virtuoso upon a violin; sometime foreman on a cattle ranch, he abandoned the saddle, lasso, spurs and branding-iron for law books. Stewart was much given to poetry as evidenced by his frequent quotations and much given to bourbon whiskey as evidenced by his frequent potations. Stewart deposited his fifteen cents on the bar and called for bourbon; Donahue set the bottle and empty glass before Stewart. According to the custom of those days the customer poured his own and did not limit the quantity. Stewart poured himself a full GOBLET—half pint—whereupon Donahue said: "That is not WATER you are pouring out." Stewart replied: "I came here for refreshment, not to be insulted." Donahue said, "And how have I insulted you?" Stewart replied, "Do I look like a man who would drink that much WATER?"[34]

In company with others, Bill Ashurst and his growing family arrived in Yavapai County by driving sheep across the Colorado River at Hardy's Ferry and spending the 1875 winter at Big Sandy River.[35] The next summer he stopped for the season a few miles south of Bill Williams Mountain, then explored farther afield.[36] Newspaper briefs, census records, and tax rolls find him all across northern Arizona, including one time at Sunset Crossing on return from a salt-mining expedition near the San Juan River.[37]

Bill settled into "Old Ashurst Ranch" on Anderson Mesa in 1878, near what became Ashurst Lake southeast of Flagstaff. Prescott was one hundred miles away and his closest neighbor was thirty miles away. Only Indians passed by, from which the family hid food and occasionally themselves in nearby lava caves. Sarah Ashurst cooked meals in a fireplace, hand sewed the garments her growing children wore, cured meat, worked the garden, and made candles, moccasins, and other necessary items when not busy teaching her youngsters to read and write. After the family moved to Flagstaff the cabin fell to ruin. It was later moved piecemeal to Pioneer Living History Village in north Phoenix near Anthem, reconstructed and furnished as it may have been, and can be visited today.

During the late 1870s, Ashurst's sheep were clipped and dipped at Phillip Hull's Mint Valley ranch. In 1885, Ashurst helped found the Mogollon Live Stock Protective Association and was later its president. In 1887 he served in the Fourteenth Territorial Legislature, where he drank brandy, smoked and chewed tobacco, dressed according to his office, abhorred off-color jokes, showed a fiery temper, and lobbied for the creation of Frisco County (Coconino County was carved from Yavapai County in 1891).

"My father first visited the Canyon in 1880," wrote his son, Andy, "after which he wintered there. He would place his horses in the various side canyons and devote his time in caring for them and prospecting." When Andy was old enough, he went along. "We were always accompanied by the assistance of Captn Hance. We endured several hardships of weather, but the Captn was never at a loss for stories to tell us, and strange enough to state he was never guilty of telling the same story twice."[38]

Andy also recalled listening as Hance reminisced with tall, slim Jack Arnold and his partner, the shorter, mild-mannered, blonde-haired "Curley" Wallace, about the Coconino basin and Little Colorado River country. They were "old associates of the Captn," he wrote, "and from the way they spoke it was quite evident the three of them had been together with the A1's [cattle operation]." Arnold and Wallace "were in partners with cattle for years. Their range was the Coconino Basin and Little Colorado River country. Curley Wallace nearly lost his right leg [when] his double action six shooter was discharged by the brush as he was chasing cattle in the Basin. The Colt tore most of the bone away. His leg was saved.... After they sold their cattle, Wallace made history gambling away his entire life savings in a single evening at James A. Vail's saloon in Flagstaff."[39]

In the 1890s, Wallace worked for the Hulls around Grandview, and later with Hance at Fred Harvey Co. One day, having assured a group of young ladies they would be perfectly safe riding mules on Bright Angel Trail, Hance appeared and "told the same girls the trip was very dangerous and that many people lost their lives every week."[40] "There, you see," remarked one woman to the other, "I knew all the time that other guide was lying."[41]

Talking to another group about Bright Angel Trail, Hance said, "You must understand that when you get down to the bottom of the Canyon

John Hance near the Grand Canyon in 1884. While the attributed date may be incorrect, this image accents Hance's strong frontier aspect. Courtesy of Arizona Historical Society, Flagstaff, AHS.0032.00007, George Hochderffer Collection.

and reach the shore of the Colorado River it is very warm. You cannot imagine how hot is. Why, I'll give you my word, I have been down there when it was so hot it melted the wings off flies!"

Inquired a lady, "How do the tourists stand it?"

"Madame," responded Hance, "I have never seen a tourist with wings."[42]

In 1917, Hance wrote that he first went to Grand Canyon thirty-three years previously, "on the 11th day of June." He was speaking metaphorically, referencing his homestead application of 1884 when he "took possession of and located as a home that certain unsurveyed Public Land of the United States."[43] Any homesteading paperwork, however, required an official government survey. By his own unintended admission, Hance was squatting on government land—no survey, no patent. Hance was peremptorily asserting ownership of the place he called Glendale Springs, but he proffered documentation by publishing his metes and bounds in the newspaper. They read remarkably like his father's Jefferson County deeds:

> Bounding lines, commencing at a pile of stones, or monument about 300 yards south of the rim of the Grand Canyon of the Colorado in the Coconino Forest, and near the place where a trail known as the 'Hance Trail' leads down into the Grand Canyon aforesaid, and running thence west one mile, on a line marked by blazes or scalps on trees to another monument of stones, thence south 1/4 of a mile by a line designated as above to a 3rd monument, thence east one mile by another line designated as above to another, 4th monument of stones, and thence north to place of beginning by a line designated above. All of which I hereby declare my intention to claim as a home under the public land law of the United States. JOHN HANCE.[44]

Surveyed or not, Hance Trail was established to some primitive yet identifiable standard—which it never got beyond—*before* Hance "filed" his homestead papers.

Canyon lore has it that Hance improved a series of ancient Indian switchbacks rising from Tonto Platform, a broad, miles-long terrace halfway to the river, and that a dim trail found at Glendale Springs put him on the scent. Just as likely, the route was a slight game path. Nevertheless, Grand Canyon is a big place—nineteen hundred square miles of surface area—and about one thousand cubic miles of missing rock define its actual below-rim enormity.[45] Hance didn't simply appear one sunny day and start to fashion a route to the river down a horrendously sheer, inverted, mile-high mountainside. To get to Tonto Platform, he would have had to carefully scour the rim for miles to identify even the most tenuous of entry points. Exploring just a few of those many steep declivities would have been an enormous undertaking, working alone as he was, going as far as he could day after day and getting nowhere except farther along the rim itself. That more than likely scenario could place his first Grand Canyon sighting in the winter of 1880, in company with Bill Hull or Bill Ashurst. Perhaps it was the three of them standing there together, gazing dumbstruck at the spectacle.

Hance did describe how he built his trail, and it's evident he was strapped for cash when leaving Verde Valley. "For two summers Hance hired out as a sheep herder" to earn money to carry out his mission, he told a newspaper writer. "With his cabin stocked with provisions, he put-in the winters constructing a narrow, winding trail down the steep sides of the cliffs toward the roaring Colorado River seven or eight miles away. He finally made a trail passable for burros [to Tonto Platform] and charged visitors a toll for using it."[46]

After completing his footpath, still living on unsurveyed land, Hance was open for business. But he also failed to record his trail—a "toll road" in era-speak—with Yavapai County. In fact, he generated no official records concerning his business dealings during his first ten years of economic activity at Glendale Springs. These oversights would cause Hance many headaches in the future.

Edward E. Ayer visited Bill Hull at Cedar Ranch in February 1884. From Chicago, Ayer would become one of America's great bibliophiles and philanthropists. In 1884, he owned one of northern Arizona's early smoke-stack industries, Ayer Lumber Co., then producing one hundred thousand board feet a day, most of it railroad ties.[47]

Thirty miles south of Grandview, Cedar Ranch was located at the northern base of the San Francisco Mountains, on the edge of a vast sandy plain spreading northward. While it was nearly the only outpost between Grand Canyon and Flagstaff, it was an enterprising enough sheep operation that wagon tracks led there from town.

Cedar Ranch, Ayer later advised a relative,

> consisted of one cattle shed, small log cabin with one room with a fire place in it, floor made of split logs, and beds of numerous sheep skins thrown on the floor with some blankets. [My companion] Col Montague and I were sitting on the floor of the cabin, on sheep skins, telling stories and all that sort of thing, when a man came in and addressed me. Bill Hull says, "Is your name Ayer?" I said, "Yes." He asked, "Be you a relative of the man that owns the mill in Flagstaff?" I replied that I was the man. He looked at me with surprise and said, "Gee whiz! I supposed you were 65 years old, 6 1/2 feet high, weighed 250 pounds and wore a plug hat." And he kept raising his words until he fairly yelled the words "plug hat."
>
> We started for the Canyon and came within thirteen miles of it the first night. The next day the snow was so deep it took us all day to go the thirteen miles. We had no tents of course, slept on the snow on the ground, felling a pine tree every night to make our bed out of pine boughs. We stayed four days at the Canyon and of course were tremendously impressed with it.[48]

If Hance was there, he later told young Amelia "Minna" Hollenback and her sister Josephine, or "Jo," all about it. They spent two weeks with John and came to trust him completely. Voracious notetakers, their letters and photographs provide a rich, intimate look at John Hance at Grand Canyon.[49]

Amelia wrote,

> If there were no Cañon and no stage line it would be worth any one's while to come here and talk to John Hance. He is the greatest man in all this part of the country, owns the whole Cañon, and everyone in it though I doubt he has a deed to any large piece of it—and is a sort of grandfather, or male, to everyone around him.
>
> Years ago he was a scout and went through all the Indian wars but took to lumbering only a few months before he might

have been killed with Custer.[50] Then a cowboy [probably Phil Hull] told him of the Grand Canyon in days when people hardly knew of its existence, and he came here in the middle of winter, and was, I think, the first white man to climb down its awful walls and stand beside the Colorado River. Now he lives here, as he has for thirteen years [since 1884] and spends the summers taking people over his trails, and I never saw a person whom I would rather trust with any number of children, on a trail, or my whole fortune, if I had one to be left somewhere.

He is as patient, kind-hearted, thoughtful and unselfish a man as you can imagine, if he does have a peculiar and original way of pronouncing his English; but oh my, what fish stories he can tell! You can depend on his word to the end, when he is serious, but it would take a mind reader to tell whether he is serious or not. That is why it is worth a long journey to hear him talk. To hear him tell his big yarns is more fun than any number of boxes of monkeys. Everyone within a radius of a few hundred miles knows John Hance . . . a genuine old-fashioned pioneer and frontiersman such as we read about but don't often come across.[51]

Ayer returned to Arizona in 1885, making three trips to the canyon that year.[52] His typed recollections of the second journey in mid-May generally agree with the *Arizona Champion*'s condensed version of the same event.[53] "I took Mrs. Ayer (and [our daughter] Lizzie 15 years old), Mrs. Johnson and Ethel Sturgis (now Mrs. Dummer)[54] to Flagstaff with me. I organized a party and went over to the Grand Canyon again. We took two wagons, six mules each, for supplies, and a six-mule wagon for water, an ambulance for the ladies"—for the ladies' comfort, not because they were injured or ill—as well as several riding horses and twenty men.

We made camp on a point sticking out into the Canyon about 4 miles east of Grandview [indicating an area at or near Glendale Springs]. Mrs. Ayer wanted to go to the bottom of it. I selected two of the strongest men I had in the party and known to be good climbers, and they, Bill Hull, uncle Henry, Mrs. Ayer and I started to go down to the bottom of the Canyon. . . . We climbed down precipices and steep slopes when a misstep would have

sent us to death many times. In time we arrived at a point immediately under our [rim] camp where there was some water [this
was, or would shortly become, Cottonwood Camp, John's rock
cabin on Hance Creek]. They could see us with a glass from the
camp. We were 3,000 feet below them and looked like small
ants on the ground, not taller than an inch or so. We there got
our lunch. By the way, it consisted of a can of tomatoes heated
up, crackers, and coffee. Leaving part of our supplies we went
on until that night and camped in a deep canyon, probably two
miles from the bottom. The next morning we went to the river
and made one or two climbs up the mountains for a particular
view and got back to our camp the same night.

We got out the next afternoon at four o'clock, thoroughly
exhausted. It was one of the hardest trips anybody ever took
for fun.

Ayer concluded by saying he'd been to Peach Springs before any of
his Grandview area activity occurred.[55]

In *Reminiscences of the Far West and Other Trips*, Ayer expanded on
this journey. "All the provisions were carried in bags on the backs of the
men," he wrote, "with the coffee pot slung above. Also on their backs they
carried rifles and a small roll of blankets, for it was necessary that their
hands should be free for the descent. Bill Hull, the adventurous cowboy
who had been down once [June 22, 1884, according to Hance's guestbook]
protested strongly against [Mrs. Ayer going]. No white woman had ever
climbed down. Bill, with a comrade, had blazed the original trail later,
but at this time there was none."[56]

Although Ayer's journey could not have been accomplished without
Hance's trail blazing, because Hance goes unmentioned his participation
comes into question. All Ayer says is that Bill Hull and his "comrade"
built the trail, but after the fact. When it's recalled that even in its heyday
Hance Trail was a precipitous, primitive route, and that in 1885 Hance
was not anyone of particular note, his lack of mention makes a certain
amount of sense.

Further clouding Hance's involvement is that in his eightieth birthday letter he recited a list of individuals who, by themselves or in groups,

The Edward Ayer party at Hance's Cove, May 1885, showing Coronado Butte (what Hance called Ayer Butte) in the right background. Although the image quality is poor, the man seated on the far right resembles John Hance. Courtesy of Grand Canyon National Park, no. 49517.

found their way to him before his guestbook came into use. He mentioned Supreme Court justices, territorial governors, high ranking Santa Fe Railway officials, Henry Ashurst, and accomplished others, but Ayer was not among them. Also, Frank Lockwood studied both Ayer and Hance with some care. He wrote a biography of Ayer and chronicled the life, character, and stories of Hance.[57] If Edward Ayer and John Hance knew each other, Lockwood would have connected the dots. He did not.

The only evidence Edward Ayer and his wife were with John Hance at Sockdolager Rapid comes from Josephine Hollenback. Hance and the Hollenback girls explored much of the East Rim, one day riding beyond Moran Point to discover an Indian ruin Hance had never seen. Jo recorded,

Mr. Hance, as excited as we were, skipped from rock to rock like a most animated chamois, and we soon [saw] that the surroundings were as new to him as they were to us. When we finally reached the top we discovered what must have been a five or six roomed cliff dwelling, the best preserved, Captain Hance admitted, of any of the ruins which he knew anything about at the Cañon. One of its fort-like walls, right on the edge of the precipice, still stands as high as my head.

Captain Hance would have heard of it, but he, who is better acquainted with the Grand Cañon than anyone else in the country, wasn't even aware there were any cliff dwellings on that point, where until that day he had never stopped. Mr. Hance went back to our horses for our cameras and the lunch, for our new discovery proved so interesting that we decided to then and there eat our luncheon in its ancestral kitchen.... The precipices right down from this ancient fort-like dwelling looked in some places to be fully 2,000 feet. Mr. Hance was actually scared at the sight in some places, and called it "Awful, sure thing!"[58]

Hance called the pinnacle Fort Hollenback for the girls. "Captain Hance was instrumental in giving names to the other points," Jo went on. "Ayres Peak [Coronado Butte] he named for Mrs. Ayer, the first and only woman who has climbed the peak, and the first one also whom Captain Hance took to the river ... and Point Moran Mr. Hance named when Thomas Moran was painting his noted picture there, for it was Mr. Hance who helped him carry his outfit, canvases etc. over to the Point, and afterwards built the trail for tourists."[59]

The first referenced journey to the river on Hance's trail seems to have occurred in June 1884, a year before Ayer's trip, and it is here that events take a curious turn. Like so many milestones in the life of John Hance, this one is known only through inference.

"First entered the Canon June 22 1884" is Bill Hull's initial entry in "John Hance's Visitors' Book," indicating his earliest transit of Hance Trail. However, Hull failed to mention the *Arizona Champion*'s special correspondent Hal (a.k.a. "the Scribe") who was also present. Led by Phil Hull to Glendale Springs, where his brother Silas Ruggles and Hance awaited them, Hal penned an account of the day that didn't appear in print until the following February, when Hance was ready for business. Hance and the others "laid the foundation for a temporary hotel," Hal wrote, "being impressed with the fact that here would come the future tourist to look out upon the 'Temples of the Gods.'" Going on to describe "spires, obelisks, plain cliffs and bold battlements, here a cathedral, there a tower, and miles away the 'little church around the corner,'" Hal concluded with the tease, "the history of our descent into the 'King of Gorges' will be made the subject of another letter."

That "descent" is what Bill Hull noted in "John Hance's Visitors' Book." However, a February 14, 1885, issue of the *Arizona Champion* detailing events of the previous June is not known to exist. If discovered, it should indicate Hance, Hull, Hal, and others reached the river in June 1884. In the February 21 issue, Hal begins a three-part series titled "The Cowboy & the Scribe," a fanciful account of his ramblings in Havasupai Canyon with an unnamed accomplice. But all is finally revealed in the last installment when the fictional Mrs. Mugwump remarks, "we'll go and live in tents on the prairies and slide down the Grand Canyon on ropes and live in the Temple of the Gods."[60]

Hal published that two months before Ayer made it to the river, but neither mentioned what they saw there—something few people have witnessed anywhere on earth, let alone at Grand Canyon. The Colorado's historic pre-dam spring floods averaged 86,000 cfs, or cubic feet of water per second. A cubic foot, "second foot" or "cu sec" in boatman-speak, is the approximate size (in volume) of a toaster oven. Grand Canyon's greatest historic flood occurred in 1884, the result of the global 1883 "volcanic winter" caused by the explosion of Krakatau in Indonesia. The Colorado River's 1884 flood has been estimated at 300,000 cfs, although some scientists put it as high as 380,000 cfs, a bit above the Mississippi's average July flow at Vicksburg.

Let's call it 333,000 cfs. Visualize 333,000 toaster ovens tumbling past you every second through a tight, tall, barren, hard-rock canyon—and what a tremendous thundering racket! The Colorado's roar would have been just as deafening and dramatic to Hal in 1884, caused by water volume and huge cottonwood trees grinding against each other, circling in violent eddies, banging into and exploding against the sheer Precambrian walls of Upper Granite Gorge. As the spate passed and the river began to drop, much of that timber was deposited far up lateral side canyons. Remnants of the event are today seen in large driftwood piles a hundred or more feet above the normal, dam-controlled waterline. Ayer would have had a difficult time finding a route to the river through the maze of

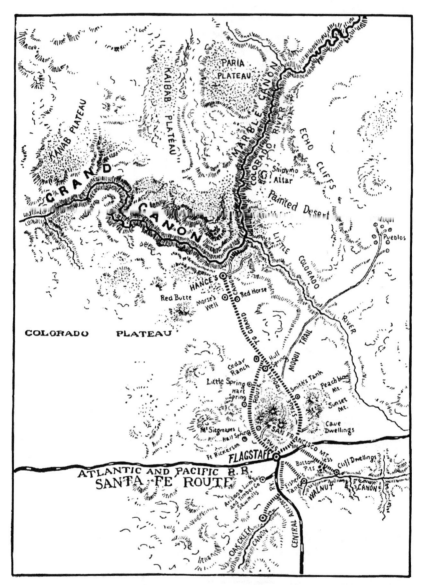

The western and eastern routes to Grand Canyon skirted the San Francisco Mountains to meet at a sheep camp called Cedar Ranch. There, they joined a road that Hance, Bill Hull, Silas Ruggles, and others carved to Glendale Springs in June 1884. This primitive wagon route connected Grand Canyon to the rest of the world, and "Hance's ranch" became an immediate tourist destination. Courtesy C. A. Higgins, *Grand Cañon of the Colorado River, Arizona* (Chicago, IL: Passenger Department, Santa Fe Route, 1892).

debris a year later. Although both dealt with it, they probably regarded what they saw as an everyday feature and did not bother mentioning it.

According to Bill Hull in his same guestbook entry, he, Hance, and Ruggles began their survey of a thirty-mile route to Cedar Ranch several days later, perhaps accounting for time spent below the rim. Their road was the slimmest of paths, barely smoothed over, laid along the shortest, easiest lines. Road making was an avocation for Hance and the others, an aspect of their frontier lives that was part of any working day. "The system of road making in this country," jotted Amelia Hollenback, "is wonderfully simple. One team drives over the hills, another drives in the first man's tracks, and that is a road."[61]

But this particular road—primitive, slow, and arduous as its passage was—connected Grand Canyon to the rest of the world. At Cedar Ranch it joined two other rugged, wagon-tracked lanes that met there. Both eventually found their separate bumpy ways to Flagstaff. The new "eastern route," developed by James Black, skirted the east side of the San Francisco Peaks past Walnut Canyon and Sunset Crater before turning north through a long series of lava domes and outcrops. There began a slow, rough, twisting, and sometimes precipitous transit across an enormous saddle of sharp-edged basaltic boulders scattered through a dense piñon forest until, finally, the road slowly descended onto the softer tablelands at Cedar Ranch.

The better-known and longer-established "western route" rounded west of the peaks past Fort Moroni and turned north across Hart Prairie and Kendrick Meadows to eventually descend northeast through piñon grasslands and reach Cedar Ranch, where, via either route, passengers spent the night before pushing on the following day.

The road to Grand Canyon stretched north at sunrise. Beneath an enormous sky it coursed broad, brushless, gentle limestone uprises before encountering a long, jarring stretch through another dense piñon forest. By late afternoon, travelers would have gained elevation and smoother passage through a shady ponderosa forest a few miles south of Glendale Springs.

Eight

GLENDALE SPRINGS

"Over the Falls at Midnight"

As the only scant water source for miles along the rim, Glendale Springs—sometimes called Canyon Spring in early literature—was John Hance's obvious choice as a base for operations. Resting in a quiet hollow two hundred yards from the precipice, it was protected from updrafts and sheltered from severe weather. The camp began with Hance, his tent, and whatever else he'd salvaged from Verde Valley.

The small ponderosa pine log cabin seen in so many photographs was most likely constructed on the foundation laid in June 1884, about the same time Hull's cabin was built, when Phil Hull established his sheep camp and supply dump a mile south of Glendale Springs. Hull's cabin was bigger and better appointed than Hance's, but both were one-room affairs similar in their saddle-notched construction and were probably built about the same time.[1]

Uncultivated and backward as it may have been, Hance's camp provided plentiful shade, fresh spring water, and a spectacular canyon overview, all eminently more inviting than Diamond Creek's scorched environs. Although Hance's creature comforts were, possibly, more primitive than Julius Farlee's, once people visited Glendale Springs they understood what the words "Grand Canyon" actually meant.

On October 4, 1884, the *Arizona Weekly Citizen* reported that visitors "to the Grand Canyon of the Colorado, in Northern Arizona, cannot imagine anything grander than the effect of gazing upon that great wonder of the world at a cash expense of $12.50 per day." Early in 1885 Hance became the subject of a newspaper debate when the *Arizona Champion*

Hance in front of his Glendale Springs cabin, well-armed and dressed, saddled to a burro and ready to ride. "Hance, Bongere & burros," 1892. Photo by William Henry Jackson, History Colorado, no. 86.200.3081.

quoted the *Weekly Arizona Miner*: "Mr. Harvey [*sic*] is the American citizen who 'squatted' on the only land by which the Grand Canyon of the Colorado River can be reached, and he charges twelve dollars to visitors for the privilege of looking at that natural wonder." Ignoring the jab at John's Confederate heritage, the *Champion* fired back: "We are surprised to find the above item in any paper printed in Yavapai County.... [There is] a strip of land where the visitor to the canyon can approach the brink of the gorge either on horseback or in a carriage. The country around these approaches [from Prescott] is a broad plateau with nothing more than gentle undulating hills over which a buckboard or common wagon can be driven without obstruction."[2]

Hance Trail, now called "Old Hance Trail," was thin, slight, and steep—and that was the easy part to Tonto Platform. Beyond and below that it

The "easy part" of Hance Trail ran almost straight downhill for its first three miles to Tonto Platform. "Hance's Trail, Canon of the Colorado," 1892. Photo by William Henry Jackson, History Colorado, no. 86.200.1441.

The lower portion of Hance Trail featured several waterfalls requiring roped descent. Hance, lower left, holds taught the line as others make their way down. "Moran's Falls," 1892. Photo by William Henry Jackson, History Colorado, no. 86.200.3110.

was a streambed stroll for a while until it dropped precipitously into the quick sheerness of Upper Granite Gorge, which necessitated a few somewhat technical roped descents with minimal finger and toeholds. None of that seems to have mattered to the first visitors to "hike" to the river, perhaps as many as three hundred by early 1894 based on comments extrapolated from Hance's guestbook.[3] Until 1891 and the installment of Bright Angel Toll Road, Hance Trail provided the only below-rim access to Grand Canyon. It *was* Grand Canyon, as widely remarked as the place itself. People had to see the trail for themselves.

About 1895, J. G. Owens, one of the trail's few remaining customers, carried his journal and lunch down "Old Hance" on a solo journey. He told it like it was—like it had always been. He "walked, ran, slid, and rolled down the [first] three miles" to Tonto Platform, where he took a long drink from Hance Creek at Cottonwood Camp. Refreshed, he descended along the creek bed through the lower exposures of sandstone and shale, "and was already several hundred feet into the [sheer, slick] granite, when [he] came to the first rope ladder." Owens made the ten-foot descent with ease. Unsure about the rope's fastness on the following fifteen-foot drop, he proceeded cautiously. Next came "a gentle slope, clinging to a rope about 40 feet long," and then a pool to swim across.

Owens had proceeded only a few steps before he "heard the roar of a heavy fall of water." The rope was on the ground fifteen feet below. The granite was extremely slick, but, "being barefoot, I found climbing rather a simple matter." He arrived safely, only to notice the rope he'd thought was on the ground was instead topping a "descent without bottom . . . the great waterfall of which I had heard Mr. Hance speak."

He cast the rope over the falls. "It hung straight in the mist of a cascade of water four feet wide and six inches deep. The rope appeared strong, and I determined to try it. The height was said to be fifty feet, but I do not think it was so much." Owens came out soaked at the bottom, undressed, found a handy spot to dry his clothes, and continued on until he reached another steep slope. "I decided the best method of descent was the one I had used years ago on my grandfather's farm in descending straw-stacks. Only one objection presented itself—the part of my costume that was missing is the one usually most relied upon on such occasions." Finally, "only one short rope remained for me, and almost leaping with joy, I found myself on the bank of the Colorado."[4]

Many women also journeyed to the river on Hance Trail. "Very often they discard their skirts and wear a bloomer-style of trousers," reported the *Abbeville Press and Banner* of South Carolina, "the better to clamber about the rocks and steep trails."[5] One group, "chaperoned by Mrs. T. J. Daggs, Flagstaff," immortalized their journey in John's guest-book with a word drawing descending crosswise down the page: "Over the Falls at Midnight. The Lost Strayed or Stolen Party."[6]

Robert Brewster Stanton recorded ladies' use of the trail when making his portage of Sockdolager Rapid in late January 1890. Stanton was attempting a transit of the river twenty years after John Wesley Powell. This was his second try, and he would succeed. Stanton's second expedition became the second successful run of the Colorado River through Grand Canyon.

His first attempt in 1889 was a disaster. Entrepreneur Frank Mason Brown, president of the Denver, Colorado Cañon and Pacific Railroad, envisioned a narrow-gauge railway coursing the river through the inner canyon not far above the waterline. Intended to deliver Colorado coal to Los Angeles, the river's overall gradient of eight and a half feet per mile made for near-perfect railway efficiency. Brown hired Stanton to draw up a preliminary survey of his railroad's course.

Ignoring the hard lessons in Powell's popular account, *The Exploration of the Colorado River and Its Canyons*, visions of inner-canyon toll roads, real estate sales, and ferry operations clouded Brown's thinking. On the human side, Powell relayed only unremitting physical toil compounded by personal conflict under starvation conditions—Brown missed that part entirely. His expedition of fifteen men rowed small, fragile, lightweight cedar boats completely unsuited to the task. Without life jackets, they were doomed from the start. In July, after losing their kitchen, cutlery, and plates—and Brown, and then Peter Hansborough, and finally Brown's black servant Henry Richards, who all drowned in Marble Canyon— Stanton assumed charge and suspended the expedition thirty-two miles below Lees Ferry at North Canyon. Hauling up the boats to the shelter of a limestone cave, they noticed Brown's corpse floating downstream along the opposite wall. The expedition's bankroll was in his pockets.

But Stanton held tight to the dream of completing his work. With remarkable efficiency he refitted with sturdy oak boats rowed by men wearing cork life jackets using honest ash oars, and the expedition was delivered overland to Lees Ferry, where Stanton ate Christmas dinner in 1889.

On January 27, 1890, Stanton and company arrived at Sockdolager Rapid. Lining his boats down the left wall just above the drop, they encountered "signs that someone had camped there.... Among the things that were left was a woman's garment."[7] Stanton gave the find more oomph: "One of the men found ... one leg of a pair of woman's embroidered drawers, and they all gave it a cheer."[8]

George Hance's fourth and final child, daughter Eva, was twenty-seven when she searched out and met her uncle John for the first (and only) time at Grand Canyon in August 1917. John's greeting, "Tell me, how is your dear mother?" must have taken her aback. Her mother was a year dead and buried by then, an untimely passing from tuberculosis. John's eyes brimmed over. To disguise his embarrassment, he replied, "I'd jest as lief youse hadn't come atal." But, after recovering from the shock, Hance invited her to his tent-cabin for a longer chat.[9]

Hance was out of touch with his brother—they lived entirely separate lives. And both John and Eva were uninformed on the latest turn in George's life. He had married Evelyn Grace Jassby that same month, after meeting her at a Masonic convention in Tucson. She was many years his junior and on the make; he was smitten with money to burn. George built his new wife a small house on the north side of the abandoned Fort Verde parade grounds, near the surgeon's quarters. Then Evelyn wanted a car, so George bought one for her and drove it to Prescott in early 1918.

George was alone that day, headed to the courthouse. His marriage had taken a wrong turn and he was pursuing a legal remedy. According to one account, "The god of love jumped [George's] job ... the 20th day of December, at which time the kitchen of the family home at Camp Verde was the scene of a pitched battle between Hance and his wife. For several days prior, Mrs. Hance had been away, and on that day, she returned and told the plaintiff that she had come home for the purpose of getting the rest of his property, and that if he did not hurry up and die from apoplexy, she would finish the job by killing him." Evelyn picked up a chunk of stove wood and knocked George to the floor, then hit his head with a granite dipper. When George tried to get up, Evelyn "made a pass at him with a butcher knife and inflicted a severe wound upon his scalp," then finished with "hammer blows upon various parts of her husband's person and left him in such a state that he had to call-in a physician."

Although the couple had been married for over five months, "the bride spent only about thirty nights at home, and on these nights, she locked herself in her bedroom and denied her husband access to her boudoir." Then she ran away. George located her in Globe, Arizona, wandering the streets, penniless. A sucker for punishment, he "promised her that if she would come home and live with him again, he would deed her a half-interest in certain real estate which he owned. She agreed, and the deeds were made, but the wife failed to keep her part of the contract" and was again on the loose. At that point George, recovered from his injuries, lost interest.[10]

A grisly story preceded George's marriage predicament by thirty years. In late April 1888, during a cattle drive on an abandoned ranch in rugged, steep, cactus-littered Lower Verde, George—somehow—made a hard landing on a dead cow's skull. He impaled himself on a horn that protruded out his groin. He withered in pain for thirty-six hours until a Fort Verde doctor arrived, administered whiskey and morphine, and removed the horn. Not expected to survive the journey to Fort Whipple hospital, George was tied on a stretcher headfirst between two mules, which brought more agony: "It worked fine until they went up the first hill when he slid up under the mule's tail and the mule crapped all over his face. On climbing up the other side he slid backward and the rear mule chewed on his toes."[11]

The incident, from which George miraculously recovered while reading his own obituary—"an old resident of the country, and universally respected"[12]—left him with an enormous hernia of abdominal contents that went nearly to his left knee. He afterward wore a truss fashioned by a Camp Verde blacksmith. It featured a spring-loaded metal plate, gauged at twenty-three pounds of pressure, which kept the sack internalized and allowed George to get around efficiently. Looking at a picture of George, you would never suspect the injury. Neither, apparently, did Evelyn.

George's oldest living descendant, blue-eyed Ruth Hance Thayer (his son Harvey's daughter), was aware of George when she was very young. When asked about the Hance brothers in her late nineties, among other

George Washington Hance. John's younger half-brother, was the "informal mayor" of Camp Verde for some fifty years. Courtesy of the Camp Verde Historical Society.

things she thought they had grown apart in the 1880s. This, she said, was because George considered himself an educated man. He read everything he could, mostly lawyerly things, rising above—he believed—John's lack of sophistication.[13] While perhaps true, they were also complete opposites. George was energized, community centered, motivated, and involved, glad-handing, backslapping, and puzzling every scheme to make a buck (which he did). George Hance died a wealthy man. John was even gabbier than George and just as energy filled, and the amount of hard labor he performed during his first seventy-five years of life is astounding. But John wasn't a Mason. John rode a mule.

George's descendants also indicate that he was "highly disapproving of his brother's lying and storytelling." That might be on target, as a sibling rivalry may have been involved. But lying is one thing, storytelling another. John *was* a liar. Everybody knew that. He was also a trusted, reliable informant. People respected John Hance because he always gave an honest answer to a sincerely thoughtful question. Minna Hollenback told it straight: "When old John Hance starts to tell you the truth, he is very exact about it."[14]

In his writings, George fails to mention his brother's Grand Canyon years, nearly half his life. George corresponded with the Prescott newspapers on Verde Valley politics, personalities, obituaries, marriages, and such, and what he wrote then is now closely studied by Verde historians. If he did record anything about John, which is probable, the information was unfortunately set ablaze in Colton, California, when his third and final wife, Fanny, got angry and burned his papers in the fireplace. What's left in the ashes is the fact that by the time John laid the Glendale Springs foundation he and George had gone in separate directions.

All that can be truly said is that John and George were together only a few known times after John left for Grand Canyon, mostly in court proceedings during the mid-1880s. These concurrent actions, possibly regarding Fort Verde contract matters, were often recited in the *Arizona Weekly Journal-Miner* as "No. 23. The U.S. vs. G. W. Hance, L. S. Knowles and Wm Schrader; U.S. attorney for the plaintiff; Rush, Wells and Howard for the defendants, and, No. 24. The U.S. vs. G. W. Hance, Arnold Ruggle and John Hance; U.S. attorney for plaintiff; Rush, Wells & Howard for the defendants."

Court daybooks indicate the same thing, only in longhand.[15] Beginning in 1884 records show continuance after continuance, in the middle of which Schrader dies. Following a break, motions are again continued for a week, month, or term, then for another term. Occasionally the defendants are awarded ninety minutes and sometimes fifteen days to reply in writing; this information was not recorded. So it goes for three years, volume by volume. The entries end abruptly in November 1888 with both actions dismissed, and there's no clue anywhere that states what it was about.

That said, George Hance's lead lawyer was Edmund William Wells. Wells worked in the Fort Whipple quartermaster and commissary departments in the mid-1860s,[16] was a Camp Lincoln clerk when Pauline Weaver died there, and had known George since they became Prescott Masons within a month of each other. Wells married George Banghart's daughter, Rosaline, while the Hance brothers farmed on Granite Creek, and Banghart's wife was Ed Peck's sister. Judging by his numerous legal appointments and rise to territorial attorney general from 1902–1904, Wells was the right man to represent George Hance et al. Providentially, he was then on break as attorney general for northern Arizona. He appears prominent to the degree he could negotiate most disputes to his desired result. That he took nearly three years to accomplish it for George Hance indicates a stubborn legal complexity.

By September 1886 John Hance had "for a long time been the guide for tourists and others to the Grand Canyon. Mr. Hance is thoroughly conversant with every trail and pathway of this wonderful place from the top to the bottom and during the Summer has been kept very busy showing visitors the different points."[17] Part of that came straight from John's first advertisement in the same issue. Compared to Julius Farlee's large, eye-catching advertisements, three years later Hance's ads were stuffed into a small box at the bottom corner of the page:

The Grand Canyon.
Being thoroughly conversant with all the trails leading to the Grand Canyon of the Colorado I am prepared to conduct parties thereto at any time. I have a fine spring of water near my house on the rim of the Canyon, of which tourists and their animals can always have free use. JOHN HANCE.

In a separate tease on the same page, the paper termed Hance "the pioneer in that section . . . perfectly familiar with all the trails and watering places," concluding with the timely suggestion that "a guide is absolutely necessary to ensure speed and safety."

Advertising publicly was just one new aspect of Hance's life. Others were also in play. On February 1, 1887, he was again in court, this time testifying for Bill Hull, plaintiff, versus Moses Casner, defendant, in a fraud case before a sworn jury. Casner prevailed that day.

Hance returned to court in early April with E. M. Sanford, an attorney from Prescott, as plaintiff against Sam Greenwood in another jury trial. "John Hance claimed the defendant Samuel Greenwood had taken and retained illegal possession of property owned by him on the rim of the Grand Canon of the Colorado."[18] The jury returned for Hance. Greenwood later claimed he'd bought half the property,[19] but there is no record in the Yavapai County archives that he did so.

Hance was still talking about Greenwood eight years later. Reported an Omaha newspaper, "For many years the bare logs of [Hance's] cabin held for him all the joys and beauties of 'Home, sweet home,'" but he was later "forced to share it with a man who had jumped his claim. For three months, with a gun or a revolver never out of reach, they eyed each other across the dead line, backed out of the single door in leaving, and by tacit agreement declared a truce every night, until a slow grinding court ejected the intruder."[20]

The Bowers brothers, their wives, and six others visited Hance in mid-1887.[21] That's not many people, but it shows a widening portrait of rim visitation. And the tourists kept coming. On June 6, 1888, "forty excursionists" left Flagstaff for the canyon,[22] and in August Hugo Richards was there with a group from San Francisco.[23]

According to Burton Holmes, "'Hance's' is on the very edge of the canyon, or within fifty yards or so of it, and yet no glimmering suggestion of the great vastness is presented to you as you stand before the long cabin in which has resided, so long, the old pioneer." Hance was quite a character, Holmes went on, with

a fine shepherd dog named "Bricktop," and a black cat rejoicing in the cognomen "Tom." The day of our arrival, whilst we were devouring some fine venison steaks, Tom came up to the table, which was composed of Hance's flat-topped trunk placed side-by-side with a dry goods box, and asked him for meat. John turned to the cat and in his quiet, drawling, nasal tones, informed him "They'll soon be some trouble between the Tom-cat family and the Hance family if you don't kinder let me alone."

The next morning at breakfast, as we enjoyed a toothsome venison stew, he said: "I've sometimes ate venison until I nearly got horns and run wild," and continuing, remarked, about wild turkeys, "Yes, I've eaten turkeys until the feathers began to grow on me and I'd wake up gobblin."[24]

By the late 1880s, Hance's storytelling was supplanting his trail's reputation. People had always remarked on his witticisms, tall tales, fabrications, offhanded reflections, and odd, pointy mannerisms, but prior to the late 1880s and the increasing use of his trail, all those characteristics never came together into a single entity universally recognized as "John Hance."

While shapeshifting from Grand Canyon's trail builder into its storyteller, he also grew "old"—Old John Hance. "There is an old fellow called John Hance who has taken up one hundred and sixty acres, and he has a house where he can accommodate travel. He is forty or fifty miles away from any white man. The only living people that he sees is some Supai Indians who are continually wandering about there hunting and fishing."[25] Hance was fifty-one that year.

An early take on the full-fledged character of John Hance was relayed by Hiram Sinsabaugh. Thirty-six hours on a train, "enlivened with song and social cheer, brought us to Flagstaff," wrote Sinsabaugh.

Here we took private conveyances to the Grand Cañon. The many little amusing and ludicrous events of those nearly six days in the wilderness ... the weary search over miles, that seemed to be leagues, for the Red Horse Tanks, until night settled down upon the thirsty, weary caravan, and [Cedar Ranch] which Billy [Hull], the cowboy, found, only a quarter of a mile further on, is an event not to be forgotten. And, that a villainous bronco slipping his bridle should delay the expedition [and] leave the company for a night without beds but for the mercy of a cowboy's cabin.

Sinsabaugh recovered, and the next day twenty-four "ladies and gentlemen appeared at the rude cabin of John Hance, the guide, the hunter, the Indian hater, the story-teller, and the owner of this approach to the valley, [who] welcomes our party to all that he has. Here we were to tent, and rest, and enjoy the supreme privilege of a lifetime."[26]

By the late 1880s, the road to Grand Canyon was well traveled and Hance's comings and goings were newspaper tidbits, like C. C. Bean's activities around Prescott. Various newspaper articles reported: "John Hance was in from the Grand Canyon a few days this week on business"; "John Hance was in town this week from the Grand Canyon and says that the country adjacent to that place never looked more beautiful"; "John Hance, the popular and experienced guide out at the Grand Canyon, paid Flagstaff a visit this week. John is a whole-souled man who makes friends wherever he goes"; "Parties who have recently visited the Grand Canyon speak in the highest terms of praise of the ability of John Hance as a guide and a genial and accommodating gentleman"; "John Hance, the Grand Canyon man, has been on quite a long visit to friends in town."[27]

But times were changing. Enterprise was creeping up on Hance from all sides, and by the fall of 1889 his adverts were full-throated. One claimed, "John Hance guarantees to enter the river in the Grand Canyon every 12 miles, for a distance of 140 miles, and will guide any party, desiring to prospect or explore, from the mouth of the Little Colorado to the mouth of the Cataract Canyon."[28] Now known as Havasupai Canyon, Cataract Canyon was originally named for its tall, dramatic waterfalls and blue-green travertine pools.

Grand Canyon was attracting not only more writers, photographers, and artists, but also an increasing number of everyday tourists. Sanford Rowe, a longtime lawman, seems to have been Hance's first competitor worth mention. Rowe lived in Williams where he operated a livery stable and raised and sold Percheron draft horses to lumber companies as a sideline.[29] With an eye toward its developing tourist appeal, Rowe determined to blaze an expeditious road from Williams to the canyon and traveled north with an Englishman named Harry Hankley to explore his prospects.

The story of how Rowe found the eponymous spring where he unsuccessfully competed with Hance has several versions. One account, authenticated by Rowe's signature, relates to Hance. While it's a circuitous tale with sometimes questionable information, it also demonstrates Hance's knowledge of the rim beyond Grandview.

In 1890 Rowe stopped at Hull barn, where Hance was breaking horses. While we don't know the precise details of that day, we do have an account of Hance working a mare and her ornery colt, the yearling always in the way of his lasso: "Whoa, Billy, whoa; nice Billy, whoa, whoa; you garl-darned hammer-headed son of your father, if it warn't for the stink you'd make, I'd shoot you."[30]

It might have been a day like that when Hance told Rowe about a place he called "Cow Tank," about fifteen miles west of Glendale Springs. Rowe hired a Havasupai man named Big Jim to take him there, found the spring, and within a day or two had posted a claim on it.[31] Between 1890 and 1892 he filed mineral locations nearby and began a marginal tourist camp.[32] That simple, ultimately noncompetitive act—outside of its location—marked the beginning of the end of Grand Canyon as John Hance knew it.

Rowe Well is a mile south of today's Grand Canyon Village, the locus of Bright Angel Trail. The story behind the making of that footpath involves two sets of brothers. One brother from the first set was killed by a stray bullet, and one brother from the second set had an unexpected shootout with Hance.

Niles and Ralph Cameron were born in Southport, Maine, Niles in 1861 and Ralph two years later. Ralph is the one who still garners press. For nearly three decades he "owned" Bright Angel Trail and Indian Garden, doggedly controlling his interests through high connections, bogus mining claims, legal shenanigans, and contentious court battles. But it was Niles that looked after Ralph's canyon affairs. Niles was Ralph's boots on the ground, his eyes and ears, collections agent, lead prospector, mine foreman, and "'guardeen' of Bright Angel trail,"[33] in death eulogized as "quiet, retiring, honorable, and upright in every dealing."[34] Niles signed "John Hance's Visitors' Book" its first year, 1891. Ralph never did, probably because by then he was busy in his initial term of three as Coconino County's first sheriff.

Although the tale of Niles having a shootout with Hance appears at first fatuous, its punchline is quite believable. In a drunken state, Niles and Hance got into an argument so nasty the only righteous way to settle it was with a duel. The problem was, they had only one pistol between them. Straws were drawn. Niles lost. He stood in the doorway awaiting his fate.

Hance fired and missed, certainly by design. Then it was Niles's turn. "Cap turned and ran, wherefore Niles from then on, after a few drinks, reminded him of the shot he had coming and called him a cowardly S.O.B."[35]

The remaining characters are John and Peter "Pete" Berry, born in Cedar Falls, Iowa. Pete was fourteen when his father died in 1872. Both he and John inherited 120 acres of farmland, but John sold out and departed for the Colorado gold fields. Pete followed later. They reunited in 1879 at Pitkin, Colorado's first mining camp west of the Continental Divide.

John Berry tired of mining and moved to Flagstaff, where, with the arrival of the railroad in 1882, he opened the San Juan Sample & Club Rooms, a bar and faro parlor across from the depot. There, John Berry, an honest, even-tempered, reputable businessman, married and fathered a son, Ralph Joseph, named after Ralph Cameron.

Five years later, back in Colorado during January 1887, Pete learned John was dead, the victim of a wayward bullet from a confrontation at his bar. The following night, vigilantes pulled John's two assailants out of jail and shot and hanged them,[36] so their fate did not concern Pete when he pulled into Flagstaff a few weeks later.

John's widow, Mary or "May," intended to sell the club rooms, but Pete took over its ownership and married May in 1888. In some popular accounts, May is said to have been a strikingly beautiful woman of questionable moral persuasion. However true that may be, she quickly departed for Tucson with her son. Pete enlisted Niles Cameron to retrieve the boy. He did, and Ralph Berry was placed with the Sisters of Charity in San Miguel, New Mexico, until he was old enough to look after himself.[37]

Pete Berry was the heavily mustached, blue-eyed, slow-tongued, quietly disposed sort, known as "the tall sycamore" because of his lanky yet muscular 170-pound, six-foot frame.[38] The only physical characteristic he shared with Hance was blue eyes. Burton Holmes compared them in the sixth volume of his *Travelogues*: "Berry is a man of few words, but those few words are always to the point. There is nothing of romance in the soul of Pete Berry; when he meets a bear, it is not the bear that does the shooting." This was an oblique reference to a story Hance told about a bear that chased him up a tree. The bear grabbed his rifle off the ground and started shooting. He was getting closer with each shot but ran out of ammo. "I do believe," Hance said, "that if they'd 'a' been another ketridge in that gun, he'd 'a' shot me sure."[39]

Between the winter of 1889 and the spring of 1890, Berry, Niles and Ralph Cameron, and others made several prospecting expeditions down Hance Trail. On Tonto Platform they worked twelve miles westward to Indian Garden and down Garden Creek to the river at Pipe Creek Rapid. Cameron and company's first recorded Grand Canyon stakes were made a quarter mile downstream of Pipe Creek, five hundred feet above the river. These were the North Star and White Elephant claims of March 25, 1890.[40]

Ralph Cameron spent a good amount of time around Indian Garden, he said, looking over the uprise to the south and studying the possibility of installing a trail to the rim from where he stood. That would avoid the lengthy, day-long commute from Hance Creek. R. A. Ferguson had expertise in trail and road surveys and thought a route possible. Interestingly, affidavits from 1903 indicate this trail did not follow or overlay a preexisting Indian route as is commonly thought.[41] According to these documents, Bright Angel Trail was constructed from scratch, carved out, and blasted into, purpose-built to access mineral claims below Pipe Creek without thoughts of tourist traffic.

Ralph was overly busy when the idea hit. A leading figure in Coconino County's creation, he was also serving extended jury duty in Prescott, so he hired H. G. Love to cover his labor.[42] Ferguson went to Flagstaff for provisions, got stuck in a snowstorm, did not return, and was replaced by Ed Gale.[43] On January 31, 1891, Pete Berry recorded Bright Angel Toll Road to the river in Yavapai County, the last entry in the county's toll road records from 1871–1891.[44] According to the same affidavits, the route was completed by year's end. It probably didn't see its first few tourists until 1892, thanks to Sanford Rowe's proximity, but Bright Angel Toll Road didn't emerge in the press until 1893, and then as a mining route.

On a second expedition along Tonto Platform three weeks later, Ferguson, Berry, Gale, Niles Cameron, and another man staked the Last Chance copper claim beneath Grandview Point. That was April 19, 1890,[45] but it lay in the background until Ralph Cameron recorded Grand View Toll Road on March 9, 1893.[46]

But, really, how did Bright Angel Trail come by its name? In 1902 Hance explained the answer to Winfield Hogaboom in the *Los Angeles Herald*.

"'Buckey O'Neill give it that name," Hance told Hogaboom, reflectively, spitting at the stove door. According to Hogaboom, "It was doubtful if the captain would proceed. Conditions had to be favorable for him to tell a story. He liked large audiences, a dozen listeners at least, and I was the only one upon this occasion."

Hance spat at the stove door again, then began. "We never did know where she come from, ner how she got here, but all to once she was here, and 'peared like she'd come to stay. She was sickly; you could see that, but she never complained none; she was allers jest as doggone cheerful as a sunshiny mornin'." He considered her beautiful, with "fluffy hair that was like a streak o' sunlight streamin' through a winder and her skin was soft as velvet, and jest white and pink, and she didn't look like a person that was intended to live on earth; leastwise in no such outlandish place as this."

"The boys all fell in love with her," he claimed:

Pete Berry, over at Grandview, an' Bass, down at the ferry, an' I guess I had a sort o' tender regard like fer her myself.

She ust t' go down th' trail nigh-on every day, walkin' slow and lookin' at th' wonderful sights in th' canyon with them big blue eyes o' hers, that was like little patches of th' sky. The boys ust t' watch her, standin' on the rim, till she'd get t' be nuthin' but a tiny spec o' bright color, movin' along th' trail. Sometimes there'd be moisture in Buckey's eyes, an' I dunno but mine, too, when we was lookin' at her, and feelin' mabbe she wasn't goin' t' last long.

Buckey ust t'say she was an angel; he knowd she was, an' he turned out t' be right, fer one day she went down th' trail an' never came back. There was a sort o' haze like hangin' in the canyon that afternoon, an' long about sundown th' light struck it slantwise and colored it up like gold. You couldn't see fer into th' canyon, but Buckey claimed he seen somethin' floatin' up through th' mist, white an' sort o' transparent like, but he know'd it was her.

There wasn't no doubt about her bein' an angel after that, an' so he named th' trail "Bright Angel trail," an' that's how it come.[47]

Nine

PROSPECTOR AND MINER

"Millions of Tons of Ore in Sight"

The story goes that John Hance went to Grand Canyon, located an asbestos mine, and built a trail to it. Quickly realizing panning tourists' pockets showed more color for a lot less work, he opened a hotel, started guiding, and garnered fame through his stories.

The pertinent aspects of that tall tale are time and place. In this case, in the early 1880s Grand Canyon tourists did not exist, nor did rim-to-river footpaths. Glendale Springs was just then coming to life—Hance Trail was under construction by 1882. That trail ended as it began, south of the river on a sandbar at the head of Sockdolager Rapid, nowhere near what came to be called "John Hance's asbestos mine" to the north.

Hance's pre-canyon occupations should be considered, since they involved only ranching, farming, freighting, and contracting to the military. References to mineral claims, mining, and prospecting activity bearing Hance's name are not found in Yavapai County records until 1890, with four Grand Canyon claims. This activity continues into Coconino County records—meaning any time after February 19, 1891—with the addition of some forty-five more canyon claims. But there's nothing on the books previous to 1890. Additionally, Hance didn't pack his Grand Canyon bags until after prospectors from Jerome began offering their stakes for sale. If Hance had been a miner in the early 1880s, he would have relocated to Cherry Creek, Squaw Peak, the Black Hills, or Copper Camp (which became Jerome) instead of Grand Canyon. Prospecting wasn't part of John Hance's résumé until nearly a decade after he left Verde Valley.

Nor was prospecting in Grand Canyon's inner depths as widespread as generally thought before Stanton's 1890 transit of the river. The dramatic uptick in Grand Canyon mineral claims after Stanton's passage clearly indicates the appeal of his newspaper writings, which began that April.

Before the 1880s, limited prospecting was underway on the Kaibab Plateau north of the river, but more so in western Grand Canyon around Grand Wash Cliffs and in a few major upstream side canyons like Diamond Creek and Cataract Canyon. Kanab Creek saw a short-lived gold rush in 1872 after Powell quit his second trip there.[1] Going by Yavapai County indexes, Cataract Canyon offered the best prospects, but not until the 1880s when nearly one hundred claims were eventually staked there.

Riparian activity of the same sort, except for the occasional outlier like placer miner Felix Lantier, whom Stanton met at Furnace Flats below Marble Canyon, was rare, even at the mouth of Cataract Creek, where less than a dozen claims are found in Yavapai County's "Index to Mines 2 1881–1889." Befitting the scenery, one was named Grand Canyon Hotel.

Stanton's newspaper reports changed that. "The steep walls of the canyon show quartz veins in places," he wrote, "and assays from specimens obtained on the trip down the river demonstrate that these veins are of remarkable richness ... and the vein matter is clearly discernible to the naked eye." He added that "all the well-known precious minerals, as well as coal, marble, iron, etc.,"[2] including placer gold, were to be found along nearly the entire length of the river. That was all any fortune hunter needed to hear, as Stanton's writings caused a "general stampede" into the canyon.[3]

Harry McDonald took Stanton at his word, deserting him halfway through their voyage at river mile 98, now called Crystal Rapid, which was barely a riffle back then. McDonald hiked overland through deep snows to Kanab, Utah, organized a prospecting expedition, and returned to Furnace Flats, where his first stakes, the American Girl and London claims, were folded into tobacco tins and tucked into rock cairns near the river on May 12, 1890. On the fifteenth he did the same thing at the Morning Star claim.[4]

Seth Tanner bore witness to several recordings made contemporaneously and in proximity to McDonald's stakes, and in September recorded his own claims in Yavapai County's books. These were the Gray

Eagle, Hover Silver, Copper King, and Yellow Pocket, all "about half way between the [Old] Hance and Tanner Trails" south of the river.[5] In canyon lore, Tanner is said to have been in the area early, seemingly before Stanton and possibly ahead of Ben Beamer who lived at the mouth of the Little Colorado River. Since Tanner had established his trail by 1890, the folklore appears marginally accurate, but Beamer never recorded a claim in Yavapai County so that part is missing. However, his probable relations worked five claims in Cataract Canyon during 1885.

The end story along the river is that few if any prospectors were certifiably active before Stanton told them where to look. Their prospects brightened so quickly in such obscure places that only a year and a half later the *Mohave County Miner* reported, "the [*Arizona Weekly Journal-Miner*] have for some time past been working themselves into the belief that mining by balloon in the Grand Canyon is feasible. They might as well talk of furnishing green cheese direct from the moon . . . as to think of working the Grand Canyon mines by this method."[6]

Bill Ashurst, John Marshall, and William Morris, none with a prior history in Grand Canyon prospecting, were on and below the West Rim before that, just two months after Stanton completed his trip and ten days before his writings began to appear in the press. Little is known of Morris, a Flagstaff justice of the peace and deer hunter not long involved with Ashurst and Marshall, whose connection went back to the latter 1870s.

Born in Nova Scotia in 1859, Marshall emigrated alone to the United States at the age of sixteen after rounding Cape Horn to land in San Francisco. He cut and hauled timber in California, worked Nevada's Comstock Lode, and prospected around Silver City, New Mexico, before arriving in Flagstaff with a group of Mormon immigrants in 1876. In Silver City he met Martha Allen, whom he married in Prescott.[7] The young couple settled in the Mogollon Mountains, tending cattle northeast of the Verde near Bill Ashurst. By the mid-1880s, Marshall was running his own brand ("K" on the left hip) and had partnered in a Flagstaff butcher shop. In 1888 he bought 160 acres of the Bob Hornbeck ranch twenty-five miles south of Flagstaff and purchased adjoining property in January 1889. So consolidated, he went prospecting with Bill Ashurst in Grand Canyon.

Ashurst, Marshall, and Morris staked the Romero and Topsy claims located "half way between the mouth of the Little Colorado River and the mouth of Cataract Cannon on the south side of the Big Colorado River in Grand Cannon" on February 15, 1890, a few days before the Cameron brothers' first claims were made below Pipe Creek.[8] Ashurst and Marshall recorded the Little Daisy, Little Joint, Morning Glory, and Blue Bell claims in the same area in March. Morris joined them for the Paymaster and Grand Cannon claims.[9]

"The discovery of gold in the Grand Canyon of the Colorado ... will undoubtedly prove to be the richest mines that have ever been unearthed," proclaimed the *Arizona Champion* in late March 1890. "The assays run up into the hundreds, and there are millions of tons of ore in sight. The ledges run from ten to thirty-eight feet in width and are exposed from three to four thousand feet up the side of the canyon."[10] At that, prospecting groups were departing Flagstaff under the cover of darkness for fear of being tailed to the mines.

The *Weekly Arizona Miner* reported that a ledge Ashurst and Marshall had staked on the south side was visible north of the river. They attempted to cross on a driftwood raft and almost drowned, but they still wanted to get at that ledge. So, a few days later Hance, Bill Hull, and others joined them riverside. Hance was just off his first prospecting expedition in the same area with Mike Kerlin, W. H. Turlow, and B. Stiles. On March 27 this group staked the Hard Rustle, "situated on the [south] side of the Colorado River about 40 miles [west] of John Hance's trail."[11] That was John Hance's first mineral claim in Yavapai County.

Behind the oars that day was red-headed Godfrey Sykes, an adventuresome Englishman whose "front yard was the six continents and the Seven Seas,"[12] the sort to call his autobiography *A Westerly Trend: Being a Veracious Chronicle of More Than Sixty Years of Joyous Wanderings, Mainly in Search of Space and Sunshine.* In 1886, Sykes, his wife, and his brother Stanley arrived in Flagstaff, and the men started a bicycle shop named Makers and Menders of Anything.[13] They also presided over an intellectual drinking club called Busy Bees, Arizona Territory's answer to New York City's Algonquin Round Table.

"The prospectors wanted to make a boat," Sykes recalled, "so they tore up the floor of the old Hull Ranch house. They took the boards out to the Canyon to make a boat—but it was not a success; no one would get into it. I now came along with the frame of a canvas boat I had made. One after the other, we went across to make locations on the ledge. On one of these trips I took John over."[14] Remembered Stanley Sykes, "It was a day or two before Hance would agree to get in the little skiff. He was very thrilled and told [Godfrey] that he had wanted to cross for a long time, and that this was the first time he had ever done it."[15]

Contrasting Sykes's account of Hance's first crossing, John offered his own version. There's nary a vestige of Hance-speak anywhere in this newspaper account, but it's not a bad yarn when edited for brevity.

"The question arose as to how I was going to cross the river without a boat, there being none at that point," said Hance. Determined to make the trip, however, Hance hunted up some driftwood logs and lashed them together with wire. "I removed my outer clothing and made a pile of it in the center of my improvised raft and securing a short stick in lieu of a paddle, pushed boldly forth on the bosom of the mighty Colorado." With the 2017 equivalent of $1,400 in the pockets of his trousers, Hance took special care that his pants were securely held between his feet.

When reaching "the center of the stream," said Hance, "where the current is very swift, it seemed impossible for me to force the raft across, and by the time I did so had been carried some distance downstream. . . . One of the logs became detached from the others, and floated off into the beyond, capsizing the others and precipitating me into the icy waters." Hance swam to the north shore. His clothes, shoes, and money had gone downstream, and his provisions and burros were on the south bank.

Hance found a log stout enough to support him and paddled back over. But he landed in an eddy choked with driftwood and again had to swim ashore, where he fashioned footwear from his undergarments. "From there on it was plain sailing, and wrapping myself in a blanket, [I] made my way to the rim and home."[16]

Reported the *Arizona Champion* a month after Hance first crossed the river with Sykes,

> on a broad level mesa above the present [mineral] locations where a good easy trail can reach it from the rim, has been surveyed and platted the town of Ashurst, which will undoubtedly be a lively camp when the owners of the various locations surrounding it begin their development work. Good clear spring water is abundant and for miles around it is the most beautiful

scenery in the canyon. As a health and pleasure resort it will have no superior in the world. Good boating on the river, fishing, hunting, and plenty of outdoor exercise climbing over and around bluffs to points of interest.[17]

In April 1890, John Marshall recorded his intent to construct the Rim Rock and River Road to Ashurst's mines. With him at the recorder's office were J. R. Kilpatrick and W. B. Vanderlip to record their Canon City Toll Road.[18] It, too, was bound for the town of Ashurst via a similar route. Also present that afternoon was James Morse who, joined by Vanderlip equipped with a third plat, filed their intentions to install "Morse's Ferry for the transportation of men, animals, vehicles, and other personal property across the Colorado River within the Grand Canyon with a terminus here described." That was the town of Ashurst, south of the river, illustrated by five symbols indicating mining claims. The town of Aztec, named for the Aztec mine (which was never recorded but clearly illustrated on Vanderlip's plat) was the north terminus of Morse's Ferry.[19] Marshall's paperwork indicated a road of six miles with a projected construction cost of $20,000. Although not to precise scale and lacking substantial cartographic detail, Marshall's road appears planned for what was later called Bass Canyon near Havasupai Point at Grand Scenic Divide.

Hance once said Grand Canyon had three liars: he was one and William Wallace Bass was the other two.[20] Born in 1849 in Shelbyville, Indiana, Bass became a train dispatcher on the Ninth Avenue Elevated in New York, where he contracted tuberculosis and took his recovery in bed at Bellevue Hospital. Thinking "good air" might help him, Bass secured railway work at the division headquartered in Williams, Arizona.[21]

Bass arrived in Williams in July 1883 when Hance Trail was under construction. Much later, he wrote of finding the site of his Havasupai Point camp in the winter of 1883–84, of making a wagon road to it from Williams in 1885, and of being the first to advertise regular Grand Canyon stage service. The overarching impression is that Bass was established at Havasupai Point in competition with Hance by about 1886.

Bass's statements, however, cannot be verified in literature or legal documentation of the era. Instead, the available information describes a different person. In newspaper reports, Bass played his banjo at a Williams gathering. "Banjo Bill" worked at Sandy's Bar dispensing "Grand

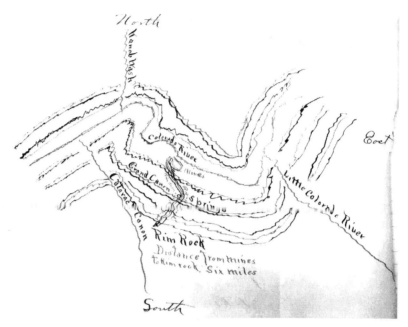

While lacking substantial cartographic detail, James Marshall's plat of his Rim Rock and River Road identifies the locations of his and Bill Ashurst's first mineral claims in Grand Canyon, halfway between the mouths of the Little Colorado River and Cataract Creek. The area is now called Bass Canyon. Courtesy of Yavapai County Records Management, RMC no. 09-2653.

Canyon cocktails"[22] and was appointed the town's constable. He searched Havasu Canyon for a lost companion he was briefly accused of murdering for his valuable pocket watch, and was arrested and acquitted for cattle theft, among other odds and ends. But unlike Hance, there's nothing in the press connecting Bass to Grand Canyon until 1890 when he and Sanford Rowe planned a stage line to connect "Cataract Canyon . . . to the grandest and most majestic part of the greatest wonder of the world,"[23] presumably the Rowe Well area.

When viewed through Yavapai County records, ranching appears to be Bass's livelihood until the latter 1880s. That fits with a May 28, 1887, *Arizona Champion* article portraying him as "a prominent rancher and stockman of Williams, one of the town's oldest citizens with one of the best ranches in that vicinity." This is all the more evident when viewed through chattel mortgages Bass made in 1888 and 1889. Both agreements offered only livestock as collateral. The first identified Bass and his associate Ed Randolph as "ranchers," and the second refers to Bass as a "stock raiser."[24]

It can't be denied Bass visited Havasupai Canyon—different from Havasupai Point, where he finally landed—soon after his Williams arrival, and it's evident he led tourists to the village of Supai. "I found [in Cataract Canyon] a strange race of red men," wrote Colonel W. H. Holabird under Bass's tutelage in August 1890. "I guess I was the second white man who ever visited their canyon. They are a peaceful people. . . . The chief of the strange tribe is an old man of sixty years named Captain Tom, a name given him by John D. Lee, the Mormon who escaped from Utah [after orchestrating the Mountain Meadows Massacre in 1857] and for six years lived in hiding with the red men. He was the first white man the Yavi-Supais had ever seen, and he taught the chief the white man's language and the use of fire arms."[25] That was, however, well off the mark, and on November 13 the *Arizona Weekly Enterprise* rebutted in kind.

Consider too that as early as 1890, when George Wharton James was selling his first Grand Canyon guidebook and lecturing in Flagstaff,[26] Bass sought schooling for Havasupai children and economic support for their elders.[27] And in the caption on the back of an old photograph,[28] he's also credited with leading a bride and her new husband down Bright Angel Toll Road that year. In truth, it is more accurate to say that Bass escorted the newlyweds to what was then becoming the trailhead.

At Grand Canyon proper, Bass came to life in the press on June 20, 1891. Wrote the *Coconino Sun*, "W. W. Bass is building a road to the Grand Canyon. . . . Mr. Bass believes that this portion of the Canyon possesses attractions which cannot be found at any other point, and that tourists will be attracted to Williams when the route is properly advertised." To garner interest in his enterprise, Bass "presented the Flagstaff Board of Trade with a liberal lot of fine wood petrifactions from the Grand Canyon."[29] This was followed by word that Bass had purchased a new passenger coach,[30] and he used it to usher "Mr. Williams and his wife, of New York, F. W. Phillips, wife and children, of Holstead, Cal., and Messrs. Duff of Williams [and] Burgess of the Arizona Republic" to the canyon that August.[31] Only a month later he anticipated the start of service from Williams.[32]

These are the first substantial indications of Bass's activities around Havasupai Point, and they come some eight years after Hance's initial ruminations near Grandview. Bass's Mystic Spring Trail, now South Bass Trail, was recorded a few weeks after he entertained the folks from New York,[33] but it wasn't until early November that his Williams road entered the books.[34]

With closer, faster access to Havasupai Point, Bass moved to Ash Fork. He realigned and sold his Havasupai Canyon water rights, buggy and harness, a team of horses, road scraper, and plow in October.[35] As the ink dried on that arrangement, he announced construction of another road, this one to connect Ash Fork and Grand Canyon, where, the brief article concluded, "a new hotel will be built."[36]

That can only mean the installation of a permanent camp at Havasupai Point, which Ashurst and his associates had left for sunnier climes. Had Bass's camp been in operation at Grand Scenic Divide previous to Ashurst's activity, it would have been used as a landmark to help indicate the locations of the Romero, Topsy, and other claims, and certainly to describe the head of Vanderlip's and Marshall's toll roads. Instead, Bass and his camp are not in evidence. He is not on the maps for the simple reason he was not engaged there in early 1890. In the only other clue to the location of Ashurst's claims outside of Marshall's plat, Morse's Ferry was identified as being some fifty miles northwest of Flagstaff on "unsurveyed lands at a great distance from any surveyed lands and incapable of further extended description."[37]

Bill Ashurst and John Marshall next appear in the territorial press in the land of John Hance, north of the Colorado River a mile below Hance Rapid, where, on January 25, 1891, Ashurst staked an immense deposit of asbestos eight hundred sheer feet above the river. He called it the Wool claim and recorded it in Yavapai and Coconino Counties, as well as in Augusta, Maine. The first recording was in Yavapai County,[38] but that portion of Grand Canyon soon became Coconino County, which is why Ashurst recorded it there. The connection to the state of Maine is curious but becomes oddly appropriate following his death.

Between February 13 and 16, Marshall and Hance staked the North End, White Buck, and Water Front claims, all near the Wool claim, and with Ashurst located the Hance Mining claim in the same area. Staked and named by Ashurst on March 23, the Hance claim became the first mineral location recorded in Coconino County's brand new "Records

Bill and Sarah Ashurst. Hance called Bill "Jake." They were the best of friends, eventually and fittingly buried near each other at Grand Canyon Pioneer Cemetery. Courtesy of Grand Canyon National Park, no. 14681.

of Mines."[39] And, after crossing the river headed back to the East Rim, Ashurst, Marshall, and Hance also staked the Grape Vine, Big Lizzard, Blue Line, and Long Rainge claims between Cottonwood Creek and Grapevine Canyon. That curious bit of John Hance's legacy goes the folkloric distance to establish him as Grand Canyon's premier prospector and miner, which he was not.

Instead, that man was Curtis McClure. Although no photographic likeness of him is known, McClure was central to canyon mining efforts during Hance's prospecting years. If he wasn't staking claims with Ashurst and Hance he did it with John Marshall, Louis Boucher, Niles Cameron, Pete Berry, a Babbitt brother, or by himself—only if he wasn't building a smelter at Rowe Well, visiting the Bradshaw Mountains, or exploring the mineral potential of Oatman, Arizona. He also owned an early share in Bright Angel Toll Road[40] and, later, like Hance, an interest in Red Canyon Toll Road.

McClure's fingers were in every mineral pie. Between 1891 and 1902 his name appears on eighty-five Coconino County claims, the majority in Grand Canyon, many with Ashurst and Hance. "The canyon is destined to become not only America's most popular resort for sight seers," he said when interviewed in Williams, "but when proper facilities for extensive mining operations have been brought into use it will be known as one of the richest districts in the country."[41] To process and move ore to the rim he envisioned riverside smelters and aerial tramways.

In February 1897 McClure staked the Corliss Quartz claim a few miles south of Rowe Well.[42] A year later he sold it to the Chicago investment firm Lombard, Goode & Co. for a one-dollar quitclaim. By then, Buckey O'Neill's Tusayan development company had obtained control of over sixty locations south of the Corliss claim. O'Neill was so enterprising that, with three separate crews, he staked ten placer locations along the South Rim in one day. Another day he filed notice on a second Bright Angel Trail, putting him in contretemps with his old boss Ralph Cameron. More significant was that, while working with editor George Young of the *Williams News*, he helped raise the funds to enlist Lombard, Goode & Co. in financing a railway to his copper mines.[43] By purchasing McClure's Corliss claim, Lombard, Goode & Co. were simply corralling rights-of-way prior to running tracks to the South Rim, where, the *New York Times* reported, an electric scenic road would be built for sightseeing purposes.[44]

Due largely to O'Neill's driving personality, the Santa Fe and Grand Canyon Railroad incorporated on July 31, 1897.[45] The Fifty-fifth Congress authorized its right-of-way through the southern reaches of Grand Canyon Forest Reserve in May 1898, and bed grading began in March 1898 under James Thurber's direction. The first rails were laid in October 1899, well after O'Neill was killed at the Battle of San Juan Hill, lionized, and buried, but not before an early route inspection by J. L. Woodward of Los Angeles, guided by Bill Hull.[46]

The rails reached milepost 45 near O'Neill's copper claims, then the end of the line and named Anita after Thomas Lombard's daughter (hence "the Anita Mines") in early 1900. Passenger service to Anita Junction began on March 15.[47]

Like its owner, "John Hance's Visitors' Book" is homey, comfortably dressed as its owner would have been. About seven inches wide by ten inches high, it would fit in a dinner jacket's waist pocket. Its sometimes coffee-spilt pages or smeared-pencil and pen-scribbled inscriptions are under a deep reddish, softly burnished leather cover embossed with a gilded title.

Between 1891 and 1900, 1,145 individuals signed John's book, some more than once. This interesting cast of characters described the next ten years of Hance's life in a "this is the adventure I had today" sort of way, like schoolboys exploring a riverbank. "John Hance's Visitors' Book" is about Grand Canyon's might and majesty, Hance and Red Canyon Trails, and the writers' reactions to the person of John Hance.

A facsimile typeset edition of John's guestbook was published in 1899. Titled *Personal Impressions of the Grand Cañon of the Colorado*,[48] it was produced and edited by G. K. Woods, a stagecoach manager and general factotum in South Rim tourist affairs around the turn of the century. *Personal Impressions* is a rare, interesting, and informative document, a translation certainly worth the read, but it fails utterly when laid beside the real thing.

Striking differences exist between the texts. Several pages, including the first two, are missing from "John Hance's Visitors' Book." The actual document doesn't begin until page three with the seventeenth signature, that of Flagstaff resident James Spamford. But Woods's facsimile edition tells us the first individual to sign and date John's guestbook—on April 20,

1891—was, remarkably, Gifford Pinchot, the man who became first director of the U.S. Forest Service. When pronounced as most would do it, "Pinchot" starts with a comfortable press of the lips, but there is spice in the "pin." The second syllable—"cho"—starts mid-tongue and finishes in a soft charcoal slide. Hance pronounced it differently, as Pinchot himself certified when describing what the missing page cannot.

Eight years after John's shuttle-haul up the Black Canyon Road, Pinchot traveled the same route to reach Grand Canyon, a three-day travail from Phoenix. Conditions had not changed during the intervening years. Pinchot "drove all night in a four-horse stage, with highly disreputable companions of both sexes. My seat was on the box with the driver. One jolt out of many threw me clear off it. I lit sprawling on the side of a cut [bank]; which was lucky, for much of the road skirted a precipice."[49]

Pinchot trekked from Glendale Springs to the river and back in ten hours. Emboldened by the power of the place, serious logistical problems encountered along the lower reaches of Hance Trail became minor difficulties. "It was a most impressive and somewhat hazardous trip," Pinchot later reflected, "partly through the gorge of a plunging tributary stream. Ropes hanging down certain unclimbable waterfalls had not been tested since the year before, for we were the first that season. The worst that happened to us was a thorough soaking."

Back on the rim, Pinchot waited out a snowstorm before moving on: "Between times John Hance impressed on us the important fact that he was the best shot, the best walker, the best boatman and swimmer, the best rider, and had the best horses and the best mines 'of any man that ever saw or read of Arizony.' Years later I learned that Hance had started a register of visitors. Mine was the first name on the list. He spelled it 'Pinchob.'"[50]

Twenty-nine of Hance's first-year signatories were members of the International Geological Congress led by "John Wesley Powell Washington D.C." Powell's fellow chaperone was Denis "Matt" Riordan, the new owner of Edward Ayer's Flagstaff lumber mill. Next was Mary Caroline Hughes of Cambridge, England. Below and to the left of her signature is a hand-drawn IGC logo with the words "Mente et Malleo" (by thought and hammer), followed by a list of scientists from Germany, Scotland, Belgium, France, Switzerland, and America.

Flagstaff's first physician, D. J. Brannen, was along to render first aid. He was nephew to Peter Brannen, a Prescott merchant and trader to the

Yavapai and Apache before they were moved to San Carlos. Peter knew Hance from Prescott, but he also had a Flagstaff store and moved into Beaverhead, so he would have seen Hance in Verde Valley as well.

Louis Boucher, another mythical Grand Canyon figure about whom little is known, also checked in. Gleaned from Boucher's entry is his former residence of Sherbrooke, Canada. Because this note is an oft-quoted lens on Boucher's life, Sherbrooke is sometimes termed his birthplace, but according to another source that was Meriden, Connecticut.[51] Like Hance, Boucher's prehistory goes mostly unaccounted for outside of hearsay. On the plains after the Civil War, he may have inscribed a Winchester rifle with the words "To Chief Spotted Tail from Louis Boucher" when possibly smuggling rifles to the Lakota.

"Rode a white mule, wore a white beard, told only white lies" is the interpretive catchphrase about Boucher recited on many river trips. "Went down Hance trail [guided by] Mr. Boucher & stayed overnight [at Cottonwood Camp] returning next day; enjoyed it immensely. Found the trail in excellent order & made the trip comfortably," recorded Horace Hovey in *Scientific American*,[52] describing Boucher as intelligent, obliging, and not very talkative. Boucher had been to Havasu Canyon, perhaps with Bill Hull. It was the Indians' custom, he said, "to roll the dead in their blankets with their guns and other personal effects, and deposit them in [crevices] between the rocky shelves under the rim. Their horses are then forced to make the awful leap from the rim to the rocks below, which are actually whitened with the bones of the sacrificed steeds."[53]

Boucher is called Grand Canyon's "hermit," as Hance is termed its "storyteller." Hermit Rest, Hermit Trail, and Hermit Shale are all named for him, as is Boucher Creek, which forms Boucher Rapid just downstream from Hermit Canyon, and the thrilling Hermit Rapid with its enormous standing waves. Boucher was the "hermit" because, as it turns out, he wasn't there between 1897 and 1900, the high-water years of pretrain tourism. Instead, he was tending sheep in Mohave County. It wasn't until the train pulled in that he started his tourism business, at least on paper. Platted in February 1902, the Silver Bell Trail led to Boucher's Dripping Springs Camp situated well beneath the rim under a shady rock overhang. Boucher had a live "waterfall" surrounded by native ferns in his living room (visited by the occasional, normally passive Grand

Canyon pink rattlesnake), and it was there he "pointed out with pride and affection" the goldfish he'd brought from Kansas in a vial, now swimming in their own little private pool.[54]

He remained at Grand Canyon until 1909 when, apparently due to interference from the Santa Fe Railroad and Fred Harvey, he packed up and drifted back into folklore, perhaps northward to Utah's coal mining district. After that, Louie is gone except for a quick visit to Pete Berry in 1912.

Hance started with the Hull brothers by shuttling people from Flagstaff in a buggy or even a grain wagon if enough customers could be had. Professional stage service to Hance's didn't begin until 1892. Before that, people got there however they could.

As late as 1891, Harriet Colton and Florence Dukes of Brooklyn, New York, one or both writing under the pseudonym of "Yucca," arrived at Hance's with other guests in mid-August. Yucca's account says much about early Grand Canyon visitation, and it is oddly fascinating to compare tourist transportation and amenities between then and now. Told here are the events of a torturously slow three-day clop-trop journey to Glendale Springs from Flagstaff at a time when Grand Canyon visitors were said to be arriving on almost every train.[55]

Heading north out of town the first morning along the "western route" in an odd conveyance of wagons and stages, Yucca's group passed the Arizona Cattle Company at Fort Moroni. Shortly after noon the vehicles "reached a lonely cabin at the foot of the mountain occupied by a Mormon family, with no trees or neighbors for miles. Here we stopped and ate our luncheon, to which our hospitable Mormon host added all the milk we could drink." It was the last house they saw that day. "All the afternoon we wandered, aimlessly it seemed to me, through forests, over prairies, up and down hillocks all alike covered with stone and malapai rock [basalt outcrops]."

Toward evening, the caravan reached a sheep camp of the stage driver's friend, perhaps Louis Boucher, where they were to spend the night.

To "tender-feet" of the "effete East," accustomed to the luxurious modern hotel, the outlook for shelter was hardly promising. A tent, somewhat the worse for wear, in which there were two cots, a pile of blankets, a rusty stove, a broken chair holding a half-burned candle in an empty whiskey bottle, was the palatial apartment we were to occupy for the night. Opposite the tent was a log-hut, used for a storehouse, and in front of this, under a roughly made porch of pine boughs, a cooking stove had been placed and here, when we emerged from the tent after removing some of the travel stain, we found the men busily engaged in cooking supper. Our table was only a few pine boards laid across a packing box, and the dishes were tin pans and cups.

But the dry Arizona air had sharpened their appetites, and they did "full justice" to the mutton and chili stew, strong coffee, and baking powder biscuits that made the meal.

The party spent its second day getting to Cedar Ranch, where a series of twenty-four stair-stepped hollow logs formed water troughs that fascinated passersby,[56] but no one was there to greet or feed them. "We made ourselves perfectly at home and in the morning started Cañon ward again."

While resting at lunch on day three, the party discovered the driver had neglected to resupply the water. "We were all thirsty and tired from our long, hot ride over a desert-like tract of country and we women were beginning to despair, as we could eat nothing with our throats in such a parched condition, when someone suggested canned tomatoes, of which we had a large supply. The juice of these we found to be quite a satisfactory substitute."

Grand Canyon was finally reached late that afternoon. "John Hance, on whose grounds we were to camp for a few days, is the guide to the Cañon and is, in his way, quite a character. His imagination, which has ample time and suitable surroundings for cultivation, is unlimited, his repertory of stories inexhaustible, and his hospitality renowned." Hance's place was "a one-roomed log cabin about fourteen feet [long]. The roof is of mud with sunflowers growing out of it and an old stovepipe answers for a chimney. There is a home-made fire-place of malapai rock at one end of the room." When Yucca returned from the rim, Hance had kindled a blazing fire and was preparing supper.

Yucca slept under the trees that night, making her bed with other ladies on one side of the campfire, the men lined along the opposite side "with the moon for a lamp and the distant howling of coyotes for a lullaby."

After the day cooled the following afternoon, they started for the river. "Jennie, a gentle little burro, belonging to John Hance, led the way, loaded with two or three Navajo blankets for bedding, a small bag containing a few toilet articles and provisions for three days." Hance followed Jennie. The others "straggled after as best we could."

Arriving at Cottonwood Camp about dusk, Yucca refused to stay there. A friend had told her about his previous night there when, following "many vain attempts to sleep had finally seated himself by the camp fire armed with a piece of wood to keep the mice at bay." Foot-sore and weary, the group trudged down the creek for another mile to camp "beside the gurgling Hance Creek" as moonshine splendor filled the canyon.

"As soon as our light breakfast was over, we proceeded down the trail. . . . We had to go over seven falls before reaching the river. I was the last one to go down the highest fall and as I started from the top, after the rope had been adjusted around my waist, John Hance said 'Now if you can't find a foothold don't be scared. Just let yourself slip.'" She did, and was slowly lowered to the bottom. Shortly, Yucca stood beside the Colorado River, "a torrent of muddy water dashing madly over jagged rocks."[57]

John Hance was Grand Canyon's original, widely remarked upon character by 1892. It wasn't just that regular stage service had begun or that Horace Carver Hovey had authored a second illustrated article in *Scientific American*. Other contemporary offerings painted Hance and his domain with more appealing detail and color, but the combined impact of these publications, as well as Bill Cody's visit in November, put Hance and Grand Canyon in front of a national audience.

Published by the Santa Fe Railroad's passenger department, *Grand Cañon of the Colorado River* was researched and written by Charles Higgins. Its frontispiece was an appealing "fuzzy caterpillar" topographic map of Coconino Forest showing the way to Hance's camp from Flagstaff—despite the routes to Rowe Well, W. W. Bass's developing imprint at Havasupai Point, and Julius Farlee's Grand Cañon Hotel, which Hovey illustrated in *Scientific American*. Hance was the only tourist operator listed on the railway's map. He was their man. And *Grand Cañon of the Colorado* was sure to reach more readers than Hovey's articles.

Higgins told Grand Canyon's human history in brief, remarkable detail, coming to rest on the "old pioneer" who lived there. "Every visitor will meet John Hance, who by virtue of his long residence, his ownership of adjacent land and of the trail, and his intimate acquaintance with every feature of the district, has established a tacit sort of proprietorship there. He is an accomplished mountaineer, a trusty guide, a genial companion, and a gentleman. Moreover, he can hold his own around the campfire, when stirring and marvelous tales are in full swing."

Hance's trail fees were also listed as follows: "'Toll, for persons descending without guide, $1.00 each; pack animals, without guide, $2.00 per day; guide and pack animals for party of six or less, $10.00 per day. Saddle horses are also furnished by Mr. Hance to parties who desire to use them in excursions along the rim.... The office of E. S. Wilcox, manager of the Grand Canon Stage Line Company, is conveniently situated on the depot platform, and visitors will find it to their advantage to apply to him immediately upon arrival and secure stage accommodations."[58]

Having turned from renting his horses, tack, buckboards, and drivers to providing the first regularly scheduled stage service to the rim, Wilcox was awarded his contract in early May, beating out A. C. Morse of Morse's Ferry fame. He also earned mention by Higgins through providing free transportation for the author and his friends. Starting May 16, 1892, his stages departed Flagstaff every Monday, Wednesday, and Friday, returning on Tuesday, Thursday, and Saturday.[59] With four changes of stock, Wilcox provided normally dependable, one-day service to Glendale Springs, becoming successful so quickly that by mid-July he owned a stage described as a city streetcar. Not intended for overland trips, it put his fleet capacity at seventy-five passengers.[60]

Higgins's first edition was illustrated with photographs by William Henry Jackson, known for his portraits of Native Americans. By the time Jackson arrived at Hance's, his images of Yellowstone had been credited with helping enable America's first national park. As at Yellowstone and to similar lasting effect, he was accompanied by the painter Thomas Moran, whose drawings illustrated the subsequent editions of Higgins's book. Moran returned Wilcox's favor of free transportation with a drawing of Hance's trailhead that Wilcox displayed in his office.[61]

The surrounds of Cottonwood Camp at the junction of east and west Hance Creeks. Hance, bearded in a white shirt, stands near his cabin. "Hance's cabin," 1892. Photo by William Henry Jackson, History Colorado, no. 86.200.3107.

Because Higgins and those in tow signed John's guest book on May 24, we know Jackson's images were exposed the same week. A third of them portray Hance, his camp, and trail, beginning with a shot of the "Stage Stop and Permanent Camp at Hance's"—a tiny log cabin with two men and one burro behind a one-rail fence, with a few tents in mid-distance, the whole of it an acre or two. Given the number of people and breadth of interpretive kiosks and services on the rim today, it is difficult to fully understand the profound truth in such an image. This is park headquarters in 1892, Grand Canyon's only year-round visitor center, hotel, restaurant, hospital, stockyard, logistics center, and administrative complex.[62]

Jackson's images also portray Cottonwood Camp, Hance's winter haunt, on Tonto Platform halfway to the river and three miles below

The interior of Hance's Cottonwood Camp rock cabin. A tarp was laced across the roof joists when weather closed in. Artist Thomas Moran leans against and blends into the right wall. "Interior of Hance's cabin at foot of the trail," 1892. Photo by William Henry Jackson, History Colorado, no. 86.200.3106.

the rim. In another image, Hance, recognizable by his beard silhouetted against a campfire blaze, tells a story as listeners sit in rapt attention.

Sam C. Taylor was at that fireside gathering. He—or perhaps Charles Higgins—was the likely "reporter" to designate himself "C" and relay, without Hance's verbiage or wry wit, a story John told that night. "C" put himself in the thick of it, relaying how he and the cap'n had captured a wild girl below the rim.

As twilight came on, their burro grew restless. Suddenly, an apparition "best told in fable . . . flitted past in the twilight. A human, wild with streaming hair, as swift as a deer . . . the wild girl that has been the talk of the country for years." Hance's dog cornered her, by which time it was dark. The next morning, they all returned to the rim, where, assisted

Published in 1892, *Grand Cañon of the Colorado River* was the first commercially available lithograph of Grand Canyon. It portrayed Sinking Ship, Coronado Butte, and Grand Canyon "as seen from John Hance's Ranch." Courtesy of Sharlot Hall Museum Library, map 0058a.

by Hance's landlady, they hoped to learn something about her. She was christened "Effie" until her correct name was known.[63]

Increased public awareness of Grand Canyon and John Hance took a second step forward that year with the publication of *Grand Cañon of the Colorado River*, the first commercially produced lithograph portraying Grand Canyon.[64] It was illustrated by Jules Baumann, an artist from Prescott, and would have been a timely complement to Higgins's *Grand Cañon of the Colorado River*, but how many people laid the two side by side is impossible to know. According to "John Hance's Visitors' Book," Baumann was at Glendale Springs in June 1891, which is when he made preliminary sketches. Back in Prescott, the finished product was large, dramatic, and colorful, rendered in an oddly distorted yet comprehensible way. All in all, it made a compelling and beautiful testament to the land of John Hance.[65]

Ten

SOW BELLY AND BEANS

"Ther Gravitation Was Peeterfied"

Hance finished 1892 with William "Buffalo Bill" Cody. Things had changed dramatically in the twenty-five years since he and Hance first knew each other. Cody now traveled with an entourage, his comings and goings widely reported. Cody's 1892 trip to Arizona formed in England as a prospective real estate venture packaged as a North Rim big game hunting preserve seeking investment. Participants included Colonel Mackinnon of the British Grenadier Guards; Major Mildway of the Queen's Royal Lancers; Colonel Frank Baldwin, twice recipient of the Medal of Honor; "Pony Bob" Haslam of Pony Express fame; photographer W. H. Broach of North Platte, Nebraska; and John M. "Arizona John" Burke, manager of Cody's Wild West show. The chef de cuisine was a Frenchman named Louis Renaud.

Stepping off the train in Flagstaff, Cody was greeted by "a cowboy contingent, fifty horses, three prairie schooners, as many mountain buckboards, and an ambulance wagon."[1] On hand to meet him were his father-in-law and Edwin Dilworth Woolley, owner of a start-up North Rim hunting camp. Magazine founder and author Junius Wells was also there, along with John Hance.[2] Off they went to Grand Canyon, stopping first to climb San Francisco Mountain, reaching Doyle Saddle on the Summit Toll Road.[3]

A photograph by Broach showing Cody and Hance together is widely known. It pictures a group of men, many with rifles, gathered on the outcrop at Hance's Cove. Directly behind Cody, alone and erect in right-center frame with his back close to the precipice, Hance faces inland,

Bill Cody and his entourage at Hance's Cove in late 1892 toast the English gentleman, highest left, who had made his first big game kill in America. Courtesy of Grand Canyon National Park, no. 05305.

upslope, with a rifle in his right hand and a bottle in his left. Most of the others in the photo have raised their glasses to the man at the extreme left, highest among them, in celebration of his first American big game kill.

A dime novel version of Cody's visit was written by party member Prentiss Ingraham. *The Girl Rough Riders* follows a troop of Girl Scouts riding sidesaddle under the leadership of a Captain Fenton on a journey similar to Cody's. Many of the real-life participants are incorporated as fictional characters back-painted with generally accurate information. John Young, for example, is described as a "young fellow, broad shouldered, and with the air of an athlete," but Fort Moroni has been renamed Old Fort Benoni.

Dan'l Seegmiller was Cody's guide for this trip, but Ingraham repurposes him as the fictional Al Huntington. Huntington's language, inflections, and stories are, obviously, channeled through John Hance.

Speaking of the petrified forest in eastern Arizona, for instance, "Huntington" offers up a Hance story.

"Everything peeterfies there, stranger," he says. "A buffalo got astray from ther herd … and just as a hunter went ter shoot him, he jumped over a peeterfied log. Scalp me if ther beast didn't peeterfy right up in ther air."

"And remained there?" another character asks.

"You bet he did."

But gravitation would have returned the buffalo to earth.

"Stranger, ther gravitation was peeterfied too."

At the rim we meet Hance himself, a man woven of verifiable facts, timely observations, and absurd fiction, someone who speaks perfect King's English. "To those who were accustomed to meeting the characters who flourish in the West," Ingraham observed, "there seemed little that was outré in his appearance. He was clad in breeches made of buckskin of his own tanning, a blue shirt, and a gray slouch hat. His was a strong face, expressive of fearlessness and determination, yet withal a rather kindly one. His beard and hair were worn long, his head showing not a thread of silver, though, as told in years, he was several steps across the threshold of fifty."

Captain Fenton's wife conversed with "Mr. Hance":

"Mister seems strange to my ears, for I have not heard it since away back before the war, when I was a young man in Tennessee," John reflected. "I have been here many years, though just how many I could only tell by looking at my calendar board, on which I have cut a mark for every day."

"So you are from Tennessee?"

"Yes, I was born in the mountain country, and learned to know her hills and valleys from childhood. I suppose I would have been there yet had not the war come. I then went into the Confederate army, was a soldier … until the end came. Then I found my kinfolks all dead, and I struck out for the far West, at last drifting here."

"And have you lived here ever since?"

"Yes," responded Hance, "here and down in the Canyon. I go there in winter."

"And you have no companions?" she inquired.

"Chickens, a cat that is growing old, and about twenty burros and ponies. [Hance traveled to Flagstaff four times a year for ammunition, flour, and other supplies.] I have a garden here, another down in the canon, and with game plenty my wants are few and easily provided for."

Hance discounts wealth here, especially the sort earned through prospecting, for wealth cannot replace life's simple pleasures. He treasures his guestbook, predicts dying in his cabin, and relays the many times he's been attacked by Indians, all of whom fell to his gun. His latest assailants had been white outlaws "who had endeavored to catch him off his guard, but they, too, found him a dangerous, deadly foe, retreating in disgust."[4]

Al Doyle ran supplies to Bill Ashurst's north side claims a month after Cody's visit. "Mrs. Doyle accompanied Mr. Doyle and crossed the river with the party, and she has the distinction of being the first [white] woman to cross the river in the Canyon."[5] That may be correct. Her only historical competitor seems to have been Nellie Powell, John Wesley Powell's niece, in 1871. Powell became the first woman to run a Grand Canyon rapid, the Paria Riffle at Lees Ferry, but Nellie ended where she began, on the north bank.[6]

Although he never signed John's guestbook, Doyle was in Hance's orbit for some fifty years, beginning in 1872 when, half-starved in his emigrant journey from Colorado, he pulled into Camp Verde and purchased supplies from Head & Co.,[7] possibly handing his money to George Hance. Proceeding to the Bradshaws, he worked at the Tiger and Peck Mines before marrying Sarah Allen and settling into Marshall Lake Ranch relatively near Bill Ashurst and John Marshall.

Like Hance, Doyle was a guide, highly regarded and widely acclaimed for his wilderness skills. Unlike Hance, he was deeply interested in public affairs (with George Hance and others he founded Arizona's Republican Party) and respected for his good judgment, genial disposition, and honest discourse. He and Sarah moved to the San Francisco Peaks[8] in 1892 and carved out Summit Toll Road, the same road Bill Cody and his party took to Doyle Saddle a few weeks later. John Hance and Bill Cody were among the first, and possibly only, customers to ride the road Al and Sarah Doyle built.

Almost a decade later, Doyle, the writer Winfield Hogaboom, Oliver Lippincott, and T. M. Chapman were aboard the first motorized vehicle, a Toledo steamer, to arrive at "Hance's Point." They anticipated a four-hour journey but miscalculated by four days, during which Doyle was poisoned when drinking gasoline-tainted water from the car's radiator.[9] Doyle also escorted Arizona historian Sharlot Hall on a three-month motoring tour of the Arizona Strip. Zane Gray called him "a wiry old pioneer, hollow cheeked and bronzed, with blue-grey eyes still keen on fire . . . tireless, willing, and when telling a story always begins 'in the early days.'"[10]

John Marshall and Buckey O'Neill autographed "John Hance's Visitors' Book" on January 25. In it, O'Neill wrote what has become a Hance mantra of sorts, "God made the Canyon, John Hance the trails. Without the other, neither would be complete." However, anticipating the legal troubles prospectors would face that year, Marshall simply wrote "Good Luck in 93." Senator Benjamin Harrison had proposed "public park" legislation for central Grand Canyon in 1882, 1883, and 1886, but his bills had never emerged from committee.[11] As president, Harrison took measures to fix that during his last year in office.

By then, Hance, Ashurst, Marshall, McClure, and Tom Frier had staked the Mineral Silk 2, 3, 4, 5, and 6 claims near the Wool claim. The core team of Ashurst, Marshall, McClure, and Hance then moved downstream to lower Pipe Creek near the bottom of Bright Angel Toll Road, close to Ralph Cameron's first claims. Using a rowboat between February 13 and 16, along with Niles Cameron and others who came and went, they located the Old Man, 600 Feet, Pipe Creek, and You Bet claims on the south side of the river, and the Red, Brown Man, Long Fiber, and Camp claims on the north side.

A month later, President Harrison issued Proclamation No. 349, "Setting Apart as a Public Reservation Certain Lands in the Territory of Arizona." This was Grand Canyon Forest Reserve, a vertical rectangle of 1,851,250 acres stretching eastward from Hundred and Fifty Mile Canyon to the mouth of the Little Colorado River. Northward, it encompassed most of Kanab Creek's drainage and much of Marble Canyon, taking in Red Butte to the south.

That day, John Hance's name was legally listed on nearly fifty mineral locations. But, important to the notion that Hance came to Grand Canyon as a prospector, only one claim—a mile up Clear Creek on the north side of the river—was staked solely by Hance, but not until 1893, well after he was involved with Ashurst. His name was on the other locations because he was Ashurst's dear friend and a vibrant element in the group's activities.

Ashurst and the others couldn't say how Proclamation 349 might affect their claims, but they worked the problem as they thought best, by recording locations as quickly as possible. It was a wise decision. Prior to February 20, Grand Canyon prospectors could drive stakes anywhere they pleased. By sundown that day, it was all over. Any claims legally recorded prior to the twentieth would be considered active unless their owners failed to perform yearly assessment work, lived outside the law, or used their stakes for illegal purposes such as moonshine operations.

Bill Ashurst held a meeting for miners at Cottonwood Camp that same day. Acting as the group chairman, with Pete Berry as its secretary, Ashurst and the rest created Grand Canyon Mining District, heretofore an area without legal description. Its boundaries were defined—locations were restricted to 1,500 linear feet of frontage—and to maintain a location's "ownership" the standards for assessment work were mandated at a yearly minimum of twenty days of labor valued at five dollars a day. By the morning of February 21, Ashurst and associates' claims were worth at least the labor expended on them. They could choose which claims to work.

A crack soon appeared in Proclamation 349's porcelain glaze, which grew into a visible fissure by early 1896. "A petition is being circulated in the northern part of Arizona, asking congress to exempt the mineral lands within the boundaries of the Grand Canyon Forest Reserve from the provisions of the reservation so that they may be worked," read the *Arizona Oasis* on January 11. The restrictions were relaxed in June 1897, but everyone knew it was coming beforehand.[12] On May 16, ahead of the announcement, Hance and Bill Ashurst staked the Red Canyon placer claim south of the river in Red Canyon, three miles from the rim, but they waited for the ordinance to take effect before recording it a month later.[13] Hance performed assessment work on that location for the remainder of his life. It was one of three claims he took to the grave.

Ralph Cameron filed his intention to build Grandview Toll Road to the Last Chance Mine, continuing on to the river below, in early March 1893. After getting as far as Grandview Mesa, the Cameron brothers, Pete Berry, and others spent six days with a block and tackle muscling a six-hundred-pound copper carbonate "nugget" up to the rim in a two-wheeled cart.[14] Berry accompanied that rock to the trailhead and from there to Chicago, where it took first prize at the Columbian Exposition for its 80 percent pure copper content.

The Last Chance Mine and nearby limestone caves quickly became attractions, putting Grandview on the map while also moving Glendale Springs toward the back burner. Berry built his first Grandview cabin that year, and by 1896 he had more than copper to mine. That October he wrote his son Ralph, "I am getting out logs to build a house 24 feet wide and 54 feet long 2 story for a hotel."[15] That was the first of several commodious, comfortable structures he built. Additionally, the expansive panorama at Grandview Point exceeded that of Hance's Cove, where any canyon view required an uphill walk through virgin ponderosa forest. In itself, that gentle stroll was not a complaint—and the view was otherworldly. But at Grandview, the spectacle was at your feet. At Grandview, you stepped away from the rim.

In the press between 1891 and 1901, Hance was as wide as Grand Canyon was deep. On the surface, reports portray him leading tourists down trails and telling campfire stories. Behind that are vague mentions of prospecting and the building of Red Canyon Toll Road. More hidden is the fact that Glendale Springs and Hance Trail were leased, sold, or bartered conditionally to three individuals during these same years. This aspect goes nearly unmentioned in the press and never by Hance's visitors. Even if James Thurber's guests were staying at Thurber's hotel and rode Thurber's stage to get there, they slept at Hance's. So far as they knew, the place was his.

Ten years after the train reached Flagstaff, Grand Canyon was known worldwide. Now, more people than Sanford Rowe were exploring its tourism potential. Lyman Henry Tolfree, of cheery, whole-souled disposition,[16] was such an individual. He and his brother James, the company overseer, operated Fred Harvey–style hotels and eating houses in Southern California. Lyman first visited Grand Canyon in 1888 and returned with his wife and two daughters, Edith Mae and Gertrude, for a closer look in July 1893. He examined the "Canyon area hotels"—meaning Cedar Ranch, Moqui Station, and Glendale Springs—for tourism potential. Hance apparently escorted the family north from Flagstaff.

After his second look, Lyman wired James, who arrived the following week and found the possibilities equally promising. Lyman would be the man on the ground. His letterhead read, "Resort at the Grand Canyon of the Colorado."[17] One of the first things he did was install a sturdy rope and wire ladder down Moran's Falls.

Also in 1893, James Willard Thurber moved with his wife, Elsie, and daughters to Flagstaff. Originally from Illinois, Thurber was involved in stagecoach tours, logging, and road and railway grading throughout the Southwest. To that list he added tour operator in northern Arizona.

In Flagstaff, the Thurber family quarters adjoined an eighty-by-one-hundred foot livery stable. Around midnight on July 4 of that year, the stables erupted in flame. Thurber and his family escaped with the clothes on their backs and, fortunately, all of his stock, but during those twenty minutes he suffered an eight hundred–dollar loss of equipment.[18]

The following April, Thurber was hoisting timber onto a railcar when the chain assembly cut loose. In an instant his lower jaw was cracked in three places and some of his teeth were gone. He was, however, filled with enterprise, determined to replace E. S. Wilcox's stages with his own vehicles, and his newspaper ads began the following month. Cast in large, bold, sans serif sentences, they read, "Grand Canyon, Cliff and Cave Dwellings, Summit of San Francisco Peaks or Oak Creek. First-Class Teams and Rigs, For Hire, For Long or Short Trips."[19]

1893 had been good to John Hance. He owned three saddle horses, two young ponies, two cattle, a harness, and $65 in homestead improvements. His tax bill was $7.62 and is of no particular interest, but this notation in Coconino County assessor's files otherwise portrays a significant event. Even though it had become delinquent by the time he paid it, it signals a reemergence, a coming out—not since the Verde had Hance been assessed or filed any sort of official paperwork except mining locations.

Hance had new mining regulations to deal with. He and the others had nothing to worry about as long as they kept up assessment work, which happened in the winter, when the tourists were gone. Come spring, as the inner canyon heat grew terrible in its blast furnace frenzy, it was time for Hance and the others to retreat to the rim and earn a living. Ashurst and Marshall would head to the Mogollon Mountains to fatten cattle for shipment to market. Animals not sufficiently aged were herded

Taking lunch near the head of Hance Rapid in the late 1890s, Hance in center back-ground. What remained of the site vanished in 1980 when a tourist burning his toilet paper caused a larger conflagration. Courtesy of The Huntington Library, Otis R. Marston Papers, V059/0098.

to the flatlands around Canyon Diablo to eat bunchgrass for the winter, then moved back to the Mogollons in the spring. And every fall, about the first of November, Ashurst and Hance would round up Ashurst's horses—twenty in 1893—and drive them down Red Canyon to winter forage on Tonto Platform. Cattle could eat Canyon Diablo's locoweed, but it had a "decided ill-effect" on a horse.[20]

Hance leased Glendale Springs and Hance Trail to Lyman Tolfree and Bill Hull for five years at three hundred dollars a year in November 1893.[21] Glendale Springs became Tolfree's Resort. Hance, John Marshall, Bill Ashurst, and Curtis McClure were near completion of what became Red Canyon Toll Road, today called "New Hance Trail," at the time.

The Red Canyon trailhead was a mile east of Hance Trail, its apparent terminus at what became Hance Rapid after a six-mile burro ride. The route, however, continued downstream for three thousand feet to Hance's landing, where a rowboat was tied above the high-water line. Travelers muscled it down to the river, rowed over to the north side, where a second boat was retrieved, and in company with the first boat returned to the south side, where the first boat was lugged back up the beach. All the participants then proceeded again to the north side in the second boat, which was again restowed, before continuing westward and downstream for twenty or more miles (well beyond the Wool claim) to eventually arrive on the North Rim via Clear Creek.

Lightly traveled, the majority of the north side of the river was thin, spare, and in places quite steep if not occasionally perpendicular. Today, the route features the remains of one particular rock-built cabin similar to but smaller than Hance's Cottonwood Camp structure, along the lower reaches of Vishnu Creek. Hance probably helped construct the cabin and may have even suggested it, but the remaining foundation and fireplace were probably not "John Hance's cabin" as it's often called. More likely, it was a community shelter, any prospector's home for a night, including Ashurst, Marshall, McClure, and Hance not a few times.

Now mostly obscure, Red Canyon Trail is barely a footnote in canyon history, but people still traverse the south side nearly every day. Its most striking remnant is Hance's hand-drawn plat on light brown wrapping paper, a diagram measuring twenty-three inches by thirty-one and a half inches. Signed by Marshall, Hance, Tom Frier, Curtis McClure, and Ashurst in descending order, it is an enticingly burnished artifact. It's also the only piece of paper known to have been wholly crafted by the hand of John Hance, whose penmanship and graphic style require a bit of study. Hance would have needed more than an hour to etch this map, describing every scant feature with remarkable candor and detail.

On Christmas Eve 1893, Bill Ashurst, his son-in-law Jimmy Pitts, John Marshall, Curtis McClure, Merit Fisher, Tom Frier (who ran the Laurel Leaf cattle brand), a soldier of fortune named Millard Love, and Niles and Burt Cameron, everyone's stomachs packed tight with "sow belly and beans,"[22] sat around a campfire perched on a bluff overlooking the Colorado at the Silver Twig claim. They listened while the river swept past below as Hance put the finishing touches on another story. As each tale ended, Ashurst tossed a small chunk of dynamite on the fire, there to furiously combust and quickly burn down. When Hance started another story, Ashurst carved another chunk off the stick. It went on like that all night.

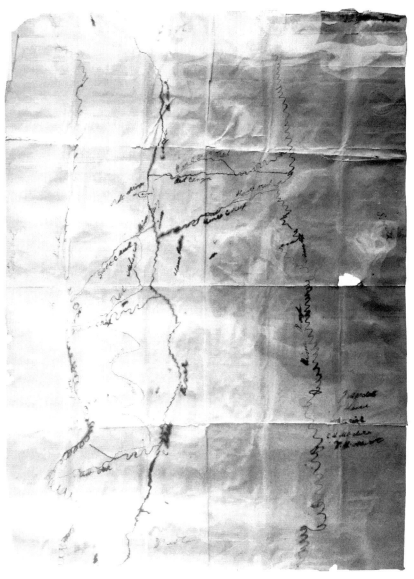

Recorded in Coconino County on January 1, 1894, Hance's plat map of Red Canyon Toll Road. Courtesy of Coconino County, Arizona.

On Christmas day, Hance, Burt Cameron, and Pitts crossed the river and butchered a steer. Hance and Cameron returned to the north side to celebrate with fresh beef, but Pitts headed home to Flagstaff, saying this trip was all of Grand Canyon he'd ever need.[23]

Hance celebrated New Year's Day 1894 in Flagstaff by recording the Red Canyon Toll Road. Even then the trailhead may have featured a notice overflowing with odd punctuation: "Toll. On. Trail, Footman. $1.00, Saddle. Animal $2.00."[24]

George Hance and Lorenzo Hickok visited John for five days that spring. Hickok had spent the winter with George at the Cienega. Obviously impressed with what he'd seen, Lorenzo inscribed in John's guestbook, "Words will not describe the Grand Canyon." George followed in his large swaying cursive without punctuation, "Arrived April 8 left April 13 George Hance Cienega Yavapai County Arizona 1894."[25]

George and Lorenzo's signatures were among only ninety-seven names recorded in John's guestbook that year, a sure indication that Pete Berry was gaining steam at Grandview. Several visitors mentioned Red Canyon Toll Road, one noting stock could be ridden nearly to the river. More curious was the fact that August featured only one name, although eight men made a "bicycle aggregation" from Flagstaff on the twenty-fourth, covering seventy miles in a long fifteen-hour day (it took twelve hours in a stagecoach).[26] Although probably unintended, these bicyclists started a Flagstaff–Grand Canyon tradition that continued into the twentieth century. The yearly rides were well promoted, featured informative milepost maps, and normally joined several clubs in a combined meet with group photos at the event's completion.

Tolfree opened Grand Canyon's first post office at Glendale Springs two weeks before the bicycle run, but because August's only confirmed visitor signed John's guestbook the previous day it's doubtful Tolfree did any postal business that month.

Flagstaff's population was 1,500 in 1895 when the Arizona Lumber & Timber Company's output reached fifty million board feet.[27] The bigger story of the summer of 1895, however, was that James Thurber's stage line had replaced Wilcox's operations.[28] By mid-March Thurber was in Denver buying supplies for his new livery station on the northwest corner of Aspen and Agassiz Streets in Flagstaff.[29] With a reporter aboard and Ike

James Thurber drives an outsized load of sightseers along the rim in the latter 1890s. Courtesy of Grand Canyon National Park, no. 04886.

Wheeler behind the reins, his first stage rumbled down the grade to Tol-free's Grand Cañon Resort at dusk on April 6. "[Grand Canyon] promises to attract more sightseers this year than any before in its history," read an early April news article. "J. W. Thurber, manager of the stage line, has already made arrangements for the transportation of several parties of tourists and townspeople. Under his management the line cannot fail to become popular. He is enterprising, accommodating, and always alive to the comfort of his patrons."[30]

In early June, Scipio Craig of the *Redlands Citrograph* spearheaded a Southern California Press Association tour. The group of twenty-three stayed at Tolfree's resort, traversed Red Canyon, and interviewed Hance at length, with resulting long coverage in the *Los Angeles Times*. The newspaper men and their wives raved over the tent furnishings of Navajo blankets, comfortable chairs, and warm beds; Tolfree's bright, hospitable, and attentive daughters; and the hotel's ample, scrumptious meals.[31] They also did a good job describing Hance, "a type of frontiersman nowhere else to be encountered except upon the very outposts of civilization in the wild and woolly West," a man with "abilities as a single-handed narrator that would put Eli Perkins to the blush."[32] Those sentiments continued into September when the Prescott paper, covering the late-August bicycling trip, complimented the service and amenities: "Mr. Tolfree has erected several commodious tents that are as well-furnished as most hotels, the table is excellent and can't be beaten in the territory."[33]

After less than a year, Hance's five-year agreement with Bill Hull and Lyman Tolfree was terminated—Tolfree and Thurber had other ideas. Thurber, for example, was eager for expansion and made his wishes known to the Atlantic & Pacific Railroad's Albuquerque superintendent H. G. Wells. Wells responded, "I shall be very glad if you and Mr. Tolfree buy Mr. Hance out, and operate the trail in partnership. You want to get your agreement with Hance as tight as the law can make it, prohibiting him from participating in the business of piloting tourists or others in and out of the Canon or along its rim, or doing business in any way in that line directly or indirectly."[34]

As indicated in the paperwork, Thurber, Tolfree, and the stage driver/ racehorse rider Ike Wheeler were "largely induced to make this purchase" by Hance.[35] Drawn on Friday, November 1, 1895, the contract was recorded the following morning, its preface stating that Hance was "well known as a guide ... in this country and in Europe, and the said Hance Trail, by my said name of Hance, is equally well known." With that mindfully historic flourish, and continuing through a torrent of legal fiction, Hance sold "his" trail, the rock cabin at Cottonwood Camp, and his "personal property used in connection with the said trail. ... Six mules in different brands and known by the names [of] Beck, Biddy, Kate, Jim, Kitty and Steve. Six horses in different brands and known by the names of Sabine, George, Aleck, Nig, Buck, and Gray Mare Kitty. Eight men's saddles, one side saddle, nine bridles, and nine saddle blankets" for $1,500, $600 of which was in hand, with the remaining balance forthcoming "in two equal payments as provided in a certain contemporaneous written agreement[36] between the parties."

While the phrase "different brands" sounds horse-thief suspicious, it is explained to some extent by vagrant stock wandering into Glendale Springs. Using newspaper ads, Hance attempted to reunite these animals with their owners: "SORRELL HORSE, flax mane and tail. Supposed to be about twelve years old. 16 1/2 hands high, thin in flesh, branded

U. S. on left shoulder, found about seventy-five miles from Flagstaff, near Coconino Forest. John Hance."[37]

Superintendent Wells prevailed. Hance would not "engage in the business of guide" within thirty miles of Glendale Springs and would not "use or permit to be used, my name as guide or in connection with the business of guiding tourists, nor in connection with any trail . . . nor to be interested, directly or indirectly, in any other trail within said distance." Hance also granted right-of-way between the hotel and his trails for ticket holders, their friends, animals, and conveyances, and he stipulated that "Red Canyon Trail . . . in which I am a quarter owner, shall not be used for other than mining purposes, and in event of my part to prevent the same being used for other than mining purposes," he would convey to Thurber et al. his interest in the Red Canyon route.[38]

The 2017 equivalent of $1,500 is $40,000. Even with all that money in his pocket, Hance was again delinquent in paying that year's taxes: $11.68.

On December 23, 1895, Wells forwarded James Thurber a letter written in longhand on stationery embossed with a dramatic red design of a stagecoach and team roaring down a hill, dust flying, accompanied by lettering that read, "J. H. Farlee, Proprietor. Comfortable Accommodations At The Canyon."

"Mr. Wells," Celia Farlee began, "The Canon Toll road and house [Grand Cañon Hotel] are for sale. The road is in good condition, the house contains 9 rooms—fairly furnished. The surroundings of the house could be made beautiful as well as grand. It would not take much to [funnel Diamond Creek's] water to the grounds . . . as the fall is about 200 feet to the mile." She was right, as Diamond Creek was, literally, within a stone's throw of the building. Farlee continued, "My husband J. H. Farlee was offered $15,000 for half interest. It was worth it if properly handled by a man with some means."

Celia continued, completely off message, "The tourist business to the Canon has not been a success at any point. It takes time, money, and a particular fitness. . . . We have offered toll road, house, and furniture for $5,000. Come and see it,"[39] she urged, concluding that her health was poor, she wanted to get away, and was anxious to close the deal.

Needless to say, Celia remained in Peach Springs. She transitioned into cattle, established her own brand, and suffered an unfortunate share

Lyman Tolfree's "Resort at the Grand Cañon" in 1896, following the Atlantic & Pacific Railroad's addition of the dining room, kitchen, and small sitting room. Arizona Historical Society, Flagstaff, AHS.0340.00010, Marjorie Flaherty Collection.

of stock thefts and cruel, criminal animal disfigurements as Julius slid farther into the background. In a final bit of irony, Julius Farlee was apparently working for James Thurber (grading a road between Prescott and Ash Fork) when he transferred his estate to Celia on March 8, 1901,[40] and died, possibly from smallpox, on the eighteenth without a death notice or an obituary. Celia's remains can be visited in Kingman, Arizona, but Mohave County's burial index contains no information on Julius's death or burial whereabouts. No photographic likeness of him is known. Additionally, no placard indicates where Grand Cañon Hotel once stood, though every vehicle traveling Diamond Creek Road to the Colorado River passes within feet of the spot.[41]

The first obvious visual change to Glendale Springs was the addition of Tolfree's dining room and kitchen building, installed in early 1896. Noted the *Arizona Republican* on March 7, the Atlantic & Pacific Railroad "have decided to build a cool weather annex to the tent hotel at the Grand

Canyon. The structure will be of logs to carry out the sylvan suggestive-
ness of the scene, and the dimensions are set at 32 x 40. There will be a
well-stocked library for the accommodation of tourists.... Not only will
the innovation add to the attractiveness of the surroundings, but it will
be a comfortable shelter for travelers when the weather happens to be
off color."

James Thurber held the contract and was done a month later. "The
[T-shaped] building is of logs, 40 x 60 feet, and contains a dining and
sitting room and a kitchen," reported the *Coconino Weekly Sun*.[42] It was
saddle-notched like Hance's cabin a few yards to the south, carrying forward the impression of old-time homespun domesticity.

The front porch and entryway roof are first seen in a whole plate
exposed in 1898 by the landscape photographer Fred Payne Clatworthy,
who also went down Hance Trail and photographed Sockdolager Rapid.
Further modifications to the roof, the porch, and the buck and rail fenc-
ing, as well as the addition of Sibley stoves in the tents, reveal other
enhancements throughout the years. Many of the images are dated, and
a fairly accurate timeline of developmental growth can be explored with
this visual archeology.

About 1895, Hance built—or, more probably, had built, courtesy of the
Atlantic and Pacific Railroad—a new cabin[43] of dovetailed, hand-milled
lumber quite similar to Bill Hull's barn, suggesting both buildings were
put up about the same time. "Hance's Point"[44] sat only feet from the rim
at the head of Hance Trail, and it appears to have been Hance's primary
residence until the early 1900s when "two old maids" lived there with him
during his last summer in it.[45] A sturdy four-season structure, it featured
at least one window, two doors, a wood-burning cook stove, fireplace, and
pitched shingle roof, substantial comfort over Glendale Springs.

Edith Sessions Tupper, whose signature was almost certainly on one
of the 1895 missing guestbook pages, described Hance at this cabin.

> In summer Hance lives in a log cabin, hanging on the very rim
> of the canyon, about a mile from the camp proper. It is the neat-
> est, cleanest place you can imagine. The walls are papered with
> pictures and lithographs of Buffalo Bill in every pose he ever
> struck. "Bill Cody!" says Hance. "Shucks! I knew him long before
> he took to play actin'."

This magic lantern slide, circa 1900, shows Thurber's hotel with Sibley stoves in some tents and the dining room's expanded porch. Courtesy of Grand Canyon National Park, no. #31398.

Hance does all his own work, and every morning his floor is scrubbed and his stove blackened until they shine and glow. Near his cabin is the corral where he keeps his pack horses which take the trail into the canyon and carry down tourists and provisions.[46]

Today, only scattered artifacts remain. A partial foundation is noticeable, and the location is verified by a photo from the Hollenback sisters featuring a juniper tree, trimmed in a certain way, adjacent to the cabin. The tree is still alive and identifiable but difficult to locate in today's dense brush. Hance Trail courses northward into the canyon alongside

Hance's spacious rim cabin at the head of Hance Trail was constructed about 1895. Photo by Amelia Hollenback, courtesy of Palace of the Governors, Photo Archives, HP.2011.26.002.

the northeast corner's remaining foundation, where the cook stove was located. After following that twisting slalom course about two hundred yards downhill it ceases to exist.

In May 1896 Thurber again wrote to Wells in Albuquerque: "Can get building for hotel with twenty-five rooms that can furnish up in first class shape. If you will do the same by me that you do with Tolfree, I think I can open up a house and give entire satisfaction."[47] Wells was supportive. Thurber ran a stage road to his new hotel at the head of Bright Angel Toll Road from Grandview Point. Sanford Rowe had already connected Williams with the Bright Angel area, and Thurber's new enterprise would not only draw business from Williams but also away from Rowe. On July 9, Bright Angel Hotel recorded its first guest signatures.[48] That Christmas, Thurber could brag—and he did—that it was his best year ever.[49] Canyon tourism belonged almost exclusively to him.

Tragedy struck at the end of July when James Tolfree's wife, reportedly in a psychotic state, committed suicide by drinking carbolic acid at their Nadeau restaurant in Mojave, California. Notices appeared in such diverse papers as the *Princeton Union*, the *Evening Star* (Washington, D.C.), and the *Wyndham County Reformer* (Brattleboro, Vermont). "She was Grover Cleveland's secretary when he was mayor of Buffalo, New York," offered the *Saint Paul Globe* on July 22.

Her death rattled the Tolfree brothers' operations. Possibly because James Thurber was squeezing him out (as they had both done with Bill Hull), and because his taxes were in arrears, Lyman had seen enough of Grand Canyon. He and Ike Wheeler withdrew their two-thirds interest in Glendale Springs and returned it to Hance with a conveyance and release on November 5.[50]

James Thurber was also present at the recorder's office that day. In a separate document he freed Hance from the restriction of guiding within thirty miles of Glendale Springs. The remainder of the original agreement, however, remained in full force. Thurber owned the lease of Hance's buildings while Hance remained accountable to Coconino County for the possessory interest fees on his homestead. But he was back to guiding on his old turf with customers supplied.

A month earlier, as Tolfree and Ike Wheeler debated handing back Glendale Springs to Hance, another drama unfolded at Hance Rapid, and Wheeler was there to see it. That day he rode down Red Canyon with Reverend George W. White, president of the University of Southern California, and a Mr. C. Kelsey. Arriving at the river, they were "startled by the appearance of a boat containing two men," George Flavell and Ramon Montéz. "They left Green River, Wyoming, on August 26th, arriving at Lees Ferry, the head of Grand Canyon, on October 16th. The trip to Hance's trail had been made without incident, and the men who have experience in other waters considered the trip an uninspiring one."[51]

Flavell (a.k.a. Clark the Trapper) packed his own tattoo kit and lived off coyote bounties in the Lower Colorado River desert. He considered this trip uninspiring, probably because the hunting and prospecting were poor and he was hungry and broke. Montéz, on the other hand, was scared out of his wits, having determined upstream in Cataract Canyon to quit the enterprise. Flavell fingered his pistol and remarked, "You can come along with me, or float down dead."[52] Ramon got back in the boat.

"The boat is an ordinary flat-bottom one, fifteen feet long and five wide, with a bow of double strength and covered with iron," stated the newspaper.[53] Her name was *Panthon*, perhaps a misspelling of "Phantom."[54]

"While we were sitting there trying to decide what to do," wrote Flavell, "we happened to look toward a little canyon that came in from the East side, and to our surprise three mounted men came up, dismounted and tied their horses. We were not over fifty yards apart.... They were much interested in the *Panthon*."[55]

After an hour's scouting, deliberation, beach pacing, river chatter, and whatnot, Flavell "decided to run the rapid (though I would not if they had not been there) and pushed off, took the east entrance which was only a small portion of the river. We had to make exact points to get through, which we failed to do, and in the flash of an eye an oar was broke, and rowlock tore out, and the *Panthon* piled up in the boulders."

They weren't in the main current. "Taking off our shoes, and pants, and with the big end of the broken oar, I pried her off, 20 feet more we came up again. Again we pried her loose. This time we whirled out in the main rapid." A second oarlock broke off and went overboard, leaving half of the boat without locks. They flounced through a narrow, crooked channel "sideways, end way, and every way, the three spectators standing on the rocks. I guess they would not of bid very high on what would be left of the *Panthon* and her crew when that rapid got through with them. Well! Luck changes! Good follows bad."[56]

Preceded only by Powell and Stanton, Flavell and Montéz became the third party to successfully navigate the Colorado River through Grand Canyon, also completing its first single-boat transit. Additionally, they were the first party witnessed navigating an inner-canyon rapid. From that journey came the first account of a canyon river event published by a nonparticipant, firsthand witness.

Flavell is also remembered as the first to run all of Grand Canyon's rapids, but there is a geographical footnote attached to his trip. In historical literature, today's Grand Canyon National Park was composed of "Marble Canyon" and "Grand Canyon." Formerly, "Grand Canyon" did not begin until river mile 60, the confluence of the main stem Colorado and Little Colorado Rivers. To say Flavell ran "all" Grand Canyon's rapids, while accurate in a historical context, ignores his portage of Soap Creek Rapid in Marble Canyon.

And, in a way, George Flavell had John Hance and his friends to thank for his place in river running history. If they had not supplied Red Canyon Trail and a few witnesses, Flavell would have portaged Hance Rapid.

Lyman Tolfree departed Grand Canyon with Ike Wheeler's assistance. Tolfree's back got wrenched packing furniture, and Wheeler went out with a carriage to fetch him. Without his direct management, though, Tolfree's post office remained open until February 2, 1897, supervised by Hance. It then lay dormant for two months until Hance reopened it under the name of "Tourist" on May 10. He was its sworn postmaster until it closed on April 29, 1899, indicating a decline in the area's visitation.

Relocating to Flagstaff, Lyman Tolfree leased the Bank Hotel across from the train depot. Remodeled and refurbished at a cost of $5,000, it was open for business by the third week of December 1896.[57] As at Glendale Springs, James Tolfree came in from the San Joaquin Valley to offer thoughts and suggestions—it was one of the last things he did. James died on January 15, 1897, in the same room where his wife had passed away. Suspicion immediately rose that he'd willfully followed her to the grave by the same method, but it was soon discovered that he went in his sleep from a massive stroke.[58]

Lyman shuttled between the Bank Hotel and the San Joaquin Valley until August 1902, when he settled into running the Weatherford Hotel at the other end of the block. When that contract expired, he managed the nearby Commercial Hotel until seven o'clock in the morning on January 4, 1905. He then retired to the bar, put a Colt .45 pistol to his temple, and pulled the trigger. Death was instantaneous. In his pocket was a note to his wife: "You know my failing. I could say more, but it is all off."[59]

Eleven

THE GREATEST LIAR ON EARTH

"It Was Plain as Day How It All Happened"

We hope when next
We visit the canons,
To find John and
Peck dearer companions.
May she put on a dress,
To cover her pants,
And change her name
To Mrs. John Hance.
May they be supplied
With plenty of bedding,
When we all come to dance,
At the Hance-Peck wedding.
John, if ever inclined
To go on a tipple,
Just go to the canon,
And behold "Peck's Nipple."

—Kansas tourists, May 31, 1897, as recorded
in "John Hance's Visitors' Book"

Annie Smith Peck, then forty-seven, was the leading mountain climber of her day and an author who lectured globally and led South American expeditions. At Grand Canyon she was on assignment for the *New York Evening World*, a frequent sponsor of her travels, yet she doesn't seem to have published anything about her trip to Grand Canyon. She spent the better part of a week at Glendale Springs but, to further confound the event, her signature isn't found in Hance's guestbook—based on the date, she would have signed page 133 or 134, pages missing from the original document.

Peck was probably the most adventuresome, no nonsense, adroit climber Hance had ever encountered, up for whatever he threw at her. This included his most ethereal, spellbinding, and intimate haunts, secret places he alone knew, and he was anxious to show her his best. Grand Canyon was the glue for those two, the accelerant being that Peck lived like Hance—home was where her trunk landed that evening.[1]

In everything known of John Hance, Annie Smith Peck is the sole reference with romantic overtones, and also one of only two or three mentions of women in his immediate sphere. Otherwise, he told jokes. "In the evening John Hance, neatly dressed and the crown of his hat trimmed with a cactus from the Canyon, amuses us. He has had—so he says—thirty-five offers of marriage, to each of which he has resolutely said 'No.' But he intends to surprise the next woman by saying 'yes.'"[2] He was married, he claimed on another occasion, but they didn't get along, so he took the house and gave her the road.

As the beacon for all things canyon, John Hance's days were closing fast. Business was alive all along the rim. Tourists no longer automatically arrived at his—though it was actually Thurber's—door every Monday, Wednesday, and Friday evening, although plenty of them still did, but no one had been down Hance Trail in years. Rather, visitors went wherever Thurber, Berry, the Cameron brothers, or W. W. Bass took them.

Hance owned ten saddle horses and made improvements to Glendale Springs (a $150 estate in 1898), but thanks to either Thurber's lease, summertime tips, horse trading, or a satisfactory roll of the dice, he was considering retirement.

Hance bought John Marshall's house on South San Francisco Street in Flagstaff that year. The newspaper reported him "improving and remodeling" the dwelling,[3] and in October he also purchased lots 23 and 24 of block 96 on the same street from the Santa Fe Railroad for $100. By November he'd constructed a small barn and was putting up a fence.[4]

At the same time, Hance's tall tales had gained such notoriety that they were ranked alongside those of the fictional German nobleman Baron Münchausen.[5] Distinct from the actual person of the same name and era, Hieronymus Karl Friedrich, the fictional Baron Münchausen rides a seahorse underwater, pilots a cannonball through the air, and camps on a church steeple during a heavy winter snowstorm. John Hance was the Baron Münchausen of the West. Homer Wood from Prescott said if Münchausen had been alive during Hance's run, he would've been John's secretary.[6]

The reprinted and edited edition of "John Hance's Visitors' Book," *Personal Impressions*, ends as it begins, with a missing signature. Though she is included in *Personal Impressions*, the signature of Annette Persis Ward, librarian of the Western Reserve Historical Society and author of a short volume entitled *Lest We Forget: Oliver Hazard Perry, the War of 1812, the Battle of Lake Erie*, is missing from the original guestbook. According to Woods's typeset edition, Ward's was the last entry in John's book, on October 6, 1898. But in the original document, Ward's thoughts and signature have been obscured by a typewritten promotion on white paper glued over them:

THE

INSCRIPTIONS IN THIS BOOK

up to and

INCLUDING PAGE 179

Have been published in book form, and the volume is now on sale at my [Woods's] office near the R.R. Station, Flagstaff, Arizona.

All visitors are cordially invited to register their names and briefly record their impressions of Grand Canyon in this book. Whatever is here written will be published in an enlarged edition of the work already in print. Let us know what you think of this surpassing wonder, this masterpiece of the ages, in order that, by uniting the first and best impressions of all visitors, we may some day secure an adequate conception of the Canyon as the best and brightest intellects of the world have regarded it.

Yours respectfully,

G K Woods

After the advert, the next signatures in John's book were written nine months later in July 1899. Several mention Pete Berry and Grandview Trail. Hance is not much remarked upon save a reunion with an old friend on page 190. The last signature in "John Hance's Visitors' Book," that of "D.D. Grass, Yankton, South Dakota," is dated January 22, 1900, on page 193.

Although Woods did not, apparently, produce a second edition of his book, *Personal Impressions* has two varieties: pages with gilt edges, perhaps intended as promotional gifts or display copies, and pages without gilt edges. There is, according to Richard Quartaroli, no distinguishable difference between the covers of either version except for the gilding. About fifteen copies are known to exist, mostly in archives. *Personal Impressions* is a collector's item with Grand Canyon aficionados. A gilded copy with wonderfully bold, detailed personal calligraphy on its inside cover recently sold for $850.[7]

Following Ashurst's discovery of the Wool claim, he and Curtis McClure filed more claims in the same area while also prospecting independently throughout Upper Granite George. Ten years later, in February 1901, Bill Ashurst was killed in a rockslide a mile downstream from Lonetree Canyon, just below Zoroaster Rapid on the south side and well above the river. From a press report, the site has always been called the "Arkansaw mine,"[8] but that name is not on the books. It was the Arkansas Traveller claim that Ashurst had staked on January 1, 1900.[9] A year later he was back, doing assessment work, when tragedy struck.

Hance told about finding Ashurst's body. They had agreed to meet on a certain date, but Ashurst failed to appear. "Fur six days I knocked aroun' an' still he didn't come [to Glendale Springs]. By that time I knew there was trouble," so Hance went in search of his friend's camp. "There it all was—his pot o' beans all dried up on the ashes of his fire where he'd let 'em to cook, his pile o' canned things an' dried up biscuits, an' flour, an' bacon, his blanket rolled up fur the day, everythin' fixed up jus' as he'd left 'em in the mornin'."

The last entry in Ashurst's diary, made on January 16, told Hance where to look: "Down the river about three miles an' twelve hundred feet or so up from it. An' o' course I knew the kind o' country where he'd be likely to look fur mineral. Sure enough, the nex' day I came acrost him,

Calligraphy inscribed in a copy of *Personal Impressions of the Grand Canyon of the Colorado*, June 1903: "Devote to Canyon and Hance, A wondering lingering glance, Say farewell to both! Though to leave them you're loth, The marvelous Canyon and Hance!" Courtesy of Mike Gulvin.

lyn' cluttered up with a big o' loose rock. There he lay with a broken hip, his face up an' his dead eyes glarin' at the sky."[10]

Hance discovered Ashurst's body about February 14,[11] and by February 16 he was in Flagstaff. On Monday, February 18, a coroner's jury "composed of John Hance, Niles Cameron, J. D. Halford, Porter Guffey, Marvin Beal, [and] Henry, Charles, and Andy Ashurst, started for the canyon."[12] Several of these names are found in the Bright Angel Hotel guest register during the following few days.[13]

Back in Flagstaff on February 21, Hance visited the Coconino County recorder's office to register a deed Ashurst sold him in 1894 for one dollar, a deed to lot 4, Brannen Division, Flagstaff. Hance had returned the favor years before in 1895 when he deeded Ashurst a one-third interest in his and John Marshall's North End claim for the same price.[14]

Two months shy of fifty years later, Andy Ashurst remembered his father's death in a letter to Lon Garrison, the first director of Albright Training Academy at Grand Canyon. The jury was led to the site by Hance, there to witness the circumstances of Ashurst's death, with the inquest that evening. "I was seated at father's last campsite. In the dark weeping very bitterly. Captn Hance was in the tent with the Coroner's Jury. And there I was obliged to pause and laugh at one of the Captns stories. Which he was at the time relating."[15]

John handled his dear friend's demise as he did similar events. However sad these sorts of things must have been for him, they did not usually color his mood except under the influence of alcohol. As Coconino Forest rancher Elizabeth Heiser told it, John Hance was normally "happy and serene—never got into the dumps. If his mule fell over the cliff and broke his leg, or the pack animal ran away, he was always calm. 'The Lord will send it back again,' he would say. Just so long as he had his coffee and doughballs, that was all he cared for." Heiser also said Hance believed in one God, but he mostly believed in John Hance.[16]

Henry Ashurst, then speaker of the Arizona Territorial Legislature, handled his father's estate. The court granted him permission to dispose of twelve locations his father and Curtis McClure had staked and maintained. Though John Hance's name does not appear on any of the paperwork associated with these locations, Henry asked the court to divide the proceeds equally three ways. The judge agreed, and the three recipients were the Ashurst family, Curtis McClure, and John Hance. All they needed was a buyer.

Susan Watts Kearny Selfridge was the daughter of General Philip Kearny, the "one-armed devil" of the Civil War and a millionaire who dreamed of riding to glory. (He did. His obituary appeared in the *Newbern Weekly Press* on September 13, 1862: shot at Chantilly, Virginia.) Selfridge was born in France in 1856. Before the turn of the century, she was briefly a correspondent of note who published interviews with conservative Prussian statesman Otto von Bismarck and former British prime minister William Gladstone.

Selfridge visited Grand Canyon and stayed at Bright Angel Hotel with two other ladies from April 10 to 12, 1901.[17] On April 11, she and one of her friends went down Bright Angel Trail, where she was photographed standing near the river at Pipe Creek with their guide. His services cost $2.50 a day, and each horse cost $3 for the trip. Another image in this series, with "Last Chance [Mine] Camp" scribbled on its verso, shows a wooden shack and four horses tethered to squatty piñons. Notes on the back of this photo indicate that Selfridge, Hance, Ralph Berry, and others were at the camp for lunch and dinner on April 15, and for breakfast and lunch on April 16.[18]

Susan Selfridge learned of "the asbestos mines for sale" from John Hance himself. She eventually gave Hance power of attorney regarding Grand Canyon matters and on June 18, 1901, filed a $6,000 four-month purchase agreement on the twelve claims for sale by the Ashurst family, McClure, and Hance.[19] However, she reconsidered in October and assigned her purchase option to George Hills of Boston. In the meantime, Henry Ashurst, holding out for more money, was going it alone. So, Hills could purchase only the McClure and Hance rights, or two-thirds interest, which he did on October 21, 1901, paying each $2,000. Before Christmas, Hills settled with Henry Ashurst for the same amount, or $6,000 total.[20]

In early February 1902, Hills transferred his title to Hance Asbestos Mining Company (HAMC) for a $1 quitclaim and other considerations.[21] HAMC had incorporated in, of all places, the small town of Kittery, Maine, the previous October. Millard W. Baldwin of New York was the company president; Hiram Thompson, Kittery, its clerk; and H. H. Palmer, also of Kittery, was a stockholder. Each owned ten shares and capital was valued at $100,000; $750 was on the books with 3,970 shares outstanding.

John Hance's name does not appear on any of the twenty-four HAMC documents known to exist.[22] Accordingly, Hance never sat on its board of directors or purchased any of its stock. Furthermore, it appears the company was named for the mines' closest geographical feature, Hance Rapid, rather than Hance himself.

Susan Selfridge later purchased one hundred HAMC shares, probably on special offer. Additionally, in separate proxies with Hance in early August 1902, she became a partner in his Lloyd and Howard claims south of the river and west of Red Canyon. A one-third interest in those locations was sold to John Penhale on August 28, 1902, for $500. Hance paid Selfridge her share of the sale, but it was an insignificant amount in the larger picture. Selfridge declared bankruptcy in 1907. Her numerous creditors included "Fidelity Trust Company of Philadelphia, as executor of B. S. Burton, $1,500 secured by 100 shares of the Hance Asbestos Mining Company" and "[Joseph] Hyde Pratt, Chapel, Hill, N.C., $1,200 for services as an expert geologist."[23]

The advice Pratt articulated to Selfridge (interestingly, around the same time Hance's HAMC co-superintendency was forever revoked) was likely bad news. Pratt would have told her transportation was key. Getting the stuff out of Grand Canyon, he would have said, *that* was the problem. What actually happened "down there" certainly needed improvement.

In this instance, burros did the work. From the asbestos mine, they were loaded with panniers weighing 80–100 pounds, or 175–210 pounds per mule.[24] So packed, the stock ambled precipitously downhill across a steep slope, headed upstream to the northside landing nearly halfway to Hance Rapid. There, the panniers were transferred to a rowboat that was rowed back and forth across the river to the southside landing, where the animals swimming behind the boat were repackaged for the six-mile journey up Red Canyon.

It sounds simple enough. In reality, however, traveling the north side involved a downhill traverse across nearly sheer terrain to the only place burros could safely navigate winter's low river flows. Additionally, the last hundred yards involved precipitous "greasy" scree. Departure from "Hance's Landing" on the south side was the same thing: an abrupt, steep rise to semi-level ground before proceeding three thousand feet upstream to the mouth of Red Canyon.

When the burros arrived on the East Rim in the evening, with twelve more miles to South Rim rail station, it's reasonable to suspect their overnight home was Glendale Springs, what the paper termed "mine manager's John Page's camp near Grandview."[25]

In the end, it must have been a sight when a freight car's worth of asbestos lashed to burros pulled into Grand Canyon depot. So far as is known, the HAMC made the trip perhaps twice. If ever authenticated, it's likely Hance led a string of thirty burros during early 1903 and another smaller train in 1904. He's also the most likely candidate to have registered the HAMC brand in Flagstaff in early 1903.[26]

On October 26, 1901, the *Coconino Sun* incorrectly noted Selfridge's payment to McClure and Hance as $6,250. Two days later, the *Arizona Republican* reported that McClure and Hance had received $10,000 from Selfridge. The figure grew and grew until it was believed that Hance toured San Francisco with the proceeds, hemorrhaging $1,000 a day on an epic ten-day bender. But even at $1,000 a day nobody took notice. The next time, Hance said, he'd take $50,000 and really wake 'em up![27]

Another version of the story puts Hance in an upscale Embarcadero hotel. His room had a bedside gas lamp that, supposedly, he did not know how to operate. Pete Berry had cautioned him beforehand to not blow out the flame, so John fanned it out with his fedora.

"I have told you," read one news tidbit, "about John Hance, the veteran guide at the Grand Canyon of the Colorado, who, with $35,000 to his credit, left there to spend the rest of his life in Honolulu, but became so homesick before he got to Los Angeles that he took the first train back to the Canyon."[28] A grain of truth is in there. Hance visited Los Angeles with Lyman Tolfree in 1896, and he toured Catalina Island with a man named Martin Buggeln in 1903 when visiting Buggeln's Los Angeles home and eating at his restaurant.[29] Hance also made trips to Albuquerque for the New Mexico State Fair (once with Buggeln), and occasionally visited Prescott for bulldogging contests at the Yavapai County Fair. However, these trips usually lasted only a week or two.

HAMC grew to sixteen claims working high-grade chrysotile asbestos originally patented in March 1903 on 325.82 acres. The enterprising company was doing well and took a silver medal at the 1904 St. Louis World's Fair.[30] But the rowboat remained on the river. On February 10, 1915, HAMC went off the books in the state of Maine.

Coconino County declared HAMC's taxes delinquent in 1930 and by 1938 had sold the property to Lawrence Mitchell for $2,500. Mitchell deeded it to the Hearst Corporation, but the paperwork went unrecorded until 1966, and it's still on the books. The mine was closed to visitation by the National Park Service due to the asbestos hazard, but photographs of the site show a coal-burning cook stove, relic building frames, beds without mattresses, location markers, shovels, picks, and other mining implements.

Martin Buggeln landed in Williams in 1885 at nineteen years of age.[31] His early Arizona years were spent delivering beef cattle to Los Angeles and, with his first wife Emma, selling shares to their placer claim near Prescott Junction.[32] He was also deputy Coconino County sheriff under Ralph Cameron.

After quitting his deputy sheriff job, Buggeln vanished from press reports for a while, but he owned work horses, saddle horses, wagons, buggies, and a piano for an estate valued at $843. Back in the newspapers by 1902, his valuation was four times that with more horses, wagons and other vehicles, safes, and Indian blankets.

James Thurber's assessor's reports and property deeds for the same period trend the opposite direction. In 1900, he sold 116 work horses to the territory, and George Woods purchased his Flagstaff stables; in March 1901, Woods assumed management of Thurber's stage line to Bright Angel Hotel. The same newspaper issue also stated that John Marshall, by now Flagstaff's first superintendent of waterworks, had men at work installing a water main to Hance's place on South San Francisco Street.[33]

In April 1901, Thurber pulled up his canyon stakes and went back to grading roads. As a codefendant with the Santa Fe Railroad and other individuals and organizations in a hostile takeover staged by Thomas Bassford, there was little else he could do. The property changing hands amounted to $150,000 cash, more money than any case previously tried in Coconino County.[34] *Thomas Bassford v. the Santa Fe and Grand Canyon Railroad* was decided in late April.[35] Thurber, the railway, and the other defendants surrendered their interests to a special master's sale.

This comprised all rights, franchises, and privileges, "including all exemptions from taxation, owned or possessed by the defendant railroad company, or which it or its assigns may or can hereafter acquire, own or possess through or under the charter of said railroad company including all grades, railroad tracks, switches, turnouts, buildings, rolling stock, locomotives, telegraph poles and lines, telephone poles, and lines."[36]

Thurber sold his Bright Angel business to Buggeln in late August 1901, a month before the train pulled in,[37] but that was only half the story. When the railway helped Tolfree upgrade Glendale Springs and, later, put up the first Bright Angel Hotel with Thurber, it came with an understanding that the railway owned the controlling interest in these buildings. Buggeln's agreement would have been a reworked version of Thurber's contract. This is seen in archival correspondence between the railway, Thurber and, laterally, Buggeln. In these letters, the company scolds each man for inconveniencing guests and gives instructions on table arrangements for certain parties, otherwise keeping affairs neat, tidy, and on schedule.[38]

The first locomotive arrived at Grand Canyon on the afternoon of September 17, 1901. Thirty passengers and one bundle of mail made the trip.[39] The news was supplanted by the assassination and funeral of President William McKinley, which filled newspaper front pages everywhere. A widely circulated photo, "The First Train to Grand Canyon," commemorates the event. Here, a group of men, women, and children stand on and around the nose of a steam locomotive. Five women are prominent; four of these are Buggeln's wife, his daughter, his sister, and her daughter.

The train from Williams had a profound effect on Grand Canyon tourism. That afternoon, Buggeln's Bright Angel Hotel became the locus of rim visitation, just as when the only road went to Glendale Springs, but this time it was much different. Two months later, on Sunday, November 10, Grand Canyon had 360 visitors.[40] This was more people than Glendale Springs saw in a year, and that day Bright Angel Trail became Grand Canyon's most traveled footpath, a title it still holds. By early 1905 the El Tovar Hotel was in full operation and Bright Angel Hotel had been remodeled. Both were close to the train depot, functioned to the respected standards of Fred Harvey Trading Co., and were near the trail.

Buggeln opened Grand Canyon post office at Bright Angel Hotel in March 1902, and that August he began negotiations with Hance for Glendale Springs. A. G. Wells had just written him, "you should turn over

Hance, decked out for a special occasion, spins a yarn. Courtesy of Grand Canyon National Park, no. 09099.

to us one-half of your net profits" from the hotel and trail rides.[41] The partnership was working beautifully, Wells said, but Buggeln was making too much money compared to the company sponsoring him.

As insurance against the railway, and to help Hance settle a debt, Buggeln offered $800 for "an undivided one-half interest" in Glendale Springs and an "undivided interest" in Red Canyon Toll Road.[42] However, Buggeln withdrew his offer the following August. By then he'd reached a deal with Wells to manage Glendale Springs for 60 percent of the proceeds. "[The Santa Fe] have assented to this feature in full belief that the concession will not induce you to unduly work business to the Hance place as against the main hotel" is how Wells painted it.[43]

Well before February 1904, Hance was "in the employ of the Santa Fe at Bright Angel Hotel and never misses being seen nor an opportunity of telling who he is."[44] Santa Fe payroll records for Hance have not been discovered. By his own account he earned twenty-five dollars a month from the railway and traveled gratis along its tracks.[45] He was also supplied with room and board by Fred Harvey, but probably wasn't fully bedded with Harvey until the company purchased Buggeln's livery operation in 1905.[46] Especially fascinating about the collection of Buggeln-Harvey transfer papers is the first animal itemized on page two of the "Horses & Mules" section. It's Darby, "a white gelding with a scar on his left fore shin."[47] And we even have a photo dated April 15, 1901, showing and naming Darby. That's when Hance was at Last Chance camp attempting to sell Susan Selfridge "his" twelve mines. Darby's in profile, but his head is out of frame.

President Theodore Roosevelt first saw Grand Canyon on May 6, 1903, after meeting with John Muir at Yellowstone. Visiting Grand Canyon was a full-day, out-and-back train ride from Williams for normal tourists—in a presidential Pullman car it was something more. Roosevelt arrived at the South Rim at 9 a.m., departed about 7 p.m., and awoke the following morning in Redlands, California. Between times he gave his famous "leave it as it is" speech to some one thousand guests gathered round the steps of Bright Angel Hotel, where W. W. Bass presented him with a large color photograph of Grand Canyon.[48] After the ceremonies, Hance led the president "and others to Grandview and back, 24 miles, Hance riding at a gallop in a loose, flapping style of equitation probably copied from the Navajo Indians."[49] Roosevelt and party enjoyed lunch at John Page's camp, where the meal was served by Martin Buggeln.[50]

Another telling of the visit between Hance and Roosevelt later emerged. While somewhat accurately describing Hance, it's also a perplexing mixture of events and places. Roosevelt and Hance were photographed together in 1903, when they first met, and again in 1911. In the 1903 photo, Hance stands behind Roosevelt and others on the rim. In 1911, the two are on horseback at a turn on Bright Angel Trail, Hance again behind Roosevelt. In literature, however, the 1911 photograph has been pasted into the 1903 event, but there's an explanation for the mixup. In 1911, Maurice Salzman, thought to be associated with Williams merchants and traders, accompanied Roosevelt's party on a trip down what he believed was "Hance's New Trail," a reference to Red Canyon Toll Road. Instead, Salzman was on Bright Angel Trail.

"During the trip to the river," Salzman wrote, "Hance and Roosevelt were talking about the problems of trade rats [pack rats] getting into food supplies, sometimes frightening ladies at camps. Hance seemed to wander off topic, saying he liked to smoke his pipe before going to bed, recalling a camp when he put the pipe on the ground beside him and dropped off to sleep."

What did that have to do with trade rats?, asked Roosevelt.

Hance replied that one morning his pipe had disappeared. "Real puzzled, I went hunting for it, and there on a hummock was the biggest, fattest, sassiest trade rat I ever saw, just sitting there smoking my pipe."

After bidding Hance farewell that evening, Roosevelt remarked, "I shall be pleased to say I have seen God's greatest and most stupendous natural wonder—the Grand Canyon. But the greatest satisfaction of all will be the remembrance of having shaken hands with the greatest liar on earth."[51]

Hance told it different. One day, he said, a stranger asked him how the deer hunting was around the South Rim.

"Why shucks," he answered, "I went out this morning and bagged three all by myself!"

"That's wonderful!" the stranger exclaimed. "Do you know who I am?"

Hance had no idea.

"I'm the new game warden around here."

"And do you know who I am?" Hance snorted. "I'm John Hance, the biggest damn liar in these parts."[52]

Twelve

TEMPEST IN A TEAPOT

"Brant and His Mob Are to Blame"

After the train arrived at the South Rim and Hance had moved to Bright Angel while occasionally working for Hance Asbestos Mining Company, Martin Buggeln remained interested in Glendale Springs. Continuing to negotiate with Hance, he made a second offer. Hance was interested, but Glendale Springs rested on unsurveyed land, and Hance had no legal patent to transfer to Buggeln. And because he never recorded Hance Trail as a toll road, Hance had no tax records to prove activity on it.

Henry Ashurst took six years to fix that, a side job during his run for U.S. Senate while in the Territorial Senate. He began in October 1902 with secondhand newspaper clippings. The General Land Office begged ignorance, advising him its survey of Grand Canyon Forest Reserve gave no mention of "Hance Hotel" or "Hance Trail." Only "Hance's Trail" (Red Canyon) was shown on reserve maps, but it was a mile east of the land in question.[1]

Ashurst's early November 1903 letter to Buggeln tells something of Buggeln's financial relationship with Hance. Glendale Springs, Ashurst wrote, should be advertised as a mortgage rather than an absolute sale.[2] Later that month Ashurst again wrote Buggeln: "I have had an interview with John Hance, and he has agreed to sign any papers you requested or wished. Now, Martin, Hance is in a humor and I suggest you get the papers in shape and Hance will sign. Of course, you will not record them," again reminding Buggeln to keep his "mortgage" quiet.[3]

Pete Berry was applying for his homestead patent at the same time. In a quickly hand-scribbled note, Ashurst relayed to Buggeln, "Mr. Berry's application will, I think, materially help us in the Hance case. A favorable report has been made on Mr. Berry's claim, but this . . . is supposed to be secret information and it might be well not to mention it."[4]

In August 1904 Ashurst corresponded with the surveyor general about the Hance and Berry homesteads, and then with Buggeln to say he'd received the government survey from Washington. He would forward the papers to Phoenix to have the approval put ahead of other things. "I do not want such a great delay if I can prevent it and will get to work with a vim to try to get this survey approved so that Hance may make his filing as soon as possible. I realize, with you, that the sooner [Hance] files the better for all parties concerned."[5]

Buggeln constructed the V—V ("V Bar V") Ranch hotel—distinct from the Verde Valley archeological site of the same name—in 1905, a monstrous two-story, seventeen-room building of milled, white-painted lumber. It completely changed Glendale Springs' homestyle presentation. Assessor's reports show an enormous one-time $3,000 expense at Glendale Springs that year. Such an outlay of cash can only indicate Buggeln's landscape-altering addition that he'd originally slated for 1903.[6] It was just as well. Hance's first patent application was rejected that year, leaving Buggeln with a hotel on no-man's-land for the next two years.[7]

Ashurst kept after it, however, working every angle until early 1906 when the Department of the Interior's Phoenix office finally requested proof of Hance's claim. Henry responded in mid-March: "It is generally understood that John Hance settled upon the land in question many years ago, perhaps over 20 years. So far as I know it has been his home . . . for the past 15 years," indicating his first visit was in 1891. "[Hance's] improvements are houses, and other buildings, and fences and reservoirs, of the value of at least $4,000," surreptitiously including Buggeln's addition, "two acres or more under cultivation upon which he raises his garden stuff, potatoes and the like, and has done so for years. The whole 160 acres are under first class wire enclosure, fence. Used mostly for pasture of his animals." He also listed references for Hance, including "Babbitt Bros, Flagstaff," where Hance's account number was 792,[8] "Jacob Salzman of Williams, William Donelson, an old resident cattleman . . . in fact almost anyone in this section of the country."[9]

Notice of action on the Hance and Berry homestead filings appeared in the *Williams News* in mid-March 1906. To certify continuous residence

Planned for 1903 but not constructed until 1905, Martin Buggeln's two-story
V—V Hotel completely altered Glendale Springs' appearance. Courtesy of Grand Canyon National Park, no. 12081.

at Grandview since 1892, Berry elected Niles Cameron, Louis Boucher,
and Hance as his witnesses. Testifying for Hance were John Marshall,
Samuel Black, Michael Riordan, and Berry. Hance and Berry traveled
together to Flagstaff to make sworn statements to a government agent
in early June.[10] Hance's testimony supporting Berry has survived. After
stating his postal address as "Grand View, Arizona," Hance responded
to over a dozen close questions concerning Berry's homestead and his
residency there. Berry would have answered identical questions for
John's claim. All was truly said, right down to the size of their vegetable
gardens.[11]

"Proof accepted and placed on record upon receipt of [John Hance's
$12] testimony fee," Ashurst wrote Buggeln on the fourteenth. "I have
got into communication with Mr. John Hance and the money will be in
Phoenix within a day or two." Ashurst also suggested Buggeln hire the
firm of Archer Ball Young to "have Mr. Young watch the case . . . so that
he can inform Hance of any developments, or should any bad features

Hance dressed immaculately after the sale of "his" mines. Courtesy of Grand Canyon National Park, no. 20340.

arise."[12] Nothing untoward transpired—except that Buggeln sold Darby to Fred Harvey and in December 1906 was off to Los Angeles.

The United States granted land patent no. 129 to John Hance on February 25, 1907.[13] On March 11, Hance assigned all of his "granted privileges thereon, along with all rights to 'Hance or Red Canyon Trail,'" to Buggeln in a warranty deed worth, on paper, $4,000.[14] "Buggeln and Hance, who for years have had business dealings," read the *Williams News*, "came to a settlement of their affairs early this week, and after deducting his advances, [Buggeln] paid Hance a handsome sum and purchased from him what has been known as the Hance place. [Hance] retires with a neat little fortune, ample to provide him for his declining years."[15]

Contradicting this impression of sudden wealth and genial comfort is that Hance's earnings made no discernible difference to his lifestyle except for clothing. A portion of his income certainly went to a haberdasher—fedora, blazer, vest, bandanna or tie, suit, gold watch, and chain, with wingtip ankle boots for special occasions. But he continued to live in Fred Harvey company housing, took "chuck" with the other wranglers, and after 1915 stayed near Bright Angel and El Tovar chatting with tourists.[16] He once told an English chap about how his gold watch was a gift worth $250 and so reliable that when he dropped it into the canyon and took three days to find it, it was still ticking away like new. "Pretty good for a 24-hour movement," the Brit replied.[17]

With Hance, occasional mentions of gambling are encountered, sometimes from questionable sources, but taken together they cast a dark shadow. One unattributed reference is impossible to ignore: "Martin Buggeln took Hance's place—Hance lost money gambling—owed Buggeln several thousand dollars."[18] When these various references are fanned out like a deck of cards across a faro table, they lend an aftertaste of gross pecuniary ineptitude. Apparently constantly in arrears, John Hance burned through money as fast as he made it.

It wasn't just his favorite racetrack, card table, or dice game that Hance loved most. He didn't know when to quit. Wrote a bystander at Grand Canyon Depot, "A few minutes before entraining for Williams, [Hance] was talking with several men and laid a five-dollar bill on the table and said: 'Will anybody cover that to say that more than 20 people will arrive on this afternoon's train?' There was no response. Then he said: 'Well, I am game. Will anybody cover it that less than 20 people will come?' There were no takers either way."[19]

"John Hance is a false profit," reported the *Williams News*, perhaps intending a double entendre, "but in order to keep up his reputation he could not be otherwise. When he last week made a bet of $25 that it would rain both at Williams and Grand Canyon on the 13th [of July 1904], some people who knew he had put up the sum began to believe him. Needless to say, it did not rain. It would seem that Hance had become so used to telling fairy stories that in this instance he forgot himself and bet $25 on his own judgment . . . and lost."[20]

With cash from the sale of Ashurst's mines in 1902, Hance offered Denis Riordan $500 to settle a debt. "Now, John," Riordan responded, "I have never bothered nor annoyed you about your indebtedness, and I have never intended to. I have believed in you and in your good intentions when many others who 'joss' and fool with you had no such confidence. I want to say to you that I admire your manly attitude, and in consideration of what you say, I will accept your proposition." Riordan's loss would not "terminate any feeling of friendship for you, or interest in your welfare, and I will always be glad to hear from you," reaffirming these sentiments when acknowledging John's payment on September 2.[21] Hance had bet against himself again, and this time he broke even, but the $500 earned from the lease of the Lloyd and Howard claims to John Penhale was used to repay Riordan.

For the purpose of writing about Hance after his death, Frank Lockwood held a sit-down to reminisce with Godfrey Sykes and D. T. McDougal, a botanist from Indiana who signed John's guestbook in 1891. They met again in 1903, after Hance had gone to work for the Santa Fe: "On this occasion I saw him in the middle of the room [at Bright Angel Hotel] talking to various people. Walking over to him, I said, 'My name is McDougal—I went down your trail some years ago.'" Hance asked what he thought of the canyon. McDougal answered, "Every time I return, it is grander than I remember it. 'Now, what do you think of that?' Hance asked triumphantly. 'Some of these old guinea hens (he waved his arms around, including the groups of tourists around him), think there's nothing to it!' 'Well, Mr. Hance,' I continued, 'how have you been?' 'Oh,' replied John, 'I have had lean years—all these years I've lived on expectations and mountain scenery.'"[22]

Hance got caught flat-footed in an Old West barroom shootout at the Fray Marcos Hotel in Williams in July 1908. He had nothing to do with it, but everything happened so quickly that men standing with him were wounded and one was even killed. Miraculously, he avoided injury.[23]

In September 1909 Flagstaff hosted the Pioneers Society of Northern Arizona's second annual picnic, reunion, and barbecue at West Park (today called Wheeler Park), located at the foot of Mars Hill below Lowell Observatory. Although rain had dominated the previous two weeks and was still coming down, some 350 people attended, including the old timers with distinctive red badges pinned to their chests. Wearing them were Sedona homesteader Jim Thompson, Williams rancher Ed Geddis, and John Hance and others from Verde Valley. There's no mention of George Hance, but Stanley Sykes traveled all the way from Maine with his family to be there.

"Pioneers wet. But Happy," reported the *Coconino Sun*. "Great tables, loaded with large amounts of good provisions, such as mutton (very fine), bread, beans, coffee, etc., and some special dishes, where we partook, with Governor [Richard] Sloan and other notables, all the luxuries, and the finest of cake, pies, peaches and grapes." Erected for the occasion, the platform was decorated with flowers, patriotic bunting, American flags, and John Hance, "the noted pioneer of Grand Canyon and the world's greatest story teller," seated beside Governor Sloan. Having ridden down Bright Angel Trail the previous day, the governor was "slightly wearied" and spoke without notes. After complimenting the organization for its "endeavor to perpetuate the memories of early days," his concluding remarks concerned Arizona's upcoming statehood.[24]

If John's gambling was passed under the table, his drinking was not. "A good drinking man and very profane" is how Camp Verde's Charlie Wingfield phrased it. In fact, most everyone who knew Hance would have echoed John Stotsenberg's assessment: "a terror when drinking."[25]

Ralph Cameron, a Republican territorial delegate, wrote Pete Berry from Washington, "I can't for the life of me see what John Hance ever expects to gain by treating you in the manner you write—the poor old phool [sic]—He should at least remember that the Harvey people never look after him when he was drunk and needed someone to look out for him, as I know you have done, and this is your reward."[26]

Hance's drinking comes up again in correspondence between Cameron and Louis Ferrell beginning in November 1908. Apparently recovering from a particular embarrassing spree, "Hance ... made a record by not taking a drink and has now been strictly sober for about six weeks." But a few months later, after a pleasure trip to Phoenix, he was desperately ill. "Old Hance ... does not seem to improve very fast and a little backset will sure finish him. He is at Bright Angel and is getting well taken care of [by Fred Harvey Trading Company]." By November 24, 1909, he was back to his old ways: "Old Hance is again hitting it up but has not yet quite got in full swing."[27]

He got there on July 24, 1914. That day, two Japanese busboys from the El Tovar Hotel climbed up Battleship Iowa (a rocky peak rising skyward from Tonto Platform, well beneath but due north of Bright Angel Hotel), where they tied a piece of white fabric with Japanese lettering to

Hance at Bright Angel circa 1904, perhaps recuperating after a night on the town.
Northern Arizona University, Cline Library, NAU.PH.568.979, Emory Kolb Collection.

the flagpole on its summit. Hance didn't like that—the "flag" had to come down, he said, insisting the boys were "bent on conquest or rebellion."[28] Hance took it to the extent that he was accorded the opportunity to make a sworn statement concerning his behavior a few days later.

The morning after the flag went up, Hance "went over from the barn where I ate and slept in my bungalow to the office of the Bright Angel at 7:00 o'clock." He informed the hotel manager, Charles Brant, "a couple of your Japanese boys went down yesterday and went on top of the Battleship, took down whatever dimension of a rag or flag that our boys had on it, and put their flag in its place. Will you have those Japanese go take that flag down and deliver it to me by 6:00 o'clock this afternoon?"

"All right, Captain, all right," Brant responded.

Hance continued, "Now, Mr. Brant, don't fail to have these boys take this down by 6 o'clock . . . and in case you fail by that time to do it, I shall be [at El Tovar], and I will see that they go with me and take it down and deliver the same to me, or I will not [have] a Japanese in your place or on the rim of the Grand Canyon, they will have to leave."

That afternoon Hance told a fellow teamster that trouble might be brewing, pledging his "sacred word and honor as a truthful man" that the flag would come down or he would be a corpse by morning. However, the flag still waved at six o'clock that evening. Hance went to his bungalow to eat supper, where he enlisted some cowboys in his crusade. They accompanied him to El Tovar to see Brant. Hance entered the building "the back way, as most of us barn fellows generally do," and proceeded to the lobby. Brant declined to meet him, sending instead his transportation chief Walter Hubbell, who suggested postponing everything until morning.

"I told him that I could not or would not give an extension of time, and that I would go myself with the Japanese boys and see they were not harmed or insulted," Hance said. Hubbell and Brant talked it over upstairs, out of earshot, agreeing to send the boys if Hance would keep his word. "This I agreed to do. I sat there a few minutes waiting for them to bring the two Japanese down, and during this time Mrs. Brant came down, and in a boisterous and loud manner said: 'Captain, what is the matter with you, are you drunk, crazy, or have you lost what little brains you ever had? And now, Cap! I tell you that the Japanese will not come down and go into the Canyon tonight.'"

Hance replied, "Hold on Mrs. Brant, under the promises and terms of this affair, they must go with me tonight." Hance would not stand down—it was now or never, he told his men. "In a short while here came the two Japanese. We walked . . . arm in arm to the head of the trail, with my men following me. The Japanese said they wanted to be friendly, that they had done wrong, and were willing to go and take the flag down and deliver it to me, and I replied that I wanted to be friendly for all times to come."

All arrived at the trailhead. Hance sent his cowboys back to their mules and the boys down Bright Angel's switchbacks. He would stand guard, he told them, until they returned. He was there an hour and a half when a man and woman appeared and wanted to explore the trail. Hance replied, "I told them there were nice drives and side walks where they could do all the walking they wanted, and that they could not go down the trail until the two Japanese boys returned. He spoke in a rather harsh manner and asked me what right I had to hold anybody on a public highway. I told him that I did not want any of his dictating or saucy talk. I told him to go back or that I would show him how to do it, and he went and that was all there was to it."

Making remarkable time, the boys returned with their flag about midnight. Hance took the prize ceremoniously, folding and then tucking it into his pocket. Ready to return to El Tovar, one of the Japanese boys asked if he could "help me up or take my arm, as I was an old man and he was afraid I would hurt myself." Right at that moment arrived

Brant with his saucy barber and several others who had secreted themselves, and way-laid me and commenced with shameful abuse on me, and Brant in particular said: "Shoot me in the back, you coward, shoot me in the back." The only word I said to him was: "Mr. Brant, if I had anything in the world against you, and if I wanted to shoot you, I would not shoot you in the back. I would step in front of you." I did not show any weapon or anything.

He told me that I must leave there, that he did not want any hoodlums or tramps there, and Mrs. Brant flew in, cursing me to a big extent, and just at that time, to my surprise, about 6 or 7 of my men who were sitting just beyond the Bright Angel office door . . . came up and asked what the trouble was about. I then said that I was somewhat relieved as I did not know how I would have been treated if it had not been for the appearance of my men. Then I says to Brant: "You old red headed Russian, damn you, I will make you jump over the rim of the Canyon and light on your head."

Just at that moment, one of my men made a rush to get hold of the impudent barber but failed to—he was too swift—and then the big stampede took place, all of them going up the walk, trying to get into the lead, and me and the boys stood there laughing at them. I told the boys to go to bed as we had won out, and they said they would not go until they had seen the flag, and I pulled it out of my pocket and showed it to them.[29]

As these events unfolded, "Captain W. W. Bass, not knowing of the surrender to Gen. Hance, had mobilized some troops from the cow-punchers and was marching to the assistance of the General."[30] Pete Berry thought the whole thing a tinderbox about to blow. He telegraphed "Captain Breen to have his National Guards ready to report at a moment's notice." Breen immediately dispatched Sheriff Thomas Pulliam to the scene. Pulliam wired the county attorney, C. B. Wilson, who departed for the canyon on the first train.[31]

Hance recalled:

The next day things ran along quietly, and not much doing, but at the same time, I suppose [Grand Canyon Railroad] were wiring for the County Attorney from Flagstaff. They decided to hold a court among themselves which they did in the big music room. There was a judge here, Justice of the Peace, duly elected by the people, for a great many years, and to do any business to be tried in the Justice Court. . . . They sent their officers two or three times for me to come, and I told them emphatically that I would not go, that it was an illegal prosecution from beginning to end, and they asked me to let them have the flag which I refused to do and did not do.

The decision of the court was for Hubbell to fire Hance, Ray Lewis, F. E. Roch, and G. W. Gardener. "Brant and his mob are to blame for all this trouble," thought Hance. "If [Brant] had stayed home and not come down there, there would have been no trouble, and the blame is all to C. A. Brant, manager of the El Tovar and Bright Angel Camp."[32]

Brant's telling contradicted Hance's: "There was no American flag lowered as there had been no flag there since the flag I had put up was blown to tatters." He'd planted that flagpole himself, shortly before July 4, 1905, with the permission of Captain Fenton of the forest reserve.[33] A gang of Brant's first El Tovar bellboys had lugged a twenty-five-foot freshly trimmed Ponderosa log down Bright Angel Trail, carrying it over a rough, rugged route through a steep minefield of boulders and cacti that eventually led across a smooth saddle to Battleship Iowa. After hoisting their log up a chimney or two, the group nailed an American flag to it and stuck it upright in a crevasse on the summit. After the holiday nobody thought much about it, and the fabric lasted only a few months in the canyon's stiff updrafts. Since then, all sorts of banners, handkerchiefs, flannel shirts, and whatnot had flown there. The boys' white cloth with the word "diamond" painted across it in Japanese was simply the latest contribution, something to show they'd made it to the top and had joined the club.

According to Brant,

Captain Hance, who I regret to say was egged on by younger people who should know better, became very much excited and said he with a dozen more fellows would break in the doors and fill the Japanese full of lead. In the meantime, the boys had started, as dark as it was, and I venture to say none of the brave fellows who were going to shoot up the two Japanese would have dared to go down and clamber over the narrow shelves of rock in daylight let alone at night. They all congregated at the head of the trail and word came to me that they were going to give the Japanese boys such a licking they would remember it all their lives. I thought I would go and see what was going to happen, and together with our clerks, Mrs. Brant and a number of dining room girls, went to Bright Angel.... Captain Hance was sitting at the head of the trail with his [pistol] to prevent anyone from going to the assistance of the boys. The Captain is old and easily influenced and I sometimes think he is in his second childhood.[34]

Now seventy-seven, his voice assuming a rough, graveled tone quite opposite the high-pitched warblings everyone knew, Hance would not back down. "Captain Hance alleges he was maliciously slandered as well as willfully abused by the manager of El Tovar, and on these grounds he declares he will institute a damage suit jointly against the Harveys and the railroad for $25,000. He says he has retained a prominent lawyer as his attorney, and the complaint will be drawn in this city in a few days, with the trial to take place in Coconino County."[35]

Elsewhere in the same edition Hance is reported to be on his way to Phoenix for private business, afterward quitting Grand Canyon and moving to Flagstaff. He wasn't gone long and he couldn't relocate—all of his Flagstaff properties had been sold. John Marshall bought back his house in 1905,[36] and Jim Hance purchased John's South San Francisco Street lots in 1906, where Hance stayed occasionally. A local headline ran "Tempest in a Teapot." The *Los Angeles Times* called it "Disturbing the Peace."[37] Either way, John Hance was out of both a job and a place to live.

He made camp at Fossil Rock, now the location of Shrine of the Ages and Grand Canyon Pioneer Cemetery. Using one of his old army wall tents, he settled in, depressed and out of circulation for the next few months, before making amends with Fred Harvey Trading Company. However, that reconciliation wouldn't have occurred until at least December, when the Santa Fe Railroad's injunction against freelance agents conducting business at Grand Canyon Depot took effect. At that point, Hance had to accept whatever Fred Harvey sent his way.

W. W. Bass corresponded with Ford Harvey (Fred's son) about Hance. Ford had taken charge of the Harvey organization after his father's death in 1901. The dispute over freelance guides working the depot had been building for thirteen years, since the first train pulled in. It came to a head in December 1914 when Grand Canyon Railway Company filed an injunction against Bass, Hance, Bert Luzon, L. Hartung, John Doe, Richard Roe, William White, Joseph Green, and James Black[38] to immediately quit "conducting and transacting [tourism-related] business" at the terminal and around the hotels' grounds.[39] Bass responded,

> The hearing on the application for a temporary injunction was had yesterday, and Mr. Hance was there and to my surprise I learned that he was charged with soliciting patronage for me on

the Station Grounds at Grand Canyon and was in my employ. This is absolutely false as he never has been in my employ in any capacity whatever and should not have been named as a defendant in the case. The poor old man feels greatly humiliated to think he must be dragged into court and be compelled to sacrifice the last few remaining dollars he had on carfare and lawyers. Now, Mr. Harvey, for God's sake try to have his name dropped from this proceeding if you can. It has stormed all the time . . . and I doubt if [Hance] will escape the ordeal without a spell of sickness. It would not take much to knock the poor fellow out.[40]

The injunction remained in effect for four years. Bass produced an enormous amount of paperwork on it, slowly gaining support. In late September 1918, well beyond the time it would have proved useful to Hance, the case was dismissed at the railway's suggestion.[41]

From there it's possible to follow Hance to his last known residence through a small batch of correspondence from Tusayan National Forest regarding "constructing and maintaining a tent house for a temporary residence." The agreement ran from September 24, 1915, through the following March when Hance could reapply, though further records are missing. By some measure, this is where the story ends: in a lone tent-cabin pegged out next to a rocking chair on fifty square feet of ground one hundred yards west of Bright Angel trailhead.

Hance celebrated his eightieth birthday in 1917. His portrait was taken, and he had a drink, maybe two. He also broadcast his pioneering achievements to the Grand Canyon community at large. Still festering from the flag incident, he believed himself maligned, forgotten, and ill-treated. After complaining that the territory, county, and state had "never contributed one cent" to his tourism efforts, Hance let it be known that he'd been denied the job of Bright Angel Trail overseer.

Hance tried for another job, believing he deserved it given his "circumstances, age and condition." "I made an effort to obtain this position, which I need very badly, but I got side-tracked. . . . The man who was appointed is a lunch counter clerk and an all-round good, clever man, but, nevertheless, I think I am more entitled to that $40.00 than he."

Hance by his tent-cabin at his last certifiable residence on the rim near Bright Angel Trail, 1915–1916. Courtesy of Dan Cassidy.

"All I have done for the Santa Fe is well known," he concluded. "I have nothing to say against them, but I shall always think I have had wrongful treatment. For every mile of the railroad I travel, I have to pay full fare."[42]

In July 1918, Pete Berry, Hance, Sanford Rowe, and others were in Flagstaff for a session at superior court. The *Coconino Sun* termed John's appearance "A MIGHTY SAD CASE. Captain John Hance, the man who obtained some notoriety by reason of having single-handed dug the Grand Canyon" to see what was inside it, "but later attaining real fame for having to shoot his wife when she broke her leg . . . was in Flagstaff yesterday as a witness in a case where he stole a horse and is prosecuting the owners for letting him do it, knowing the present high cost of feed."[43]

John Hance on his eightieth birthday in 1917. Courtesy of Grand Canyon National Park, no. 03676.

Hance en route to the hospital in Flagstaff, "completely done up" after a series of strokes in late 1918. Northern Arizona University, Cline Library, NAU.PH.568.6469, Emory Kolb Collection.

By the time that article was published Hance was laid up at the Fray Marcos Hotel with "a slight wound on a finger, which has resulted in an infection which bothers his neck, making him quite ill."[44] A fortnight later he paid a week-long visit to Flagstaff seeking medical attention for "some kind of scalp disease."[45]

Hance won the primary election for Grand Canyon constable in September. Letters immediately poured in seeking his endorsement for the governor's race, but Hance didn't respond. He couldn't. He had suffered a stroke. "Hance was quite ill during the latter part of 1918," wrote Dama Margaret Smith in *I Married a Ranger*. "[He was] worn out and broken down and toward the last became quite helpless. As he grew feeble, he seemed to long for the quiet depths of the gorge." Realizing the end was near, Hance wanted to die at his Red Canyon placer mine. According to Smith, "One night ... he escaped the vigilance of his friends and with an old burro that had shared his happier days started down the trail." A forest reserve ranger named West followed Hance, finding him "where he had fallen from the trail into a cactus patch and had lain all night exposed to the raw wind."[46]

Hance was transported to Flagstaff on Monday, December 2, "in a delirious condition caused by some infection of the head which has been troubling him for some time past."[47] In the same edition appeared notice of Niles Cameron's death from Bright's disease in San Diego.

After being sheltered at the Commercial Hotel for a few days,[48] Hance was admitted to Coconino County Hospital for the Indigent on December 9.[49] The hospital where John Hance died is now the Arizona Historical Society Pioneer Museum on Highway 180, one mile north of what's now called "Old Town" Flagstaff. During his last days on earth Hance attempted "at least two" escapes, getting so far as the road leading to Grand Canyon[50] before ultimately passing away on the afternoon of January 6, 1919. Teddy Roosevelt died the same day in Oyster Bay, New York.

The death certificate read "Senility [and] Endocarditis."[51] Babbitt Brothers Trading Company handled the arrangements, billing George Hance for $277. John was laid to rest by the standards of the day. He was shaved, embalmed, dressed in new clothing, and placed in an $85 casket packaged in its own private Pullman car.[52]

Edgar Whipple and John Marshall accompanied Hance to his canyon. Flagstaff's Episcopal minister accompanied the party and conducted the service on the afternoon of Saturday, January 11, under the shed of the railroad platform. "All of Hance's friends at the Grand Canyon turned out to honor his memory. He was buried in the little cemetery east and north of El Tovar Hotel," near his after-the-flag-incident camp at Fossil Rock. "Prominent men and women who had known and enjoyed him made up a fund to buy a bronze plate for his grave. Remembering the size of his yarns, whoever placed the enormous boulders at his head and feet put them nine feet apart."[53]

Thirteen

ONE MAN'S LEGACY

All Fact and Mostly Fiction

Twenty years earlier John Hance's passing would have received national coverage. In 1919, his death notices were not published so far afield as might be expected. Only the *Coconino Sun*, *El Paso Herald*, *Mohave County Miner*, *Arizona Republican*, *Albuquerque Morning Journal*, *Spanish American* (Mora, New Mexico), and *Rolla Herald* covered it in more than a few sentences.

George Hance did not attend the service, sending word that "owing to influenza illness," the Spanish flu that had nearly killed him and from which he was slowly recovering, he was unable to leave Camp Verde.[1] He did, however, administer John's estate. George made several trips to Flagstaff that year and the next, declaring John intestate. Outside of three mining claims, the Red Canyon placer mine, and no. 13 and no. 14 mill sites, John Hance owned nothing but household furniture.[2] That probably meant his rocking chair, his old wooden kit-box with its leather latch, and a Dutch oven.

George published a reminiscence in the *Weekly Journal-Miner* on January 15 and was quoted in another article the same day. On January 17 he offered "A Brief History of Captain Hance," inadvertently published in John's name, in the *Coconino Sun*. In both versions, George rambled on about the early years, about crossing the plains with Jerry Sullivan and battling Indians with the Hickok boys. George considered John "a man full grown ever since I can remember," a compelling tribute to a brother he hadn't seen since 1901, when they both had visited Jim when he was sick in Williams.

Hance's footstone and headstone at Grand Canyon Pioneer Cemetery were placed far apart to represent the enormity of his lies. Author photo.

From Albuquerque, Arizona state historian James McClintock published Hance's most thorough obituary. While he described his subject using a questionable timeline and was sometimes mistaken on other details, he nonetheless offered an honest, heartfelt, and telling reminiscence of the man he'd known since May 24, 1897.[3] "John Hance, Builder of the First Grand Canyon Trail, Dies. Noted Story Teller, Known to All Grand Canyon Visitors," ran his lede.

"With the passing of John Hance," McClintock began, "Arizona has lost her most picturesque pioneer, one known to many thousands of tourists as a very guide of guides within the Grand Canyon region. . . . For most of the long period of his southwestern residence, John Hance lived within or on the lip of the Grand Canyon," exploring its every recess until the gorge held no secrets from him. "The Old Hance Trail, directly north of Flagstaff, was the first avenue into the Canyon opened for the sightseer who cared to use it . . . down a waterway for a part of the distance, where ropes were needed and where horses had to be abandoned. . . . Hance's memory will be kept green by the remembrance of his tales. They were unique, and in a way colossal, in keeping with the character of their environment." Near the conclusion, McClintock wrote that Hance's "greatest joy was in the finding of a good listener."[4]

From birth, Hance was extraordinarily fortunate to have the American frontier at his feet. His Civil War travels showed him a good portion of the eastern part of the country. Then he moved west to the vast Kansas plains, to New Mexico's piñon-juniper woodlands and red sandstone mesas, and finally to the spectral wonders of Arizona Territory's Colorado Plateau. But the primal elegance of Grand Canyon stopped him cold. With its "vastness and terrible sublimity,"[5] it was the consummate place for an outlier of John Hance's frontier ways and mindset to call home. In this, he should be remembered as the first white American to have been so powerfully grabbed by what he termed the "mighty miracle"[6] that he clung to the area, like moss to stone, for the remainder of his life. That's what his tombstone says: "First Locator on Grand Canyon."

Grand Canyon National Park was created February 26, 1919, less than two months after John Hance passed away. During his lifetime the number of canyon tourists grew from John Hance—just John Hance— to thirty-eight thousand souls the year he died. By 1928 that number was one hundred and fifty thousand.[7] Visitation now runs over five million people annually and exceeded six million in 2017. The majority of these folks are short-timers on tour buses who usually spend less than an hour on the rim before going off to the next attraction.

Today, John Hance couldn't be found in the crowd. The gentle press reminders of days gone by, notes such as, "John Hance, the guide, has been climbing through and exploring [Grand Canyon] for ten years, and every day he finds new beauties in it. He regards the Canyon as being under his special care and takes a proprietary interest in it that is quite amusing to see,"[8] are long gone. They portray an unknown person in a place time unimaginably foreign when viewed through the large picture windows of El Tovar's stately dining room. That transition took place after the train arrived, when the crowds started coming. Comments in the hotel's guestbook back then ranged from: "As compared with Randolph Street, Chicago—well—forget Randolph Street"; "I feel like a child grappling mentally with an arithmetic problem"; "I came. I saw. I diminished"; and (in 1912) "I've followed lots of trails before but the one I followed to-day is beyond me, but the 'Guide' wasn't."[9] Perhaps the guide was John Hance.

The only South Rim structures that Hance would recognize today would be El Tovar Hotel and stables, Lookout Studio, Hopi House, Hermit's Rest, the railway depot, part of Bright Angel Hotel, Buckey O'Neill's cabin, the Kolb brothers' studio, and the Hull Cabin Historic District.

Camp Verde still fosters a rural, hometown aspect, modestly advertising itself as "the center of it all," which is appropriate since it's just a hair off the geographic midpoint of Arizona. But much has changed in Verde Valley since the 1870s. As Charles Douglas Willard remembered, "wild game was everywhere, and the grass was knee high and plentiful. The land was like a sponge and when it rained the water was absorbed into the ground immediately, so very little ran into the river channel and the small amount that did . . . stood in pools which became stagnant and polluted with malaria germs, consequently many people were stricken with malaria, but they had to administer their own medication, such as calomel and quinine, because there were no [civilian] doctors available."

After the Yavapai-Apache Removal, however, "most everybody that came to Verde Valley brought cattle, horses, or sheep with them, and the stock soon trampled the spongy land down to solid ground, thus causing the rain water to run into the river channel, which was then only about 100 feet wide and the flood waters often rose to six or seven feet high, causing the river to cut into banks, change the course of the main river channel and the river bed spread half a mile wide in places."[10]

Today, Verde Valley's recreational opportunities include vineyard tours, float trips, horseback rides, jeep tours, multiple hiking trails, and exceptional national monuments and state parks. But the only buildings Hance would know are the military armory, the well-maintained grounds and remaining buildings of Fort Verde State Historic Park, Head's store (which is now a restaurant called Sutler's Steakhouse), and the stage stop and hotel across the street with its small courtyard. Joe Melvin's adobe house remains occupied. "Boss" Head's limestone home two hundred yards downslope from his store, a few irrigation ditches, and the ancient Native American salt mine near town, would also be familiar to Hance. But the site of Camp Lincoln became a housing development years ago. Hance's former homestead on the Verde River now lies adjacent to several elegant, deeply shaded homes with manicured lawns on East Quarter-horse Lane. The remains of George Hance's Cienega Ranch amount to a few awkward piles of stones; the barn fell down years ago. Nor could John or George climb up ladders to explore Montezuma Castle's ancient cliff-side rooms or bathe in Montezuma Well's reliably consistent freshet of carbonated water as they once did, long before both sites gained national monument status.

Glendale Springs was still there physically when Hance died but gone emotionally to all but a few. Almost forty years after he built it, the little log cabin with its sod roof was seeing its last days as Martin Buggeln's chicken coop. By 1957, when Buggeln's V—V Hotel was dismantled and the area cleared by the U.S. National Park Service because vagrants had taken up residence there,[11] Hance's cabin was gone. Only a few foundation stones remain, but it is both interesting and fitting to know where some of the stones went. "I made a visit to all the old camp sites," wrote Andy Ashurst from Asusa, California, in early 1948, "and collected fragments of stone from the chimneys of each old cabin to put in my garden."[12]

Glendale Springs isn't mentioned in Grand Canyon National Park's everyday handouts. This is understandable given the pace and interests of today's visitors, but alongside other historical characters portrayed on the rim Hance and his exploits remain in the background. On the East Rim at Lipan Point, with a magnificent overview of Hance Rapid, there's a photo and brief description of Hance on a park kiosk, but he's better told in the second display in the Verkamp building on the South Rim. There's also mention of Hance in literature available at the Backcountry Office about hiking Old Hance and New Hance Trails. And Hance occasionally returns from beyond when told by NPS "Ranger Ron" Brown, a stout, long-bearded fellow in period costume who tells Hance stories to appreciative park audiences.

Had Hance been focused and forward thinking, continually expanding and improving his accommodations, trails, services, and menu, Glendale Springs would now be Grand Canyon's premier resort hotel. But he wasn't wired that way, unlike the Tolfree brothers, James Thurber, Pete Berry, or, in truth, anyone else. John Hance started and ended as a bare-bones mule skinner. He moved supplies and people; he cooked stews, washed dishes, and told stories; he led mule trips; he shod and fed burros; and he prospected and maintained a few mining claims. But he didn't sell maps. Or Navajo rugs like Martin Buggeln or jewelry like Louis Boucher, or, so far as is known, anything except a few postage stamps, a bed in a tent, and a challenging trail with ropes down tall waterfalls.

He got on day by day, breaking horses at Hull's barn, leading trail rides, and telling yarns. When sober, he was busy, forthright, down to earth, gracious, easy to get along with, and reliable to a fault, as Gertrude Stevens noted in Hance's guestbook in July 1892: "This is a warm place. I fainted when I saw this awful looking Cañon. I never wanted a drink so bad in my life. Captain, I won't forget you for bringing me the oyster-can full of water."

Another time, Hance and others were discussing the road between Heber (Arizona) and Fort Verde. Hance "horrified them with the assertion that it was 'a hundred long miles and a hell of a road.'" Nobody believed him, so they made a special trip to Heber and back to see for themselves. "The old man told the truth," they reported. The road "proved to be a hundred miles of boulders and malapai."[13]

John Hance lived during a time—and in a fashion—that today remains the contextual setting of countless Old West movies. As a movie character, however, he has never been portrayed in a Hollywood production. The best Hance seems to have done in this regard is a half-page profile photo, seated on an unnamed white horse in the *Moving Picture News*.[14] The only known films containing him were titled *Capt. John Hance Telling About His 14th Wife, Grand Canyon, Arizona* and *Capt. John Hance Telling His Famous Fish Story, Grand Canyon, Arizona*, 35mm black and white shorts produced by Burton Holmes and Oscar Depue. A few stills from *Fish Story* are seen in Holmes's *Travelogues*, volume 6, but these moving pictures are not included in the Burton Holmes Archive, a repository of Holmes's work.[15]

Hance told plenty of fish stories, and occasionally one got told on him. He enjoyed informing people of the salmon he always caught in the river and once took a party down Red Canyon to show them how he did it. Arriving at the head of Hance Rapid, Hance "picked up one of the lines and gently pulled it toward him. The line was slack and the supposed tenderfoot of the party, who had done quite a little salmon fishing," told Hance that unless the line was kept taut, he'd lose the fish. "The line came in all the faster, and soon a big three-foot salmon was thrown upon the bank. But the stench that arose from that fish was too great, and the party broke and ran, leaving Captain Hance to bury it as best he could."[16]

In another tale, Hance stands at the head of Bright Angel Toll Road, some meat in his hand, and offers a witty rejoinder when someone tries to stump him. "I'm goin' down to feed my pet fish," he told a lady from Boston. "Some years ago I was fishin' down there in the Cañon in the Colorado River. I wasn't havin' much luck, but all of a sudden I seen a commotion in the water, and a tolerable-sized fish riz up and looked at me." The fish was angry and jumped through the air at Hance, who ducked. "He went clean over me and landed in a pool in the hollow of the rocks behind me [in] a considerable pond of water. He couldn't get out, and he's there yet. Him and me is fast friends now, and I go down twice a week an' feed him." When asked how long ago that was, Hance responded seventeen years. The lady remarked that the fish must be quite big by now.

"Oh," Hance quipped, "not so much! Last time I put the tape on him he was only twenty-seven feet long. He ain't got his full growth yit."[17]

It is something of a curiosity that many people around Verde Valley have never heard of John Hance, while, at Grand Canyon, so few know

The left-side interior of a cabin Hance is said to have lived in on the rim, a mile west of Bright Angel stables. The American flag has forty-six stars, indicating this was 1907 or later. Courtesy of Grand Canyon National Park, no. 04465A.

anything of George Hance. Both were the patriarchs of their communities. George aspired to that. John did not.

As a practical matter, John Hance's story boils down to John Hance's stories, some of them photographic. It's commonly understood, for instance, that Hance lived in log cabin on the West Rim near Charles Bryant before the flag incident, information otherwise unattributed. However, given the arrangement of the fireplace and kitchen flu as well as the build style and timber cuttings, this structure does not correspond with any known exterior images of places Hance called home.

Story-wise, Hance embellished his reliable old standards, never telling them the same way twice. Nearly everyone heard the one where his wife breaks her leg down in the canyon and he can't get her out, so has to shoot her. Next, she falls from the rim, five thousand feet 'twas 'fore she landed an' done broke 'er leg.[18] But John's rifle was only good up to three thousand feet, so he sent her two bullets from that gun at the same time.[19] Another version finds the poor woman repeatedly bouncing up and down, up and down—she'd slipped off the rim wearing rubber boots!

The right-side image of the same cabin with the calendar indicating October 1903.
Courtesy of Grand Canyon National Park, no. 04465B.

But that required only one shell, you see. Or, after relaying how his mate
fell off the trail in a thunderstorm and he had to put her out'n 'er misery,
someone gasped, "You shot your wife?" "Na," he replied, "I was talkin'
'bout my mule."[20]

Nor is it possible to forget the cap'n bound for the North Rim across
thick fog by snowshoe (or sometimes ski) and getting stuck on a peak
halfway over when the fog lifted—'bout starved to death 'til the fog come
back! In the next version he's made it across, evidenced by the campfire
you'll see burning over there tonight.[21] Or, the time when he used his
old pair of expensive field glasses to bring the Colorado River so close
that Darby could drink from it right there on the rim. Oh yes! First time
'twas 'bout five gallons. And dadblameit if that hos didn't love 'em ham
sandwiches—with mus-taad![22]

While these events never happened, they embody the life of John
Hance to a remarkable degree. By example, and not to overshadow the
encompassing deplorable events with a seemingly insignificant diver-
sion, for two brothers to work on both the Navajo Return *and* the Verde

Removal was an incredible occurrence. Not only does that small chunk of information add enormously to John Hance's story, it also makes for astonishingly rich archetypal American history.

So does another true tale. In 1908 Niles Cameron retrieved what was left of Bill Ashurst's body from deep in the canyon. Arriving back on the rim, someone asked if he'd found the remains. "Yes," he replied, "got him right here," patting the gunny sack on one of his burros.[23] What was left of Bill Ashurst was interred near the head of Bright Angel Trail, but photographs of the gravesite do not indicate a location identifiable today. In 1937, eighteen years after Hance passed on, Henry Ashurst requested his father's remains be moved to Grand Canyon Pioneer Cemetery. Grand Canyon National Park agreed,[24] and Bill Ashurst's bones were laid to rest beneath a small headstone a few feet west of his best friend's grave.

John Hance played an integral role in America's westward expansion during the latter 1800s. In retrospect, it's fair to say he was among those to have defined the era. For about fifteen of those years Hance was among its most-remarked citizens, a near-cult figure who was widely known in America and abroad. He was the Southwest's equivalent of Daniel Boone or David Crockett—Hance even fought Indians, just like them. Boone was a colonist who set a westward path through the mountains. Hance, growing up an hour's drive south of Cumberland Gap, did the same thing at Grand Canyon with his trail. But he was also a longhunter like Crockett, raised under remarkably similar conditions only fifty miles from Crockett's birthplace. Both also fought in wars that define American society today.

Beyond his own fanciful imagination, there was nothing "epic" or "great" about John Hance. He was, in all regards, a man who chewed tobacco, spit out its juice, and wiped his whiskers on his pants. While he pondered Grand Canyon's creation, believing it was formed by the river rising up from beneath, he was not otherwise a noted conservationist like John Muir, a man of letters like Mark Twain, or a nurseryman or proselytizer such as John Chapman. On paper, not much remains except "John Hance's Visitors' Book," his map of Red Canyon Toll Road, some voter registration signatures, and an obscure notation in a Head & Co. ledger.

Red Canyon and Bright Angel Trails have been nominated for National Register of Historic Places designation, but Arizona Route 64 (coursing Glendale Springs near Buggeln Picnic Area) and Hull Cabin Historic District are as close as Old Hance Trail is likely to get to that list. The omission is understandable but also regrettable. John Hance's legacy rests solely on the word fantasies he created rather than the physical toil he endured to build the first trail in Grand Canyon and carve the first road to the rim, where he operated its first hotel. His was the founding role in Grand Canyon tourism.

BOARD ON GEOGRAPHIC NAMES (BGN) REGARDING HANCE PLACE NAMES

Hance Rapids*
BGN ID 5536 Lat 360245N Long 1115513W Elevation 2566; US Geological Survey 15' Quadrant Map Cape Royal.

Hance Canyon, with Hance Creek
BGN ID 42725 Lat 360245N Long 1115709W Elevation 2539; USGS 15' Quadrant Map Cape Royal.

Hance Trail
BGN ID 5537 Lat 360113N Long 1115549W Elevation 3750; 15' Quadrant Map Cape Royal.

Hance Spring, Yavapai County, AZ—relating to George Hance
BGN ID 29714 Lat 343419N Long 1120149W; USGS Map Cherry.
BGN ID 29713 Lat 343336N Long 1114423W; USGS Map Walker Mtn.

*Hance Rapids was designated May 4, 1932, by the BGN following the U.S. National Park Service nomination on July 10, 1930. The BGN citation reads, "Named for John Hance, local pioneer." Hance is one of ten canyon rapids studied to remarkable degree and beautifully illustrated in *Hydraulic Maps of Major Rapids: Grand Canyon, Arizona, Miscellaneous Investigation Series, Map I-189* by Susan Kieffer.

NOTES

CHAPTER 1

1. Hugo Richards and W. S. "Boss" Head, Camp Verde sutler's store ledgers, 1871–1886, RG 99, Subgroup 09, Arizona State Library, Archives and Public Records; Accession number GRCA-005861, Grand Canyon National Park Museum Collection.

2. D. T. McDougal to Frank Lockwood, "John Hance, Philosopher, Early Day Canyon Guide," *More Arizona Characters*, University of Arizona Bulletin (July 1942): 44 (author's paraphrase).

3. C. H. Tyler Townsend, "A Wagon Trip to the Grand Canyon of the Colorado River," *Appalachia* 7 (1893–1895): 60 (author's paraphrase).

4. Joseph A. Monk, *Arizona Sketches* (New York, NY: Grafton Press, 1905), 144–47.

5. Possibly the mother of William Randolph Hearst. See Joe Lee, "My Wonderful Country," submitted by Gladwell Richardson, *Frontier Times* (Feb–Mar 1974), Otis "Dock" Marston Manuscript Collection, THL.

6. Larry Winter, "November 7, 2004, Grand Canyon Hikers Recall the Greatest Canyon Liar of Them All," courtesy Richard Reddick.

7. Williston Fish, "Memories of West Point 1877–81," unpublished manuscript, U.S. Military Academy, West Point.

8. Sheila Stubler, personal correspondence with author, spring 2016.

9. William Swilling Wallace, ed., "Lieutenants Pershing and Stotsenberg Visit the Grand Canyon: 1887 [*sic*]," *Arizona and the West* 3, no. 3, (Autumn 1961): 265–84.

10. Ibid.

11. Donald Smythe, "'Black Jack' Pershing's Brilliant Career Almost Ended in an Attempt to View Arizona's Awesome Grand Canyon in 1889," *Montana: The Magazine of Western History* 13, no. 2 (Spring 1963): 11–23.

12. Edith Sessions Tupper, "In the Grand Canyon of the Colorado," *Frank Leslie's Popular Monthly* 41, no. 6 (June 1896), 679. See also "In Grand Canyon," *St. Paul Daily Globe*, August 19, 1895.

CHAPTER 2

1. Jefferson County, Tennessee, recorder's records.

2. Hance family tree, CVHS.

3. Or possibly Johann Hance according to research by Jen Walker.

4. See the inflation calculator at https://westegg.com/inflation/ to determine today's value for amounts given in the text.

5. Jefferson County, Tennessee, recorder's records.

6. "Brief History of Captain Hance," signed "John Hance" but written by George Hance, *Coconino Sun*, January 17, 1919.

7. Jean Patterson Bible, *Bent Twigs in Jefferson County* (Rogersville, TN: East Tennessee Print Company, 1991), 43.
8. Josephine Hollenback, letters regarding northern Arizona tour, summer of 1897, Fray Angélico Chávez History Library, Photo Archives, box 1, folder 16, Santa Fe, New Mexico.
9. Marshall Trimble, *Arizoniana: Stories from Old Arizona*, (Phoenix, AZ: Golden West Publishers, 2002). See also "Gallery of Rogues and Characters," *Arizona Republic*, May 20, 1990.
10. Bob Jarnagin, personal correspondence, fall 2013.
11. Phelps County Genealogical Society, Rolla, Missouri.
12. George Hance's cousin, George Washington Hance of Dandridge.
13. MS 1065 F.46A, NAUSCA.
14. "Recently, while on a visit to the Grand Cañon, I met an old resident who told me that during the past few years he had seen several small flocks of passenger pigeons in the timber of the mesa lands along the Colorado River. He said he had seen and killed many 'back East' when he was a boy, and that he knew well the difference between the 'banded tailed' or 'wood pigeon' of the West, and the passenger pigeon." James H. Cook, "Wild Horses of the Plains," *Natural History* (January 1919): 104.

CHAPTER 3

1. George Wharton James, "Hance, and the Grand Canyon," *Southwestern Empire* (May 1895): 35–37.
2. "46th Arkansas Infantry (Mounted)," *Wikipedia*, last revised October 10, 2019, https://en.wikipedia.org/wiki/46th_Arkansas_Infantry_(Mounted).
3. "Bob Fix reports on John Hance: July 1948," GRCA.
4. Jim McGhee, *Guide to Missouri Confederate Units, 1861–1865* (Fayetteville, AR: University of Arkansas Press, 2008), 168.
5. James, "Hance, and the Grand Canyon," 35–37.
6. John Hance, CMSRs, NARA.
7. Hugh Simmons, personal correspondence, fall 2013.
8. Kiosk, Prairie Grove Battlefield State Park, Arkansas.
9. Ibid.
10. Robert L. O'Connell, *Fierce Patriot: The Tangled Lives of William Tecumseh Sherman* (New York, NY: Random House, 2014), 77.
11. Hugh Simmons, personal correspondence, fall 2013.
12. "Battle of Helena," *Online Encyclopedia of Arkansas History and Culture*, last modified September 4, 2018, www.encyclopediaofarkansas.net.
13. James, "Hance, and the Grand Canyon," 35–37. Hance was apparently unaware he was attacking Helena, mistaking it for Vicksburg, as indicated in his reference to General Howard.
14. John Hance, CMSRs, NARA.
15. Colonel L. Adams, "Experiences in Northern Prisons," *Memphis Daily Appeal*, April 18, 1864.
16. Hugh Simmons, personal correspondence, fall 2013.
17. Lonnie R. Speer, *Portals to Hell—Military Prisons of the Civil War* (Lincoln, NE: University of Nebraska Press, 1997), 70.

18. Ibid., 46.
19. Ibid., 143.
20. Hugh Simmons, personal correspondence, fall 2013.
21. John G. Wilson, letter to the *New York Times*, June 18, 1867.
22. John Hance, CMSRs, NARA.
23. Captain John Sterling Swan, "Prison Life at Fort Delaware," transcribed by Neil Allen Bristow, online diary, June 26, 1876, last updated June 3, 2005, http://freepages .genealogy.rootsweb.ancestry.com/~greenwolf/coombs/swann-js.htm.
24. John Hance, CMSRs, NARA.
25. "Capt John Hance Spinner of Hance Spinner of Yarns," *Williams News*, April 20, 1916.

CHAPTER 4

1. "Brief History of Captain Hance," signed "John Hance" but written by George Hance, *Coconino Sun*, January 17, 1919.
2. "Cheerful Chirps," *Coconino Sun*, October 20, 1922.
3. George Hance, "Interesting History of Arizona Pioneer," *Coconino Sun*, February 9, 1912.
4. "We were unable to locate any entries for John Hance." NARA, #RD-DC-12-01844-ABH.
5. "A Brief History of Capt. Hance," signed "John Hance" but written by George Hance, *Coconino Sun*, January 17, 1919.
6. Joseph G. Rosa, *They Called Him Wild Bill: The Life and Adventures of James Butler Hickok* (Norman, OK, University of Oklahoma Press, 1974), 17.
7. Letters of Howard L. Hickok and Lydia Hickok Barnes, State Historical Society of Missouri.
8. Hamlin Garland, "Were Drunk on Water," *Anaconda Standard*, November 8, 1896.
9. George Hance, letter to John Duke, October 22, 1929, CVHS.
10. Not to be confused with the California-based Butterfield Overland Mail.
11. Manuscript review by Don Lago, fall 2018.
12. Henry Morton Stanley, *My Early Travels and Adventures in America and Asia*, vol. 1 (New York, NY: Charles Scribner's Sons, 1895), 89.
13. Mark Twain (Samuel Clemens), *Roughing It* (Hartford, CT: American Publishing Company, 1872), 23.
14. Evan S. Connell, *Son of the Morning Star—Custer and the Little Bighorn* (New York, NY: North Point Press, 1997), 170.
15. George Hance, letter to John Duke, October 22, 1929, CVHS.
16. This is, apparently, the only known instance of Lorenzo threatening another man with death.
17. Excerpts of a letter from Frances Hance Rose to Lon Garrison, July 31, 1948, GRCA.
18. George Wharton James, "Hance, and the Grand Canyon," 35–37.
19. McFarland and Poole, via Joy Fisher, USGenWeb Archives, uploaded March 7, 2005, http://files.usgwarchives.net/az/yavapai/bios/gbs93sullivan.txt.
20. "What Correspondents Say of Arizona," *Weekly Arizona Miner*, October 17, 1868.
21. Alexander M. Bielakowski, ed., *Ethnic and Racial Minorities in the U.S. Military: An Encyclopedia* (Santa Barbara, CA: ABC-CLIO, 2013).
22. William Haas Moore, *Chiefs, Agents & Soldiers—Conflict on the Navajo Frontier 1868–1882* (Albuquerque, NM: University of New Mexico Press, 1994), 33.

23. George Hance, letter to J. F. Mahoney, September 9, 1931, CVHS.

24. Neal Ackerly, citing the *Semi-Weekly Review*, July 7, 1868, in *A Navajo Diaspora: The Long Walk to Hwéeldi* (Silver City, NM: Dos Rios Consultants, Inc., 1998).

25. George Hance, *Coconino Sun*, January 17, 1919.

26. Roscoe Willson, "Bacon Was Scarce Those Days," *Arizona Days and Ways Magazine*, December 24, 1972.

27. Unknown, snippet found in Sharlot Hall Museum archives and attributed to Roscoe Willson.

28. See *Arizona Republic*, April 15, 1931: John Hance, Geo W. Hance, Wm. D. Breed, John T. Bullard, Joseph Boyer Hurley, "Negro Ben" McKinney, John M. Branaman, Mrs. B. Branaman, Stonewall Jackson Branaman, John Branaman Jr., Dan McSwiggen, Jerry W. Sullivan, James Flynn, Alexander Graydon, Ned Powers, Robert Duncan, John Stanley, Dennis May, London Sayer, Sam Renslow, William Parker, Jim Foy, and John McMinn.

29. SHMA, DB10, folder 1, item 11.

30. According to George Hance. Jerry Sullivan called it the Sullivan-Hance party.

31. "Capture of a Pack Train by the Coyotero Apaches," *Weekly Arizona Miner*, November 14, 1868. See also Hayden Library, Pioneer Biographies Index for Solomon Barth.

32. "Arizona Pioneers Days—Doyle Remembers Things Too," *Coconino Sun*, June 5, 1908.

33. Platt Cline, *They Came To the Mountain—The Story of Flagstaff's Beginnings* (Flagstaff, AZ: Northland Press, 1976), 86.

34. George Hance, *Coconino Sun*, June 5, 1908.

35. Ibid.

36. "Bacon Was Scarce Those Days," SHMA, under R. G. Willson, December 24, 1972.

37. SHMA, DB19, folder 1, item 11.

38. Aztlan Lodge 177, Prescott, Arizona, membership records.

39. McFarland and Poole, via Joy Fisher, USGenWeb Archives, uploaded March 7, 2005, http://files.usgwarchives.net/az/yavapai/bios/gbs93sullivan.txt.

CHAPTER 5

1. George Hance folder of writings, CVHS.

2. Glenda Farley, "1865 Settlement: Exploring and Building the Fort," *Verde Independent*, July 14, 2012.

3. Lonnie Underhill, "Dr. Edward Palmer's Experiences with the Arizona Volunteers," *Arizona and the West* 26, no. 1 (Spring 1984): 49.

4. Glenda Farley, "Verde Heritage," *Verde Independent*, June 22, 1972.

5. "Local Intelligence—Thursday," *Weekly Arizona Miner*, August 2, 1878.

6. *Tripsacum dactyloides*, a warm season grass suitable for most livestock.

7. "Verde, Agua Fria Ruins, Montezuma Well, Etc.," *Arizona Weekly Miner*, December 17, 1875.

8. YCAzRR.

9. "The Country North," *Weekly Arizona Miner*, April 30, 1870.

10. "What Our Farmers Have Put in the Ground," *Weekly Arizona Miner*, August 27, 1870.

11. "Dreadful Work of the Indians," *Weekly Arizona Miner*, October 31, 1868.

12. Mike Burns, *The Only One Living to Tell: The Autobiography of a Yavapai Indian* (Tucson, AZ: University of Arizona Press, 2012), 70.

13. Douglas V. Meed, *They Never Surrendered: Bronco Apaches of the Sierra Madres 1890–1935* (Tuscon, AZ: Westernlore Press, 1993), 12.

14. "Local Intelligence—Another Indian Outrage," *Weekly Arizona Miner*, October 9, 1869.

15. "Brief History of Captain Hance," *Coconino Sun*, January 17, 1919.

16. "Local Intelligence—Thursday," *Weekly Arizona Miner*, October 19, 1877.

17. Ibid.

18. "Our Situation," *Weekly Arizona Miner*, January 23, 1869.

19. YCAzRR.

20. Two hundred dollars in 2017.

21. James, "Hance, and the Grand Canyon," 35–37.

22. Stewart Rosebrook, personal correspondence, summer 2016.

23. C. H. Orme, "History of the Quarter Circle V Bar," Orme School Yearbook, 1949–1950.

24. "Local Intelligence—Loss by Fire," *Weekly Arizona Miner*, May 20, 1871.

25. "Local Intelligence—Crops at the Verde," *Weekly Arizona Miner*, September 23, 1871.

26. George Hance, letter to J. F. Mahoney, September 9, 1931, SHMA.

27. *Weekly Arizona Miner*, November 2, 1872.

28. George Hance, letter to J. F. Mahoney, September 9, 1931, SHMA.

29. Camp Verde Historical Society Newsletter, May–July 2014.

30. George Hance, "Highlights of Territorial Indian Wars Recalled by Noted Pioneer of Arizona," *Arizona Republic*, April 15, 1931.

31. "Local & Miscellaneous," *Weekly Arizona Miner*, October 29, 1873.

32. Ibid., December 31, 1874.

33. Letter from Albert Schroeder to Lemuel Garrison, November 18, 1948, GRCA.

34. Ibid. See also *Arizona Weekly Miner*, December 10 and 15, 1875. Al Sieber chased the thieves to within a few miles of San Carlos, where he found the animals slaughtered.

35. Letter from Albert Schroeder to Lemuel Garrison, November 18, 1948, GRCA.

36. John G. Bourke, *On the Border with Crook* (Glorieta, NM: Rio Grande Press, 1892), 217.

37. George Hance, "Highlights of Territorial Indian Wars Recalled by Noted Pioneer of Arizona," *Arizona Republic*, April 15, 1931.

38. Fort Verde State Historic Park, microfiche post returns.

39. Vincent Randell, personal correspondence, spring 2017.

40. Fort Verde State Historic Park, microfiche post returns.

41. Dan L. Thrapp, *Al Sieber: Chief of Scouts* (Norman, OK: University of Oklahoma Press), 168–69.

42. William T. Corbusier, *Verde to San Carlos: Recollections of a Famous Army Surgeon and His Observant Family on the Western Frontier, 1869–86* (Tuscon, AZ: Dale Stuart King, 1969).

43. Bonnie Peplow and Ed Peplow, eds., *Pioneer Stories of Arizona's Verde Valley* (Camp Verde, AZ: Verde Valley Pioneers Association, 1972), 147–48.

44. "Lynk [*sic*] and Adda Smith interview," George Babbitt Collection, OH. 57. 29, NAUSCA.

CHAPTER 6

1. Thrapp, *Al Sieber: Chief of Scouts*, 200.

2. "Verde, Agua Fria Ruins, Montezuma Well, Etc," *Arizona Weekly Miner*, December 17, 1875.

3. CVHS folklore.
4. "Local Intelligence—Thursday," *Weekly Arizona Miner*, April 5, 1878.
5. Ruth Hance Thayer, personal correspondence, summer–fall 2015.
6. George Hance files, SHMA.
7. "George W. Hance by Eva Hance," February 22, 1982, SHMA.
8. George Hance files, SHMA.
9. Ibid.
10. George Hance folder, CVHS.
11. "Bob Fix Reports on John Hance: July 1948," GRCA.
12. "Bradshaw, William David," Arizona State University Archives, https://www.asu.edu /lib/archives/azbio/bios/BRADSHAW.PDF.
13. *Los Angeles News*, December 17, 1864.
14. "Mining Intelligence," *Weekly Arizona Miner*, August 20, 1870.
15. "Mines and Mining," *Weekly Arizona Miner*, May 27, 1871.
16. "Court Proceedings," *Weekly Arizona Miner*, July 11, 1879.
17. "Local Intelligence—Monday," *Weekly Arizona Miner*, November 7, 1877.
18. "Mining Intelligence," *Weekly Arizona Miner*, November 16, 1877.
19. "The route was considerably different than today's I-17 except in some places in the lower elevations and between Mayer and Humboldt in the north. It can be replicated by driving south out of Mayer the back way to Old Cordes southwest of Cordes Junction, then proceeding down Antelope Hill and through Bumblebee to the I-17 access road; if equipped with 4wd, continue south to Black Canyon City, exiting Maggie Mine Road." Stuart Rosebrook, personal correspondence, fall 2015.
20. "Finished—The new road . . . ," *Weekly Arizona Miner*, November 1, 1873.
21. "History of Maricopa County," *Phoenix Herald*, July 19, 1883.
22. "The Grand Canyon," *Arizona Republican*, August 29, 1905. See also "John Hance's Visitors' Book," August 31, 1895, MS 0054 (Rare), Arizona Historical Society Library and Archives, Tuscon, Arizona: "JOHN Y.T. SMITH [and daughter]. Phoenix, Arizona. To Mr. John Hance:—My Old Friend: I am delighted to meet you on the rim of the Grand Canon of the Colorado River, after a score or more of years since our last meeting."
23. NARA, ATL-18 6/17 and ATL-18 7/17, Riverside, California.
24. Ibid.
25. *Portrait and Biographical Record of Arizona: Commemorating the Achievements of Citizens Who Have Contributed to the Progress of Arizona and the Development of Its Resources* (Chicago, IL: Chapman Publishing Company, 1901), 43–44.
26. "Local Intelligence," *Weekly Arizona Miner*, June 29, 1877.
27. "Light Bidding," *Weekly Arizona Miner*, December 21, 1877.
28. "Local Intelligence," *Weekly Arizona Miner*, July 31, 1877.
29. Hugo Richards and W. S. "Boss" Head, "Ledger IV," page 144, Camp Verde sutler's store ledgers, 1871–1886, RG 99, Subgroup 09, Arizona State Library, Archives and Public Records, Phoenix, Arizona.
30. YCAzAR.
31. Charlie Wingfield letter, May 20, 1948, CVHS.
32. David Rumsey, online map collection, https://www.davidrumsey.com.
33. "The Deepest Canyon in the World," *Weekly Arizona Miner*, April 9, 1880.
34. Earle Spamer, personal correspondence, winter 2017.

35. "Local Intelligence—Thursday," *Weekly Arizona Miner*, May 3, 1878.
36. *Arizona Weekly Journal-Miner*, July 12, 1899; anonymous, personal correspondence, summer 2017.
37. Steve Ayres, "A Real Whodunit: Camp Verde's 1899 Wingfield-Rodgers Murder," *Verde Independent*, March 24, 2009.
38. The *Weekly Arizona Miner* has changed names several times throughout its history. In 1874 the name was changed to *Arizona Weekly Miner*, reverting back to the original in 1877. In 1885 the paper merged with the *Arizona Weekly Journal* and became the *Arizona Weekly Journal-Miner*, which was changed to *Weekly Arizona Journal-Miner* in 1903.
39. "Local Intelligence—Wednesday," *Weekly Arizona Miner*, September 17, 1880.
40. Hance never recorded a mark or brand in Yavapai County. "Marks and Brands," inventory papers with two boxes of actual samples, YCAzRR.
41. "Indenture," John Hance to Murray McInernay; John Hance, last Verde assessment, 1881, YCAzRR.
42. "To Day's News," *Weekly Arizona Miner*, July 8, 1881.
43. On July 17. Sheila Stubler, personal correspondence, winter 2017.
44. "Camp Verde Abandoned," *Weekly Arizona Miner*, July 29, 1881.
45. "Local Intelligence—Wednesday," *Weekly Arizona Miner*, July 15, 1881.

CHAPTER 7
1. Hance etched "John Hance" into the rocks at the mouth of Hance Creek. Helen Ranney, personal correspondence with photos, winter 2019.
2. James, "Hance, and the Grand Canyon," 35–37.
3. Colleen Holt, Jerome Historical Society, personal correspondence, spring 2013.
4. "Ruggles, Silas," Arizona State University Library Archives, https://repository.asu.edu /items/47425.
5. "John Hance's Visitors' Book," MS 0054 (Rare), 9.
6. YCAzAR.
7. James R. Fuchs, "A History of Williams, Arizona, 1876–1951," *University of Arizona Bulletin: Social Science Bulletin* 24, no. 5 (November 1953): 50–51.
8. "Local Matters," *Arizona Champion*, February 21, 1885.
9. George Wharton James, forward to *Adventures in the Canyons of the Colorado* by William Wallace Bass (Grand Canyon, Arizona: self-published, 1920), 5.
10. Day Allen Willey, "Hance of the Grand Canyon," *Outing Magazine* 56 (April–September 1910), 30–31. According to George Wharton James, W. W. Bass made the same claim, one of several of his "first sighting" accounts.
11. "Territorial Items," *Arizona Weekly Citizen*, May 22, 1881.
12. "Grandest Scenery in the World," *Arizona Weekly Miner*, May 4, 1877.
13. *Arizona Weekly Miner*, April 20, 1877.
14. "Death of Capt John Moss," *Arizona Weekly Miner*, April 23, 1880.
15. "Grandest Scenery in the World," *Arizona Weekly Miner*, May 4, 1877.
16. "Death of Capt John Moss," *Arizona Weekly Miner*, April 23, 1880.
17. First advertisement for "Young & Farlee," *Mohave County Miner*, January 28, 1883.
18. "Hackberry," *Mohave County Miner*, March 25, 1883.
19. "A Trip to the Grand Canyon," *Mohave County Miner*, September 14, 1889.
20. "The Winter Resort," *Arizona Champion*, October 13, 1883.

21. Frederick Trautmann, ed., "Germans at the Grand Canyon: The Memoirs of Paul Lindau, 1883," *Journal of Arizona History* 26, no. 4 (Winter 1985): 387.
22. Mary Wager Fisher, "A Day in the Grand Cañon," *Outing Magazine* 22, no. 4 (July 1893), 261–64.
23. Ancel Taylor to Robert Morrow, letter dated March 22, 1969, Mohave Museum of History and Arts Library.
24. Tracy, S. M., *Report of an Investigation of the Grasses of the Arid Districts of New Mexico, Arizona, Nevada, and Utah*, U.S. Department of Agriculture, Botanical Division, bulletin 6, page 5–29. Tracy's transcription of Asa Gray's list of plants in Farlee's register appears on page thirteen.
25. Earle Spamer, "Demons at the Farlee Hotel," *The Ol' Pioneer* 29, no. 4 (Fall 2018). See also Félix Frédéric Moreau, *Aux États-Unis: Notes de Voyage* (Paris, France: E. Plon, Nourrit et Cie, 1888).
26. Earle Spamer, personal correspondence, summer 2018; Nancy Brian and Earle Spamer, "Knowlton Hop-Hornbeam Revisited (*Ostrya knowltonii* Cov.)," *Bartonia*, no. 60 (2000): 49–56.
27. Mary Wager Fisher, "A Day in the Grand Cañon," 263.
28. *Arizona Republican*, October 10, 1901.
29. Susan Deaver Olberding, *Fort Valley Then and Now: A Look at an Arizona Settlement* (Flagstaff, AZ: Fort Valley Publishing, 2002, revised 2007), 23.
30. Cline, *They Came To the Mountain*, 135.
31. Andy Ashurst, letter to Lon Garrison, "Azusa California December 22, 1951," GRCA.
32. Oral history interview with Senator Henry Fountain Ashurst, May 19, 1959, and October 9, 1961, NAUSCA, OH.57.15.
33. "Local and Personal," *Mohave County Miner*, January 16, 1897.
34. "Senator Ashurst Recalls Fond Memories," *The Sun*, March 27, 1959.
35. George Babbitt interview with Charley Clark, NAUSCA, OH.57.21.
36. Fuchs, "A History of Williams, Arizona," 50–51; Cline, *They Came To the Mountain*, 90.
37. "Local Intelligence—Been After Salt" *Weekly Arizona Miner*, August 2, 1878.
38. Andy Ashurst, letter to Lon Garrison, "Azusa California December 22, 1951," GRCA.
39. Ibid.
40. "Comments by E. M. Ennis, March 19, 1948," GRCA.
41. J. Donald Hughes, 1968 manuscript, NAUSCA.
42. "No Winged Tourists," *Coconino Sun*, August 28, 1908.
43. John Hance's eightieth birthday letter, GRCA.
44. Homestead notice, *Arizona Champion*, October 30, 1886.
45. Wayne Ranney, *Carving Grand Canyon: Evidence, Theories, and Mystery* (Grand Canyon, AZ: Grand Canyon Association, 2012), 17.
46. "Nature's Mighty Crevice," *Omaha Daily Bee*, February 23, 1896.
47. "The Ayer Lumber Company," *Arizona Champion*, February 23, 1884.
48. Edward E. Ayer, "Trip to Grand Canyon 1883–1884 and After," Otis R. "Dock" Marston Manuscript Collection, box 10, folder 9, THL.
49. Amelia and Josephine Hollenback, letters regarding northern Arizona tour, and album 1, summer of 1897, photographs of northern Arizona tour, box 1, folder 16, the Fray Angélico Chávez History Library, Photo Archives.

50. Because Hance was known to Custer in Kansas, it's possible Custer requested his services in 1876. The message would have been delivered to Camp Verde by military telegraph.
51. Amelia Hollenback, letters regarding northern Arizona tour, and album 1, summer of 1897, photographs of northern Arizona tour, box 1, folder 16, the Fray Angélico Chávez History Library, Photo Archives.
52. *Arizona Champion*, February 7, May 23, and November 21, 1885.
53. "The Ayer Trip to the Grand Canyon," *Arizona Champion*, May 23, 1885.
54. Ethel Sturgis Dummer (1866–1954) became a social welfare leader, philanthropist, and author. In 1885 she had just graduated from Kirkland School, Chicago.
55. Ayer, "Trip to Grand Canyon 1883–1884 and After."
56. Frank C. Lockwood, *The Life of Edward E. Ayer* (Chicago, IL: A. C. McClurg & Co., 1929), 98–100.
57. Frank C. Lockwood, "More Arizona Characters," *University of Arizona Press Bulletin*, July 1, 1943.
58. Josephine Hollenback, letters regarding northern Arizona tour, box 1, folder 17, the Fray Angélico Chávez History Library, Photo Archives.
59. Ibid.
60. *Arizona Champion*, March 7, 1885.
61. Amelia Hollenback, letters regarding northern Arizona tour, and album 1, summer of 1897, photographs of northern Arizona tour, box 1, folder 16, the Fray Angélico Chávez History Library, Photo Archives.

CHAPTER 8
1. Shane Murphy, "John Hance and the Dovetailed Joins," *The Ol' Pioneer* 29, no 3 (Summer 2018): 3. Hull Cabin Historic District is administered by the Kaibab Ranger District, U.S. Forest Service, Williams, Arizona. Hull Cabin is available for overnight rental during the summer. It's also possible to reserve the historic Buckey O'Neill cabin, circa 1895–96, now incorporated into the Bright Angel Lodge complex at Grand Canyon Village and also on the National Register of Historic Places. Named for a revered Yavapai County figure, O'Neill's place comes with electricity, tap water, toilet, and hot shower. Souvenir shops, an ice cream service bar, and several dining rooms are within crawling distance. Hull Cabin is quite the opposite. There's not a restaurant or store within fifteen miles, with several of those miles on gravel roads. Cell phones don't work there. Visitors are on their own, tasked with supplying their own bedding, food, and toiletries, just like John Hance would have done.
2. *Arizona Champion*, February 21, 1885.
3. Shane Murphy, proceedings, 2019 Grand Canyon History Symposium.
4. Shane Murphy, "I've Got to Tell Stories," *Journal of Arizona History* 56, no. 4 (Winter 2015), 425–58.
5. "The Grand Canyon," *Abbeville Press and Banner*, August 3, 1892.
6. "John Hance's Visitors' Book," 7.
7. Tom Martin, ed., *From Powell to Power: A Recounting of the First One Hundred River Runners through the Grand Canyon* (Flagstaff, AZ: Vishnu Temple Press, 2014), 143–44.
8. Expedition diary, Robert Brewster Stanton Papers, 1846–1960, New York Public Library.

9. Eva Hance, letter to Herald Lantis, October 1, 1982, CVHS.

10. "Young Wife is Defendant in Divorce Case," *Weekly Arizona Journal-Miner*, January 23, 1918.

11. Ralph Palmer, *Doctor on Horseback: A Collection of Anecdotes Largely but Not Exclusively Medically Oriented*, chap. 8, CVHS.

12. "Local Notes," *Arizona Weekly Journal-Miner*, May 9, 1888.

13. Shane Murphy, "Ruth Hance Thayer with Amanda Thayer, personal correspondence," CVHS.

14. Amelia Hollenback, box 1, folder 15, the Fray Angélico Chávez History Library, Photo Archives.

15. ATL 18 6/17 and ATL 18 7/17, NARA, Riverside, California.

16. Platt Cline, *They Came To the Mountain*, 85.

17. "The Grand Canyon," advertisement in the *Arizona Champion*, September 11, 1886.

18. *Arizona Champion*, April 9, 1887.

19. *Arizona Champion*, September 1, 1888.

20. "Nature's Mighty Crevice," *Omaha Daily Bee*, February 23, 1896.

21. "Local Notes," *Arizona Weekly Journal-Miner*, June 22, 1887. Hance is not mentioned, but Bowers's line of travel indicates his destination, and he certainly knew Hance.

22. "Local Notes," *Arizona Weekly Journal-Miner*, June 6, 1888.

23. "Local Notes," *Arizona Weekly Journal-Miner*, August 1 and August 15, 1888.

24. George Wharton James, "Hance, and the Grand Canyon," *Southwestern Empire* (May 1895): 35–37.

25. "The Atlantic & Pacific and the Grand Canyon of the Colorado," *Arizona Weekly Journal-Miner*, July 4, 1888.

26. "In Wonderland," *Los Angeles Times*, July 1, 1888.

27. "Local Matters," *Arizona Champion*, April 20, July 6, August 24, August 31, and September 28, 1889.

28. "Local Matters," *Arizona Champion*, October 26, 1889.

29. "Local Matters," *Arizona Champion*, December 17, 1887; James Kintner, letter to Ray S. Page, June 24, 1969, GRCA.

30. "God's Temples," *Arizona Republican*, September 16, 1894.

31. "Location of Rowe Well," in folder "Articles on Ralph Cameron, J. W. Thurber's Stage Line, Grandview, Peter Berry, and More," GRCA, no. 108309.

32. Michael F. Anderson, *Polishing the Jewell: An Administrative History of Grand Canyon National Park* (Grand Canyon, AZ: Grand Canyon Association, 2000), 4.

33. "How's This?" *Williams News*, March 8, 1913.

34. "Niles J. Cameron Passes at Sand Diego," *Coconino Sun*, December 6, 1918.

35. "Bob Fix Reports on John Hance: July 1948," GRCA.

36. Roscoe G. Willson, *No Place For Angels: Stories of Old Arizona Days* (Phoenix, AZ: The Arizona Republic, 1958), 66–70.

37. Debra Stuphen, "Too Hard a Nut to Crack: Peter D. Berry and the Battle for Free Enterprise at the Grand Canyon, 1890–1914," *Journal of Arizona History* 32, no. 2 (Summer 1991): 154–55.

38. "Great Register," Grand Canyon Precinct, 1914, CCAzRR.

39. Burton Holmes, *Travelogues*, vol. 6 (New York City, NY: The McClure Company, 1901).

40. YCAzRR. Pipe Creek is named in these documents.
41. "Arizona Territory vs. Ralph Henry Cameron, 1903," GRCA, no. 19936. Certifying that no previous route existed along the proposed path were Godfrey Sykes and Lyman Tolfree.
42. "The Territory of Arizona, Plaintiff—VS—R.H. Cameron, Defendant," affidavit of Ralph Cameron, February 25, 1903.
43. Ed Gale, letter to Martin Buggeln, GRCA, no. 80085.
44. Yavapai County toll road records, 1871–1891, 40–42, YCAzRR; plat in Coconino County recorder's files, map no. 901364.
45. YCAzRR.
46. CCAzRR.
47. W. C. Hogaboom, *Coconino Sun*, December 27, 1902.

CHAPTER 9
1. George H. Billingsley, Earle Spamer, and Dove Menkes, *Quest for the Pillar of Gold: The Mines and Miners of the Grand Canyon* (Grand Canyon, AZ: Grand Canyon Association, 1997), 50–52. An archaeological site called the "Movie Set" (or sometimes "Hollywood Set") from this era features handmade rocker and sluice boxes, flatware, plates, and an Old West coffee pot.
2. "Grand Canyon Mines," *Arizona Champion*, April 19, 1890.
3. "Gold in Grand Canyon," *St. John's Herald*, April 24, 1890.
4. YCAzRR.
5. S. B. Tanner and F. B. Jacobs, September 12, 1890, YCAzRR.
6. *Mohave County Miner*, September 26, 1891, referencing "Baloon Mining," *Arizona Weekly Journal-Miner*, August 15, 1891.
7. Platt Cline, *They Came To the Mountain*, 103. Martha Allen was the sister of Sarah Allen, who married Al Doyle.
8. Yavapai County "Records of Mines," book 29, page 263, YCAzRR; see also Yavapai County toll road records, 1871–1891, 34–35, YCAzRR.
9. Yavapai County "Records of Mines," book 29, page 375–80, YCAzRR.
10. "The Comstock," *Arizona Champion*, March 29, 1890.
11. YCAzRR.
12. Frank Lockwood, foreword to *A Westerly Trend: Being a Veracious Chronicle of More Than Sixty Years of Joyous Wanderings, Mainly in Search of Space and Sunshine* by Godfrey Sykes (Flagstaff, AZ: Arizona Pioneers Historical Society, 1944), vi.
13. Diane Boyer, personal correspondence, summer 2016.
14. Frank Lockwood, "More Arizona Characters," 46.
15. Diane Boyer, personal correspondence, summer 2016.
16. "Captain John Hance Relates a Story," *Williams News*, June 9, 1906.
17. "The Grand Canyon," *Arizona Champion*, May 3, 1890. This plat has not been located.
18. Yavapai County toll road records, 1871–1891, 34–37, YCAzRR.
19. Ibid., 35–39; see also *Arizona Weekly Journal-Miner*, April 16, 1890.
20. Bert Lauzon, NAUSCA, no. 107304.
21. "Fraser's Notes," Otis R. "Dock" Marston Manuscript Collection, box 14, folder 12, THL.
22. "Local Matters," *Arizona Champion*, March 7, 1885.

23. "The Journal-Miner Says," *Mohave County Miner*, March 15, 1890.
24. W. W. Bass and Ed Randolph, letter to Frederick Siemer, November 9, 1888; W. W. Bass, letter to Cormick E. Boyce, November 5, 1889, found in the Coconino County recorder's vault under the title "Water Rights Record Transcribed from Yavapai County," with stickers on the volume's spine identifying its contents, 314, 451.
25. "The Supai Indians," *Arizona Weekly Journal-Miner*, August 27, 1890.
26. *Arizona Champion*, July 17 and August 30, 1890.
27. "To Commissioner of Indian Affairs," July 12 and September 11, 1890; October 16, 1891, Otis "Dock" Marston Manuscript Collection, box 14, folder 12, THL.
28. PH.660.121, NAUSCA.
29. "Local Matters," *Coconino Sun*, July 18, 1891.
30. "Local Matters," *Coconino Sun*, August 8, 1891.
31. "Territorial News," *Arizona Republican*, August 13, 1891.
32. "Local Matters," *Coconino Sun*, September 5, 1891.
33. Promiscuous records, book 1, page 7, CCAzRR.
34. Ibid., page 16, CCAzRR.
35. W. W. Bass, letter to S. M. McCowan and John F. Gaddis, October 18, 1893, CCAzRR.
36. *Arizona Weekly Journal-Miner*, December 20, 1893.
37. "Yavapai County Toll Roads, 1871–1891," 38–39, YCAzRR.
38. Yavapai County "Records of Mines," book 30, page 89, YCAzRR.
39. "Record of Mines," book 1, page 2 (page 1 is blank), CCAzRR.
40. Quitclaim deed, "C. H. McClure and Robt. A. Ferguson to R. H. Cameron," March 17, 1902, CCAzRR.
41. "Canyon's Mineral Wealth," *Arizona Republican*, February 22, 1898.
42. CCAzRR.
43. "Promiscuous Records," book 1, page 114; "Record of Mines," book 1, page 569–78, CCAzRR; Rudy J. Gerber, *The Railroad and the Canyon* (Gretna, LA: Firebird Press, 1998), 48.
44. "Cars to the Grand Canyon," *New York Times*, August 6, 1897.
45. Al Richmond, "The Grand Canyon Railway: A History," *Journal of Arizona History* 27 (Winter 1986): 425–38.
46. "Local and Otherwise," *Coconino Sun*, April 29, 1899.
47. Gerber, *The Railroad and the Canyon*, 50.
48. G. K. Woods, ed., *Personal Impressions of the Grand Cañon of the Colorado Near Flagstaff, Arizona: As Seen through Nearly Two Thousand Eyes, and Written in the Private Visitors' Book of the World-Famous Guide* (San Francisco, CA: The Whitaker & Ray Company, 1899).
49. Gifford Pinchot, *Breaking New Ground* (Washington, D.C.: Island Press, 1987), 41.
50. Ibid., 43.
51. "The Grand Canyon: Pioneers of the Canyon," *The Mentor* 3, no. 16, serial 22 (1915).
52. Horace Carter Hovey, "On the Rim and in the Depths of the Grand Canyon," *Scientific American* (August 1892): 87–89.
53. "The Grand Canyon: Pioneers of the Canyon," *The Mentor* 3, no. 16, serial 22 (1915).
54. Margaret Armstrong, "Canyon & Glacier," *Overland Monthly* 59, no. 2 (February 1912): 95–99.
55. "Territorial News," *Arizona Republican*, August 13, 1891.

56. Richard Mangum and Sherry Mangum, *Grand Canyon-Flagstaff Stage Coach Line: A History and Exploration Guide* (Portland, OR: Hexagon Press, 1999), 66–117.
57. "Yucca," "A Woman's Trip to the Grand Canon," *Goldthwaite's Geographical Magazine* (July 1892): 258–67.
58. C. A. Higgins, *Grand Cañon of the Colorado River* (Chicago: The Henry O. Shepard Company, 1892), 13, 31.
59. "Grand Canyon Gateway," *Coconino Sun*, May 12, 1892.
60. Richard Mangum and Sherry Mangum, *Grand Canyon–Flagstaff Stage Coach Line*, 18.
61. Ibid., 25.
62. While this timeframe respectfully ignores W. W. Bass at Havasupai Point, as well as Sanford Rowe's fledgling enterprise, it must be said that Bass was nowhere close to Hance in reputation, drawing power, or appeal. Additionally, Rowe's personal impact, outside of his location near Bright Angel, appears insignificant overall. In fact, by the time Bass and Rowe were coming to life in the press, Hance had almost singlehandedly invented Grand Canyon tourism and had stepped away from its everyday transportation and accommodation aspects.
63. "A Wild Girl Captured," *Coconino Sun*, May 26, 1892.
64. Lucy Bowditch, "Interpreting 19th and Early 20th Century Photographs of the Grand Canyon: Religion, Science, Art History, and Tourism," February 23, 2019, Grand Canyon History Symposium.
65. See SHMA, map 0058a. The four captions read: "Panoramic view of the Grand Canyon as seen from John Hance's Ranch on the South Rim"; "Hance Canyon, looking east 1.5 miles from its mouth into the main Colorado canyon"; "Looking north across the main canyon from the rim of Hance Canyon"; and a bird's-eye view of "Flagstaff and the San Francisco Peaks from the south."

CHAPTER 10
1. *Salt Lake Tribune*, September 26, 1892.
2. Ernest Goppert, "God Bless the Hands That Made Them Custard Pies: William F. Cody's North Rim Adventure," *Points West* (Winter 2003): 24–29.
3. Maps and plats, book 1, 24–27, CCAzRR.
4. Prentiss Ingraham, *The Girl Rough Riders: A Romantic and Adventurous Trail of Rough Riders through the Wonderland of Mystery and Silence*, with illustrations by L. J. Bridgman (Boston, MA: Dana Estes & Company, 1903), 124.
5. "Local Brevities," *Coconino Weekly Sun*, December 1, 1892.
6. Richard Quartaroli, personal correspondence, winter 2016.
7. "Doyle Remembers Things Too," *Coconino Sun*, June 5, 1908.
8. *Coconino Sun*, June 9, 1892.
9. "Automobile Trip," *Coconino Sun*, February 8, 1902.
10. Matt Dodge, "Arizona's Forgotten Guide," *Real West Magazine* (May 1979): 20.
11. Anderson, *Polishing the Jewell*, 7.
12. Ralph Cameron, letter to Peter Berry, June 17, 1897, GRCA, no. 14823.
13. Record of mines, book 1, page 391, CCAzRR; see also *Arizona Silver Belt*, June 24, 1897.
14. William Edwin Austin, ed., *Interview with Bert [sic] Cameron, June 21, 1959*, GRCA, no. 015232.

15. Peter Berry letter, October 31, 1896, GRCA.
16. "Sudden Ending of Life," *Coconino Sun*, January 7, 1905.
17. MS 162, box 1, folder 16, NAUSCA.
18. "Local Matters," *Coconino Sun*, July 6, 1893.
19. Advert, *Coconino Sun*, May 31, 1894.
20. Andy Ashurst, "Exhibit 1" letter, GRCA.
21. Agreements, book 1, 31, CCAzRR.
22. "Famed Pioneers Held Xmas Party in Grand Canyon In '93," clipping dated December 24, 1948, GRCA.
23. J. A. Pitts, letter to Andrew J. Ashurst, July 30, 1947, GRCA. Pitts accompanied at least three canyon prospecting expeditions with his father-in-law.
24. GRCA, no. 50004. The interpretation is open to debate; the sign is heavily worn and mostly unreadable.
25. John Hance's "Visitors' Book," 72.
26. *Coconino Weekly Sun*, August 23, 1894. See also Richard Mangum and Sherry Mangum, *Grand Canyon–Flagstaff Stage Coach Line*, 74–79.
27. "The Tour of the Editors," *Los Angeles Herald*, June 16, 1895.
28. "Ho for the Grand Canyon," *Coconino Weekly Sun*, March 14, 1895; see also MS 162, box 1, folder 16, NAUSCA.
29. Richard Mangum and Sherry Mangum, *Grand Canyon–Flagstaff Stage Coach Line*, photo, 27.
30. "The Glories of Nature," *Coconino Weekly Sun*, April 11, 1895.
31. "To the Grand Canyon," *Los Angeles Times*, June 2, 1895.
32. Ibid.
33. "They Enjoyed the Trip," *Arizona Weekly Journal-Miner*, September 4, 1895.
34. H. G. Wells, letter to James Thurber, October 17, 1895, MS 162, box 1, folder 16, NAUSCA.
35. Agreements, book 3, page 436–38, CCAzRR.
36. Whereabouts unknown.
37. "Estray Horse," *Arizona Champion*, May 22, 1886.
38. Agreements, book 3, page 436–38, CCAzRR.
39. MS 162, box 1, folder 16, NAUSCA.
40. "Bill of Sale, Thurber's Camp #1 Mch 8-1901," MCR.
41. In this same regard, every effort should be made to determine the whereabouts of Farlee's large bottle of calling cards.
42. "The Stage Line Open," *Coconino Weekly Sun*, April 2, 1896.
43. "To the Grand Canyon," *Los Angeles Times*, June 2, 1895.
44. Richard Mangum and Sherry Magnum, *Grand Canyon–Flagstaff Stage Coach Line*, 29.
45. Geo. A Reed, "Bearhide Camp, August 15, 1948," to Lemuel A. Garrison, GRCA.
46. Edith Sessions Tupper, "In the Grand Canyon of the Colorado," 677–84.
47. GRCA, no. 14641.
48. Bright Angel Hotel register, MS 25, MNA.
49. "Nuggets of Territorial News," *Arizona Republican*, November 12, 1896.
50. Agreements, book 4, page 56–57, CCAzRR.
51. "Down the Colorado," *Coconino Sun*, October 29, 1896.

52. Shane Murphy, *Ammo Can Interp: Talking Points for a Grand Canyon River Trip* (Flagstaff, AZ: Canyoneers, Inc., 2007), 123.
53. "Down the Colorado," *Coconino Sun*, October 29, 1896.
54. Marieke Taney, "Elusive & Remarkable: Stories, a Few Facts and Many Speculations; George F. Flavell's 1896 Colorado River Voyage," Grand Canyon Historical Society Symposium prospectus, 2016.
55. Tom Martin, ed., *From Powell To Power*, 171.
56. Ibid.
57. Bank Hotel advertisement, *Flagstaff Sun-Democrat*, January 14, 1897.
58. "Tragedy at Mohave," *San Francisco Call*, January 17, 1897.
59. "Lyman Tolfree Suicide," *Williams News*, January 7, 1905.

CHAPTER 11
1. Brook Sutton, "Historical Badass: Annie Smith Peck" *Adventure Journal*, November 6, 2014.
2. July 13, 1895, MS 006, folder 1, Bechtel Collection, Slusser Memorial Philatelic Library, Tucson, Arizona.
3. "Brief Locals," *Coconino Sun*, February 26, 1898.
4. "Arizona Day by Day," *Arizona Republican*, November 20, 1898.
5. "Canyon's Mineral Wealth," *Arizona Republican*, February 22, 1898.
6. "Charlie Wingfield. Prescott Ariz. May 20, 1948," CVHS.
7. *Personal Impressions* has seen a limited print-on-demand run. See Billie Jane Baguley Library, Heard Museum, Phoenix, Arizona.
8. "Killed by Falling Rocks," *Coconino Sun*, February 23, 1901
9. "Record of Mines," book 2, page 370, CCAzRR.
10. "The Arizona Pioneer," *Topeka State Journal*, July 2, 1903.
11. "Killed by Falling Rocks," *Coconino Sun*, February 23, 1901.
12. Ibid.
13. Fred Harvey Bright Angel Hotel, register of guests, October 29, 1900–August 13, 1901, RC 39 (10):17, Heard Museum Archives; see also Bright Angel Hotel register, 1896–1901, MNA.
14. "Deeds," book 1, page 445, CCAzRR.
15. Andy Ashurst, letter to Lon Garrison, December 22, 1951, GRCA.
16. Frank Lockwood, *Desert Magazine* 3, vol. 9 (July 1940), 15–18.
17. Bright Angel Hotel, register of guests, Heard Museum archives.
18. Photographs of Selfridge in Grand Canyon with descriptions on verso, auctioned on eBay in January 2017, screen captures.
19. "John Hance et al and Susan W. Selfridge, June 18, 1901," CCAzRR.
20. Curtis McClure and John Hance, letter to George E. Hills, "Record of Mines," book 10, CCAzRR; Henry F. Ashurst, letter to George E. Hills, "Record of Mines," book 10, CCAzRR.
21. George E. Hills, letter to Hance Asbestos Mining Company, February 5, 1902, CCAzRR.
22. Xerox copies, courtesy of the state of Maine, secretary of state's office.
23. *The Sun*, June 13, 1907; June 30, 1908. The New York District Court discharged this action in mid-1908.

24. "The Asbestos Deposits," *Williams News*, July 1, 1905.
25. "Arizona's Guest for a Day," *Williams News*, May 9, 1903.
26. "New Brands Applied For," *Coconino Sun*, January 31, 1903.
27. Frank Lockwood, "More Arizona Characters."
28. "Fascinates Men," *Evening Star*, August 23, 1905.
29. "Grand Canyon Items," *Williams News*, September 19, 1903.
30. "We Fared Pretty Well," *Williams News*, December 3, 1904.
31. Mrs. C. B. Wilson Collection, MS 162, NAUSCA; GRCA, no. 108309, no. 44601; *Williams News*, November 23, 1939.
32. "Index to Locators," YCAzRR.
33. "Local Brevities," *Coconino Sun*, March 23, 1901.
34. "An Interesting Case," *Coconino Sun*, December 8, 1900.
35. "Judge's Opinion," *Coconino Sun*, April 10, 1901.
36. "Notice of Special Master's Sale," *Coconino Sun*, June 22, 1901.
37. Bill of sale, J. W. Thurber to Martin Buggeln, August 28, 1901; General index to deed records, 666, CCAzRR.
38. Thurber and Buggeln files, GRCA.
39. Marjory J. Sente, "No Fries 'Til Mail: How Tourism Brought Mail Service to the Grand Canyon," in *A Rendezvous of Grand Canyon Historians: Proceeding of the Third Grand Canyon History Symposium*, January 2012, edited by Richard Quartaroli.
40. *Arizona Silver Belt*, November 28, 1901.
41. Buggeln-Harvey correspondence, August 6, 1902, GRCA, no. 80085.
42. "John Hance to Martin Buggeln," "Deeds," book 13, page 229, CCAzRR.
43. Buggeln-Harvey correspondence, August 12 and 20, 1903, GRCA, no. 80085.
44. "The Grand Canyon," *Williams News*, February 20, 1904.
45. John Hance's eightieth birthday letter, GRCA.
46. "The Grand Canyon," *Arizona Republican*, August 29, 1905.
47. "$59," Buggeln-Harvey correspondence, GRCA, no. 80085.
48. "From Friday's Daily," *Weekly Arizona Journal-Miner*, May 6, 1903.
49. James McClintock, *El Paso Herald*, January 10, 1919.
50. *Williams News*, May 9, 1903. See FP FPC-1, box 6, folder 05, 004, and 010 for photos of Hance associated with this event, Rare Books and Manuscripts, Arizona State University Library, Tucson, Arizona.
51. C. L. Sonnichsen, ed., "John Hance Champion Liar," in *Arizona Humoresque: A Century of Arizona Humor* (New Orleans, LA: Pelican, 1992), 51.
52. Marshall Trimble, "John Hance, Grand Canyon's Windjammer," *True West Magazine* (August 19, 2016).

CHAPTER 12

1. MS 162, box 1, folder 16, NAUSCA.
2. Ibid.
3. MS 162, box 1, folder 1, NAUSCA.
4. MS 162, box 1, folder 16, NAUSCA.
5. MS 162, box 1, folder 1, NAUSCA.
6. *Mohave County Miner*, July 25, 1903.
7. "Department of Interior, United States Land Office, Prescott," MS 162, box 1, folder 2, NAUSCA.

8. Babbitt Brother Trading Company ledgers, November 1896, June 30 and July 6, 1900, MS 83, series 2, volume 5, NAUSCA.
9. MS 162, box 1, folder 2, NAUSCA.
10. "Local News," *Williams News*, June 2, 1906.
11. GRCA, no. 20849.
12. MS 162, box 1, folder 2, NAUSCA.
13. CCAzRR.
14. "Deeds," book 32, page 599, CCAzRR.
15. "Some Local Items," *Williams News*, March 16, 1907.
16. Homer Wood, quoting Bob Fix, May 1948, CVHS.
17. "Charlie Wingfield, Prescott Ariz. May 20, 1948," CVHS.
18. Unattributed clipping, GRCA.
19. Charles H. Edwards, letter to the editor, *Desert Magazine*, August 1940.
20. "Local News," *Williams News*, July 16, 1904.
21. Wilson Collection, MS 162, box 1, folder 9, NAUSCA.
22. Frank Lockwood, *Prescott Evening Courier*, June 27, 1942.
23. "Negro Murders Deputy Mora in Duel," *Weekly Arizona Journal-Miner*, July 22, 1908.
24. "Pioneers Wet but Happy," *Coconino Sun*, September 10, 1909.
25. Wallace, "Lieutenants Pershing and Stotsenberg Visit the Grand Canyon" (Tuscon, AZ: University of Arizona Press, 1961), 280.
26. June 1909, GRCA, no. 14966. See also "Charlie Wingfield. Prescott Ariz. May 20, 1948," CVHS.
27. Louis Ferrell, letters to Ralph Cameron, MS 006, folder 1, Bechtel Collection, Slusser Memorial Philatelic Library, Tucson, Arizona.
28. "Canyon Guide Is in Trouble," *Los Angeles Times*, December 29, 1914.
29. "Statement of Captain John Hance, in Regard to the Trouble between He and Several Other White Employees, and the Management of the El Tovar Hotel," GRCA, no. 22788. See also *Williams News*, September 24 and October 1, 1914.
30. "American-Japanese War in Arizona," *Williams News*, July 30, 1914.
31. Ibid.
32. "Statement of Captain John Hance," GRCA, no. 22788.
33. "Tempest in Teapot Flag Story a Fake," *Coconino Sun*, August 7, 1914. This may be the Captain Fenton characterized by Prentiss Ingraham in *The Girl Rough Riders*.
34. Ibid.
35. "Capt. Hance May Sue Harveys for $25,000," *Weekly Arizona Journal-Miner*, August 5, 1914.
36. "Flagstaff 'Gems' and 'Sun' Beams," *Williams News*, January 7, 1905.
37. "Tempest in a Teapot," *Coconino Sun*, August 7; "Canyon Guide Is in Trouble," *Los Angeles Times*, December 29, 1914.
38. "Complaint," December 10, 1914, MS 1065, NAUSCA.
39. "Injunction Suit Granted," *Coconino Sun*, December 25, 1914.
40. "Williams, Arizona," December 19, 1914, MS 1065, NAUSCA.
41. "Superior Court Notes," *Coconino Sun*, September 27, 1918.
42. John Hance's eightieth birthday letter, GRCA.
43. "A Mighty Sad Case," *Coconino Sun*, July 12, 1918.
44. Ibid.
45. "Local Brevities," *Williams News*, August 2, 1918.

46. Dama Margaret Smith, *I Married A Ranger* (Project Gutenberg, 2006), 98.
47. "Captain Hance Ill," *Coconino Sun*, December 6, 1918.
48. Jennifer Walker, personal correspondence, summer 2019.
49. Babbitt Brothers Trading Company, MS 83, series 18, volume 7, NAUSCA.
50. Grace Moore manuscript, 56, GRCA, no. 36066.
51. Certificate of death, no. 9858, Arizona State Board of Health.
52. Babbitt Brothers Trading Company, MS 83, series 18, volume 7, NAUSCA.
53. Dama Margaret Smith, *I Married A Ranger*, 98.

CHAPTER 13

1. "Brief History of Capt. Hance," *Coconino Sun*, January 17, 1919.
2. Probate no. 321, December 31, 1919, microfiche, Coconino County Superior Court.
3. "John Hance's Visitors' Book," 131.
4. John Hance, Builder of the First Canyon Trail, Dies," *El Paso Herald, Home Edition*, January 10, 1919.
5. "Grand Canyon," *Arizona Weekly Citizen*, December 1, 1888.
6. Bruce Dinges, "Book Notes," *Journal of Arizona History* 32, no. 4 (Winter 1991): 451.
7. Hal K. Rothman, "Selling the Meaning of Place: Entrepreneurship, Tourism, and Community Transformation in the Twentieth Century American West," *Pacific Historical Review* 56, no 4 (November 1996): 525–57.
8. "Nature's Greatest Wonder," *Coconino Weekly Sun*, June 9, 1892.
9. El Tovar Hotel guest registers, 1909–1911, Fred Harvey Company Collection, 1900–1996, box 20, folder 110, NAUSCA.
10. Charles Douglas Willard, Phyllis Lindner Collection, privately held.
11. Don Lago, personal correspondence, summer 2017.
12. Andy Ashurst, "Asusa, California, January 2, 1948," GRCA.
13. "After a Bath," *Arizona Republican*, September 16, 1894.
14. *Moving Picture News*, January 6, 1912, 19.
15. Burton Holmes Archive, burtonholmesarchive.com
16. "Local Brevities," *Flagstaff Sun-Democrat*, July 15, 1897.
17. Charles Frederick Holder and David Starr Jordan, *Fish Stories Alleged and Experienced: With a Little History Natural and Unnatural* (New York, NY: Henry Holt and Company, 1909), 14–15.
18. Author's paraphrase, provenance unknown.
19. Lonnie E. Underhill, *Hamlin Garland, John Hance & the Grand Canyon* (Gilbert, AZ: Roan Horse Press, 2015), 24.
20. Author's paraphrase, "Bob Wingfield Comm'l Co. Camp Verde," May 20, 1948, CVHS.
21. J. Donald Hughes, "John Hance's Grand Canyon Tales," August 1968, unpublished manuscript, NAUSCA.
22. Paraphrasing J. Donald Hughes, "John Hance's Grand Canyon Tales," NAUSCA; see also Emory Kolb and Burt Lauzon files, NAUSCA.
23. Diane Boyer, personal correspondence, relative's undated monograph. Niles Cameron is misidentified here as Hance. See also Kern Nuttall, *In A Better Place: Cemeteries & Gravesites of Grand Canyon* (Flagstaff, AZ: Vishnu Temple Press, 2016), 82.
24. Nuttall, *In a Better Place*, 82.

SELECT BIBLIOGRAPHY

Anderson, Michael F. *Polishing the Jewell: An Administrative History of Grand Canyon National Park*. Grand Canyon, AZ: Grand Canyon Association, 2000.
——. "Grand Canyon National Park Toll Roads and Trails." Proceedings of the Inaugural Grand Canyon History Symposium, January 2002. Grand Canyon Association.

Armstrong, Margaret. "Canyon & Glacier." *Overland Monthly* 59, no. 2 (February 1912), 96–99.

Ayres, Steve. "A Real Whodunnit: Camp Verde's 1899 Wingfield-Rodgers Murder," *Verde Independent*, March 24, 2009.

Bible, Jean Patterson. *Bent Twigs in Jefferson County*. Rogersville, TN: East Tennessee Print Company, 1991.

Billingsley, George H., Earle Spamer, and Dove Menkes. *Quest for the Pillar of Gold: The Mines and Miners of the Grand Canyon*. Grand Canyon, AZ: Grand Canyon Association, 1997.

Bourke, John G. *On the Border with Crook*. Glorieta, NM: Rio Grande Press, 1892.

Cline, Platt. *They Came To the Mountain—The Story of Flagstaff's Beginnings*. Flagstaff, AZ: Northland Press, 1976.

Cody, William F. *The Life of Hon. William F. Cody Known as Buffalo Bill: The Famous Hunter, Scout and Guide*. Hartford, CT: F. E. Bliss, 1879.

Connell, Evan S. *Son of the Morning Star—Custer and the Little Bighorn*. New York, NY: North Point Press, 1997.

Cook, Mary Jean Straw. *Immortal Summer: A Victorian Woman's Travels in the Southwest: The 1897 Letters & Photographs of Amelia Hollenback*. Santa Fe, NM: Museum of New Mexico Press, 2002.

Corbusier, William T. *Verde to San Carlos: Recollections of a Famous Army Surgeon and His Observant Family on the Western Frontier, 1869–86*. Tuscon, AZ: Dale Stuart King, 1969.

Dodge, Matt. "Arizona's Forgotten Guide." *Real West Magazine* (May 1979): 16–21.

Fish, Williston. "Memories of West Point 1877–81." Unpublished manuscript, West Point Military Academy.

Fisher, Mary Wager. "A Day in the Grand Cañon." *Outing Magazine* 22, no. 4 (July 1893).

Fuchs, James R. "A History of Williams, Arizona, 1876–1951." *University of Arizona Bulletin: Social Science Bulletin* 24, no. 5 (November 1953).

Gerber, Rudy J. *The Railroad and the Canyon*. Firebird Press, 1998.

Goppert, Ernest. "God Bless the Hands That Made Them Custard Pies: William F. Cody's North Rim Adventure." *Points West* (Winter 2003).

Higgins, C. A. *Grand Cañon of the Colorado River.* Chicago, IL: The Henry O. Shepard Company, 1892.

Holder, Charles Frederick, and David Starr Jordan. *Fish Stories Alleged and Experienced: With a Little History Natural and Unnatural.* New York, NY: Henry Holt and Company, 1909.

Holmes, Burton. *Travelogues,* vol. 6. New York City, NY: The McClure Company, 1901.

Hovey, Horace Carter. "The Grand Canyon of the Colorado," *Scientific American* (June 1892).

———. "On the Rim and in the Depths of the Grand Canyon." *Scientific American* (August 1892): 87–89.

Hughes, J. Donald. "John Hance's Grand Canyon Tales," August 1968, unpublished manuscript, Northern Arizona University Special Collections and Archives, Flagstaff, Arizona.

Ingraham, Prentiss. *The Girl Rough Riders: A Romantic and Adventurous Trail of Rough Riders through the Wonderland of Mystery and Silence,* with illustrations by L. J. Bridgman. Boston, MA: Dana Estes & Company, 1903.

James, George Wharton. "Hance, and the Grand Canyon." *Southwestern Empire* (May 1895): 35–37.

Lockwood, Frank C. *The Life of Edward E. Ayer.* Chicago, IL: A. C. McClurg & Co., 1929.

———. "More Arizona Characters." *University of Arizona Press Bulletin,* July 1, 1943.

———. Foreword to *A Westerly Trend: Being a Veracious Chronicle of More Than Sixty Years of Joyous Wanderings, Mainly in Search of Space and Sunshine.* Flagstaff, AZ: Arizona Pioneers Historical Society, 1944.

Magid, Paul. *The Gray Fox: George Crook and the Indian Wars.* Norman, OK: University of Oklahoma Press, 2015.

Mangum, Richard and Sherry Mangum. *Grand Canyon–Flagstaff Stage Coach Line: A History & Exploration Guide.* Portland, OR: Hexagon Press, 1999.

Martin, Tom, ed. *From Powell to Power: A Recounting of the First One Hundred River Runners through the Grand Canyon.* Flagstaff, AZ: Vishnu Temple Press, 2014.

McGhee, James E. *Guide to Missouri Confederate Units, 1861–1865.* Fayetteville, AR: University of Arkansas Press, 2008.

Meed, Douglas V. *They Never Surrendered: Bronco Apaches of the Sierra Madres 1890–1935.* Tuscon, AZ: Westernlore Press, 1993.

Monk, Joseph A. *Arizona Sketches.* London, UK: Grafton Press, 1905.

Moore, William Haas. *Chiefs, Agents & Soldiers—Conflict on the Navajo Frontier 1868–1882.* Albuquerque, NM: University of New Mexico Press, 1994.

Moving Picture News 5, no. 1 (January 6, 1912), 19.

Murphy, Shane. *Ammo Can Interp: Talking Points for a Grand Canyon River Trip.* Flagstaff, AZ: Canyoneers, Inc., 2007.

———. "I've Got to Tell Stories." *Journal of Arizona History* 56, no. 4 (Winter 2015).

———. "A Few Words from Cap'n Hance." *The Ol' Pioneer* 27, no. 3 (2016).

———. "Old Hance Trail." *The Ol' Pioneer* 27, no. 4 (2016).

———. "The Arizona Pioneer." *The Ol' Pioneer* 28, no. 1 (2017).

———. "John Hance's Asbestos Mine." *Boatman's Quarterly Review* 30, no. 2 (2017).

———. "Concerning Havasupai Point." *Boatman's Quarterly Review* 29, no. 4 (2017).

———. "Julius Farlee, John Hance, W. W. Bass, and the Birth of Grand Canyon Tourism, 1883–1893." Proceedings of the Grand Canyon Historical Symposium, 2017.

———. "Hance's Trail." Proceedings of the Grand Canyon Historical Symposium, 2019.

———. "The Camp Verde Ledgers." Proceedings of the Arizona Historical Society, Prescott, 2019.

———. "The Hance Brothers in Yavapai County." Sharlot Hall Museum presentation, 2019.

Nuttall, Kern. In A Better Place: Cemeteries & Gravesites of Grand Canyon. Flagstaff, AZ: Vishnu Temple Press, 2016.

O'Connell, Robert L. Fierce Patriot: The Tangled Lives of William Tecumseh Sherman. New York, NY: Random House, 2014.

Olberding, Susan Deaver. Fort Valley Then and Now: A Look at the Arizona Settlement. Flagstaff, AZ: Fort Valley Publishing, 2002, revised 2007.

Orme, C. H. "History of the Quarter Circle V Bar." Orme School Yearbook, 1949–1950.

Palmer, Ralph. Doctor on Horseback: A Collection of Anecdotes Largely but Not Exclusively Medically Oriented, Camp Verde Historical Society, Camp Verde, Arizona.

Pinchot, Gifford. Breaking New Ground. Washington, D.C.: Island Press, 1987.

Pratt, Joseph Hyde. "Asbestos Deposits of the Grand Canyon, Arizona," Geological Society of America 20th Annual Meeting.

Quartaroli, Richard D., ed. "A Gathering of Grand Canyon Historians: Ideas, Arguments, and First-Person Accounts." Proceedings of the Grand Canyon Historical Society Symposium, 2012, 2016, and 2019.

Ranney, Wayne. Carving Grand Canyon: Evidence, Theories, and Mystery. Grand Canyon, AZ: Grand Canyon Association, 2012.

Richards, Hugo and W. S. Head. Camp Verde Sutler's Store ledgers. Arizona State Library, Archives and Public Records.

Rosa, Joseph G. They Called Him Wild Bill—The Life and Adventures of James Butler Hickok. Norman, OK: University of Oklahoma Press, 1974.

Rothman, Hal K. "Selling the Meaning of Place: Entrepreneurship, Tourism, and Community Transformation in the Twentieth Century American West." Pacific Historical Review (1996): 525–57.

Sente, Marjory J. "No Fries 'Til Mail: How Tourism Brought Mail Service to the Grand Canyon." In A Rendezvous of Grand Canyon Historians: Proceeding of the Third Grand Canyon History Symposium, January 2012, edited by Richard Quartaroli.

Sides, Hampton. Blood and Thunder—The Epic Story of Kit Carson and the Conquest of the American West. New York, NY: Anchor Books, 2006.

Smith, Dama Margaret. I Married A Ranger. Project Gutenberg, 2006.

Smythe, Donald. "'Black Jack' Pershing's Brilliant Career Almost Ended in an Attempt to View Arizona's Awesome Grand Canyon in 1889." Montana Magazine 13, no. 2 (Spring 1963): 11–23.

Sonnichsen, Charles L., ed. "John Hance Champion Liar." In Arizona Humoresque: A Century of Arizona Humor. New Orleans, LA: Pelican, 1992.

Spamer, Earle. Raven's Perch Media. https://ravensperch.org.

Speer, Lonnie R. Portals to Hell—Military Prisons of the Civil War. Lincoln, NE: University of Nebraska Press, 1997.

Stanley, Henry M. *My Early Travels and Adventures in America and Asia*, vol. 1. New York, NY: Charles Scribner's Sons, 1895.

Stuphen, Debra. "Too Hard a Nut to Crack: Peter D. Berry and the Battle for Free Enterprise at the Grand Canyon, 1890–1914." *Journal of Arizona History* 32, no. 2 (Summer 1991).

Taney, Marieke. "Elusive & Remarkable: Stories, a Few Facts and Many Speculations; George F. Flavell's 1896 Colorado River Voyage." Grand Canyon History Symposium prospectus, 2016.

Thayer, Ruth Hance. *Fact or Fiction? The Hance Brothers of Yavapai and Coconino Counties, Arizona*. Master's thesis, 1963, Northern Arizona University Special Collections and Archives.

Trimble, Marshall. *Arizoniana: Stories from Old Arizona*. Phoenix, AZ: Golden West Publishers, 2002.

Thrapp, Dan L. *Al Sieber: Chief of Scouts*. Norman, OK: University of Oklahoma Press, 1995.

Trautmann, Frederick, ed. "Germans at the Grand Canyon: The Memoirs of Paul Lindau, 1883." *Journal of Arizona History* 26, no. 4 (Winter 1985).

Tupper, Edith Sessions. "In the Grand Canyon of the Colorado." *Leslie's Popular Monthly* 41, no. 6 (June 1896): 677–84.

Twain, Mark (Samuel Clemens). *Roughing It*. Hartford, CT: American Publishing Company, 1872.

Underhill, Lonnie E., *Hamlin Garland, John Hance & the Grand Canyon*. Gilbert, AZ: Roan Horse Press, 2015.

———. "Dr. Edward Palmer's Experiences with the Arizona Volunteers." *Arizona and the West* 26, no. 1 (Spring 1984): 49.

Wallace, William Swilling. "Lieutenants Pershing and Stotsenberg Visit the Grand Canyon: 1887 [*sic*]." *Arizona and the West* 3, no. 3 (1961).

Willey, Day Allen. "Hance of the Grand Canyon." *Outing Magazine* 56 (April–September 1910).

Willson, Roscoe G. *No Place for Angels: Stories of Old Arizona Days*. Phoenix, AZ: The Arizona Republic, 1958.

———. *Pioneers and Well Known Cattlemen of Arizona*, vol. 2 (Phoenix, AZ: Mcgrew Commercial Printery, 1951).

Woods, George W., ed. *Personal Impressions of the Grand Canon of the Colorado Near Flagstaff, Arizona: As Seen through Nearly Two Thousand Eyes, and Written in the Private Visitors' Book of the World-Famous Guide*. San Francisco, CA: The Whitaker & Ray Company, 1899.

"Yucca," "A Woman's Trip to the Grand Canon." *Goldthwaite's Geographical Magazine* (July 1892).

INDEX

Locators in italics indicate images

A-1 cattle operation, 80, 82
advertisements. *See under* Grand Canyon;
    Hance, John, and Grand Canyon
Alexander, Catherine, 62
Ali, Hadji, 58
Allen, Martha, 114
Allen, Sarah, 136
Alton Federal Military Prison, 23–24
Anderson, William, 18–19
Anita Mines, 123
Apache Indians, 38, 40, 41–54, 63. *See also*
    hostilities, Native American
Arizona Historical Society Pioneer
    Museum, 186
Arizona Territory, 35–36, 67–68
Arnold, Jack, 82
Arnold, Wales, 42, 44, 46, 58
asbestos mine, Hance, 2, 112, 120, 161–63
Ash Creek Homestead, 47–48, 60–61
Ashurst, Andy, 80, 82, 160, 191
Ashurst, Henry Fountain, 80–81, 160–61,
    169–72, 196
Ashurst, Sarah Bogard, 80–81, *121*
Ashurst, William Henry "Bill," 80–82, 85,
    121, 140–42, 196; death of, 158–62;
    prospecting of, 114–15, 120–21,
    137–38, 158
Ayer, Edward, 85–99, *89*
Ayer, Mrs. Emma, 87–90, *89*

Babbitt Brothers Trading Co., 186
Banghart, George, 39, 43–44
Banghart, Mary, 43–44
Bankhead, Henry, 30
Barnitz, Jennie, 34

barracks, 24–25, *25*
Barth, Solomon, 38, 62, 63
Bass, William Wallace, 117–19, 156, 167,
    179, 181–82
Bassford, Thomas, 164
Battle of Muchos Canyones, 51–52
Battleship Iowa, 175, 177–81
Baumann, Jules, 132
Beale, Edward "Ned" Fitzgerald, 38
Beamer, Ben, 114
Bean, Curtis Coe, 39–40, 58, 61–62, 64, 68
Bean, Mary "May" Bradshaw, 61–62
Beecher Island, Battle of, 30
Berry, John, 109
Berry, Mary "May," 109
Berry, Peter "Pete", 109–11, 126, 138–39,
    156, 175, 179; homestead filings,
    169–72
Berry, Ralph Joseph, 108, 109
Big Creek flood (1867), 34
Black, James, 93
Black, Samuel, 171
Black Canyon Road, 48, 62, 124
boat making, 115–16
Boone, Daniel, 196
Bosque Redondo, 36–37
Boucher, Louis, 125–26, 171
Bourke, Gregory, 52
Bradshaw, William, 60–61
Brannen, Peter, 124–25
Brant, Charles, 177–80
Brant, Mrs., 177–78, 181
Breed, William, 38
"Brief History of Captain Hance, A"
    (George Hance), 187
Bright Angel Hotel, 151, 160, 164–67, *176*
Bright Angel Toll Road, 110

Schoepf, Albin Francisco, 24
Schrader, William, 103–4
Selfridge, Susan Watts Kearney, 161–63
Sherman, William Tecumseh, 36
Shivers, David Wesley, 43–44
Shuttlepan, Apache chief, 52
Sieber, Al, 53, 58, 64
Simmons, Hugh, 26
Sinsabaugh, Hiram, 106–7
Sloan, Richard, 175
smallpox, 23, 148
Smith, Abraham Lincoln "Linc," 54
Smith, Edmund Kirby, 22, 27
Smith, Edward, 53–54
Smith, John Yours Truly, 62–63
Smith, Margaret, 185
Smith, Ulysses Grant, 54
Smoky Hill Trail, 32
snakes, 78–79
Sockdolager Rapid, 2, 89, 99–100, 113, 149
Southern California Press Association tour, 145–46
stage services, 126, 129, 140, 144–45, 145, 151
Stanton, Robert Brewster, 99–100, 113
Steen, Alexander, 19–20
Stevens, Gertrude, 192
Stewart, Mickey, story of, 80–81
Stoneman, George, 45
Stotsenberg, John, 6–7, 7, 175
Sullivan, Jeremiah, 37–40, 46, 58, 68, 187
Summit Toll Road, 136
Supai Indians, 6, 44, 106
surveying, land, 10–11
sutler's store. See Camp Verde sutler's store
Swetnam, James, 41
Sykes, Godfrey, 115–16
Sykes, Stanley, 116, 174

Tanner, Seth, 113–14
Taylor, Sam C., 131–32
Tenth Consolidated Regiment, Missouri Volunteer Infantry, 27
Thayer, Ruth Hance, 101–2
Thompson, Jim, 174

Thurber, Elsie, 140
Thurber, James, 139, 140, 144–52, 145, 156, 164–65
Tiger Mine, 61
Tolfree, Edith Mae, 139
Tolfree, Gertrude, 139
Tolfree, James, 139–40, 152, 154
Tolfree, Lyman Henry, 139–40, 141, 146–50, 152–54
"Tom" Hance's cat, 105–6
Tonto Platform, 84–85, 95, 110
tourism, Grand Canyon: early, 74–93; Hance competitors, 76–78, 107–8, 117; Hance inventing, 8, 197; then and now, 126–28, 130, 156, 189–90
Trail of Tears, 10
Tupper, Edith Sessions, 149–50
Twain, Mark, 33–34, 196

Union Pacific Railroad, 33
Upper Granite Gorge, 98

Verde Removal, 52–53, 195–96
Verde Valley, 41–54, 191. See also Camp Verde
Visitors' Book, John Hance's, 90, 99, 108, 137, 144, 157–58; physical copy, 123–24; messages in, 155, 190
Vulture Mine, 50
V—V Ranch Hotel, 170, 171, 191

Wallace, "Curley," 82
Ward, Annette Persis, 157
Wells, A. G., 165–66
Wells, Edmund William, 104
Wells, H. G., 146–48, 151
Westerly Trend, A (Sykes), 115
Wheeler, Ike, 146, 154
White, George W., 152–53
Whiting, Charles, 37
Wickenburg, Arizona, 50
Wilcox, E. S., 129
Willard, Charles, 190
Williams Road, 119–20
Willey, Day Allen, 74
Wilson, John G., 25–26

Wingfield, Charlie, 175
Wingfield, Clint, 69
Woods, G. K., 123–24, 157–58, 164
Wood, Homer, 157
Wool claim, 120–21, 137, 142, 158

Yavapai Indians, 44–47, 52–53, 119, 190
Yellowstone National Park, 129
Young, Archer Ball, 171–72
Young, H. J., 76
Young, John Willard, 79–80, 134
Yucca (writer), 126–28